Praise for The Essence of Tantric Sexu:

"This beautifully written, yet scholarly book makes available the true meaning of Tantra, its origins, and how the very words from Tantra's past have led to our present-day thinking. *The Essence of Tantric Sexuality* dispels many of the popular myths about Tantra while offering readers a way to begin to incorporate some of the wisdom of the East into their daily lives."

—Alice K. Ladas,
coauthor of *The G Spot and Other Discoveries about Human Sexuality*

"Dr. Jonn Mumford (Swami Anandakapila), on whose illuminating and experiential work this book is based, represents the very best of his tradition and lineage. The authors, Mark Michaels (Swami Umeshanand Saraswati) and Patricia Johnson (Devi Veenanand), write with uninhibited lucidity, erudition, and humour. Everything is a gateway, an entry point to the potentiality of Life, for the Tantric. The authors have made a magnificent contribution to both the classical and contemporary literature of Tantra. This book is indeed a revelation of the essence of Tantric sexuality!"

—Yogacharya Swami Ajnananda Saraswati (Paul Skye),
author of *Mastery of Stress*

"Mark Michaels (Swami Umeshanand Saraswati) and Patricia Johnson (Devi Veenanand), using the strong light of Dr. Jonn Mumford's (Swami Anandakapila) 1976 Gnosticon lectures, illuminate deeply into the cave of ancient Tantra and share with us how vitally relevant Tantra is for today . . . With this work we are given passwords to access knowledge, understanding, and power that were formerly available only to the selected few. The reader will find immediate and engaging access to the Tantric world of spirit and sexuality for men and women of all sexual orientations. This work is destined to be the dog-eared reference book for generations of serious students of Tantra."

—Bruce Anderson,
author of *Tantra for Gay Men*

About the Authors

Mark Michaels (Swami Umeshanand Saraswati) and **Patricia Johnson** (Devi Veenanand) are a devoted married couple who have been teaching Tantra and Kriya Yoga together since 1999. Their popular workshops have been featured in several publications, including the *Village Voice, NOW* magazine, and *Breathe* magazine.

The two seek to combine a traditional, lineage-based approach with the best contemporary, Neo-Tantric methods. Their approach includes breath work, meditation, chanting, and *puja* (a type of Hindu devotional ritual), and their "initiated Kriya yoga" practices aim to lay a spiritual foundation for bringing the heightened awareness and pleasure of sex into everyday life.

The authors are senior students of Dr. Jonn Mumford (Swami Anandakapila Saraswati) and have been named lineage holders of the OM-Kara Kriya® system for the Americas and Europe. Sunyata, coauthor of *The Jewel in the Lotus*, named Michaels his lineage holder in 2001. Michaels and Johnson have studied Bhakti Yoga with Bhagavan Das and Tantra with Dr. Rudy Ballentine, and they have been featured in Dr. Judy Kuriansky's *The Complete Idiot's Guide to Tantric Sex*.

Michaels is a graduate of New York University School of Law, is a member of the Bar in New York State, and holds master's degrees in American Studies from NYU and Yale. A playwright and translator, he translated and adapted Goldoni's *The Mistress of the Inn* for New York's Roundabout Theatre Company and cowrote *The Thrill of Victory, The Agony of Debate,* which premiered at New York's Primary Stages. Patricia Johnson is a professional operatic soprano who tours extensively throughout the United States, Europe, and South America and has performed with the New York City Opera, the Houston Grand Opera, and the Berlin Komsiche Oper.

They make their home near New York City.

The Essence of Tantric Sexuality

Mark A. Michaels & Patricia Johnson
(Swami Umeshanand Saraswati)   (Devi Veenanand)

Foreword by Rudolph Ballentine, M.D.

Llewellyn Publications
Woodbury, Minnesota

First Edition
First Printing, 2006

Author photo by Julie Betts Testwuide
Book design and layout by Joanna Willis
Cover painting by Kailash Raj / © www.exoticindia.com
Cover design by Gavin Dayton Duffy
Illustrations by Llewellyn art department on pages 27, 36, 99, 110, 127, 167
Illustrations by Mary Ann Zapalac on pages 26, 29–30, 39, 50, 73–74, 88–91, 98, 100–102, 107–108, 110, 113, 115, 120, 122, 124, 126–127, 131–134, 136, 140–141, 143, 151–152, 154–155, 157, 159–160, 168, 175

Photo Credits:
The photograph of the homunculus model is reproduced by permission of the Natural History Museum, London.
The photograph of the relief from the temple at Khajuraho in central India is reproduced by permission of K. L. Kamat/www.kamat.com.
The publisher gratefully acknowledges Kailash Center for Personal Development, Inc., for the use of photographs from Dr. Jonn Mumford's personal collection as well as permission to reference audiotapes and other material from Dr. Mumford's personal archives.

Llewellyn is a registered trademark of Llewellyn Worldwide, Ltd.

Library of Congress Cataloging-in-Publication Data
Michaels, Mark A., 1959–
The essence of tantric sexuality / Mark A. Michaels & Patricia Johnson; foreword by Rudolph Ballentine.
         p. cm.
Includes bibliographical references.
ISBN-13: 978-0-7387-0900-0
ISBN-10: 0-7387-0900-X
   1. Sex—Religious aspects—Tantrism. 2. Tantrism. 3. Sex instruction. I. Johnson, Patricia, 1964–
II. Title.

HQ64.M53 2006
306.77—dc22   2006040866

Llewellyn Publications
A Division of Llewellyn Worldwide, Ltd.
2143 Wooddale Drive, Dept. 0-7387-0900-X
Woodbury, MN 55125-2989, U.S.A.
www.llewellyn.com

 Printed in the United States of America on recycled paper

To Gurudev Dr. Jonn Mumford (Swami Anandakapila Saraswati)
with deepest affection and respect. OM Maharaj. It certainly has been a wild ride!

Contents

Illustrations

Foreword

We all owe a debt of gratitude to Dr. Jonn Mumford (Swami Anandakapila) for his independent-mindedness and courage when he gave the original lectures on which this book is based. Having known and worked with them over several years, I am also pleased by the skill and understanding shown by Mark Michaels (Swami Umeshanand) and Mark's wife, Patricia Johnson (Devi Veenanand), in turning the lectures into this concise and yet flowing book. There is much in it to appreciate.

First, I am relieved to see an honest discussion of the difference between "Neo" (or "California") Tantra and the classic tradition that preceded it in India. Something erupted when Tantric teachings, however modified and diluted, reached the West Coast, and its momentum is not all to be celebrated. As this book makes clear, at its best, this American Neo-Tantra provides a helpful, if limited, antidote to the fearful, taboo-ridden, moralistic (and, at the same time, prurient) sexuality that so dominates our country. But at its worst, it subtly colludes in the perpetuation of it.

The tone Swami Anandakapila set in these lectures back in 1976, on the contrary, clears the air. It is nonmoral, and yet it bows with deep reverence before the numinous phenomenon of fully conscious sexuality. A space is created by this discussion, wherein we can look with awe and with joy at the body and at its potential for ecstasy as obvious and natural assets in the spiritual quest, rather than as evil saboteurs of it. In this space, we can discuss matter-of-factly, for example, the use of masturbation as a rich path of sexual/spiritual unfoldment or, as another example, the holy imperative to be playful and to experiment in this temple of mysteries. And with such a safely sane arena to talk within, the book can even broach that most forbidden of topics, anal sex, and explore its wonder and potential.

There is also an elegance and simplicity in the explication of technique that is gratifying. The systematic treatment of the erogenic zones—and how and in what order they are best aroused—is a gift for everyone who wishes to make love (to self or others). The Tantra-oriented massage outlined in chapter 14 is a solid asset for Tantric aspirants, and the use of the Masters and Johnson stages of sexual arousal to clarify the importance of steadily and patiently building excitement and energy (i.e., remaining in Phase 1) makes the Tantric approach to sex seem commonsensical and powerful, rather than merely frustrating.

And perhaps most enticing for me is how the book cracks the door to the *inner* work with the masculine and feminine and, though it is not the subject of the present work, peeks at the possibility that that inner work might continually, step by step, amplify and catalyze the *outer* work between a man and a woman—or, once this connection is made, between any two persons who are Tantric partners.

And there is much more than these specific topics, which are so thoroughly explored. In fact, from the opening concise and informative history of Tantra in the West to the final discussion of the Tantric Mass and the secrets of Amrita—even if (and maybe especially when) they don't conform exactly to the reader's (or my) own understanding—a series of juicy bits of information and ideas, of quirky new ways to come at ancient teachings, leave a lasting trail of luminescent little pearls running through our minds, which continue to challenge and delight.

RUDOLPH BALLENTINE, M.D.

Preface

This book is an unusual collaboration; it is based, for the most part, on a series of lectures that Dr. Jonn Mumford, Swami Anandakapila Saraswati, delivered at Gnosticon 5, an extended conference hosted by Llewellyn Publications in 1976. Gnosticon brought together experts from a variety of occult backgrounds and disciplines. A taped set of Dr. Mumford's lectures was available from Llewellyn for a number of years. Today, copies are virtually impossible to find, and Dr. Mumford (who will be referred to throughout the text as "Swamiji," a title of respect and affection and a reference to his initiation as a Swami of the Saraswati Order, one of the ten traditional Indian orders) was content to let the information languish, because he had doubts about whether some of the more explicit material should ever appear in print.

In 2004, my wife and teaching partner, Patricia Johnson (Devi Veenanand), suggested that we approach Swamiji about the possibility of writing a book based on the Gnosticon lectures. She felt that the material was too valuable to be allowed to lapse into obscurity and that it was important to ensure that Swamiji's contribution to the development of contemporary Tantra receives the recognition it deserves. Much to our surprise, he agreed to support us in undertaking the project. Our company, Kailash Center for Personal Development, Inc., had acquired the rights to most of Swamiji's material some time before, but we would not have dreamed of going forward with this project without his blessing. I can only hope that, in keeping with the ancient tradition, Devi Veenanand and I have conveyed the teachings effectively.

We first met Swamiji on his tour in 1999, shortly after beginning to study with him by correspondence over the Internet. We were very fortunate that his itinerary on that tour included New York, since he is unlikely to return to the United States. Today, he is content to remain in Sydney, conducting his online programs (which it is now our privilege to sponsor) and making the occasional trip to Pondicherry, Tamil Nadu, India, where he serves as a guest teacher at Ananda Ashram, founded by one of his Gurus, Dr. Swami Gitananda Giri Guru Maharaj. Since meeting Swamiji, we have continued to study with him both online and in person, in Sydney and Pondicherry. Our visits with him in Sydney are always filled with surprises.

Swamiji has an amazing capacity to discover the delightful in virtually anything and to instill this sense of wonder and amusement in his students. We have had some truly remarkable experiences just sitting and enjoying coffee with him in his apartment. He has been called one of the "laughing Swamis" of Australia, and the title suits him. But along with the laughter, he is serious about teaching, and his commitment to helping students find "faith, hope, and courage" within themselves is one that we share and strive to embody in our own work.

Swamiji has a rare gift for placing authentic Hindu Tantra, including its sexual aspects, within a conceptual framework that makes it accessible for Westerners. He manages to do this without overemphasizing sexuality, watering down the teachings, or coating them with New Age trappings, however appealing such modifications might be to Western seekers. We became his students because we were seeking something deeper and more authentic than what popular American Tantra had to offer, and that is exactly what we found. It is truly a privilege to learn from him, and he has shared more knowledge than we can ever hope to absorb completely.

The history of Tantra in the Western world is a checkered one indeed. Early accounts depicted Tantra as scandalous, depraved, and tantamount to black magic. By the early twentieth century, there were somewhat more serious attempts both to understand the Tantric tradition and to explain it to Westerners in objective and even respectful terms. Sir John Woodroffe (1865–1936), also known as Arthur Avalon, was a key figure both in providing the West with a more enlightened perspective on Tantra and in making classical texts available in English. Woodroffe, who served as a judge in colonial India, was a Tantric initiate and, with the help of several Indian collaborators, collected and translated numerous Tantric texts. He wrote extensively on the philosophical underpinnings of Tantra and various aspects of Hindu philosophy; he was also a prominent supporter of and advocate for Indian independence. Western scholars do not generally admire Woodroffe's work, but his were among the first translations of Tantric scriptures to become available to general readers, and they remain both important and influential to this day.

An American known as Pierre Arnold Bernard (popularly called Oom the Omnipotent) was a near contemporary of Woodroffe's. Bernard is a rather mysterious figure who probably never left the United States, despite his claims to the contrary, but who seems to have been instructed in Tantra by an Indian-born Syrian named Elias Hamati. Bernard combined authentic teachings with large doses of charlatanism and fraud. He fabricated an intellectual pedigree and spent the early part of his career dodging criminal charges on both coasts.

Bernard founded an organization called the Tantrik Order in America that attracted not only adherents from the upper crust of New York society but also, interestingly enough, some people with significant knowledge of the Hindu tradition, including Swami Bodhananda, leader of the Ramakrishna Order in New York at the time. It appears that Bernard gave instruction in Vama Marga practices during his early years as a teacher, though it is impossible to discern what this entailed or whether the teachings were in any way authentic; at one point, he seems to have had an organization known as the "Bacchante Club." In 1910, there was a sexual scandal, and Bernard was charged with kidnapping but acquitted when key witnesses against him failed to appear. In 1918, he left New York City and established a retreat center known as the Clarkstown Country Club in West Nyack, New York. This center had a profound influence on the popularity of Yoga in America, and a diverse array of luminaries, including Kurt Weil, Dr. Ida Rolf, Sir Paul Dukes, and Cyril Scott, were associated with the C.C.C.

It seems that Bernard was hesitant to engage in public discussion of Vama Marga Tantra in the years after the scandal, and by the 1920s, he was deemphasizing the term "Tantra" and stressing "Yoga" instead. A police raid on the C.C.C. in 1919 "found his followers doing simple exercises," according to the *New York Times*. The C.C.C. closed in the late 1940s, and Bernard died in 1955 at the age of eighty. After his death, one of his disciples wrote that Bernard was "ahead of his time, as are most pioneers, and therefore was misunderstood and persecuted by the ignorant and the envious, and by the sensational press."[1]

While Yoga had by no means entered the American mainstream, it enjoyed gradually increasing popularity from the 1920s through the 1950s, as the career of Paramahansa Yogananda makes evident. By the '50s, there were a number of books on Hatha Yoga available to the general public, including an outstanding one by Pierre Bernard's nephew Theos Bernard, a pioneering academic and an early Western initiate in Tibetan Buddhism. Celebrities like Aldous Huxley and Christopher Isherwood embraced Advaita Vedanta; however, Tantra, especially Vama Marga Tantra, was virtually unknown and little examined, even in academic circles.

During the 1960s, popular interest in India and many aspects of Hinduism grew rapidly. Swamiji's own *Psychosomatic Yoga* (1962) appeared in advance of an emerging mass-culture phenomenon. In 1964, Omar V. Garrison published a book entitled *Tantra: The Yoga of Sex*. This was perhaps the first twentieth-century book to focus on the sexual aspects of Tantra, and Garrison's title helped shape a popular misconception that persists to this day. Garrison clearly had some knowledge; however, his book is filled with inaccuracies and reflects a fundamental misunderstanding of the meaning of Tantra. Also during the 1960s, Agehananda Bharati, possibly the first Westerner initiated as a Swami, wrote a very important book, *The Tantric Tradition*, which describes Vama Marga practice in considerable detail and depth; the book is highly scholarly in its approach and certainly was not intended for a popular audience. During the same period, the forced exile of many important Tibetan Lamas, most notably Chogyam Trungpa Rinpoche, brought Buddhist Tantric teachings to a vast number of Western seekers.

In the early 1970s, there was still very little popular knowledge that Vama Marga Tantra even existed. The 282-page *Catalog of Sexual Consciousness* (1975) devoted a mere four pages to the subject, and the only available sources of teachings it identified were Trungpa Rinpoche's organization and Bhagwan Shree Rajneesh Centers in Watertown, Massachusetts, and New York. Nevertheless, the book's very publication suggests that in the aftermath of the "sexual revolution," there was considerable interest in sex as a tool for consciousness expansion. It was

---

1 From an anonymous letter by "D.H.W." pasted inside *Life at the Clarkstown Country Club,* a promotional book published by the C.C.C. in 1935. Interestingly, the authors have three copies of the book, and each of them contains the letter, which was clearly written after Bernard's death in 1955.

at this very moment that Llewellyn published Swamiji's second book, *Sexual Occultism* (1975), and that he delivered his seminal lectures on Vama Marga at Gnosticon in 1976.

Swamiji's adventures in India predated those of the '60s generation. He was an accomplished Yogi by the late 1950s and had studied with many Indian masters. He met Paramahansa Satyananda Saraswati in the late 1960s. His studies with Paramahansaji culminated in a residence at the Bihar School of Yoga and his initiation as Swami Anandakapila Saraswati at the BSY Silver Jubilee Celebration in 1973. Swamiji was one of two Westerners initiated that year.

The lectures on which this book is based were perhaps the first public discussion of Vama Marga Tantra delivered to an American audience by a Western teacher with authentic Indian training in a lineage-based system. Some of the material that Swamiji presented at Gnosticon was almost entirely unknown outside of India, and Swamiji's Gnosticon lectures inspired succeeding generations of Tantra teachers, whether they realize it or not.

Most Western teachers of Tantra have also been influenced by Rajneesh (Osho), but Rajneesh did not teach traditional Tantra and had not been through a traditional process of training and initiation. He was a popularizer who blended a theoretical knowledge of Tantra with methods based in Western psychotherapy, as well as other spiritual disciplines, thereby transforming Tantra into a kind of healing modality or quest for personal growth, an approach that is, at best, remote from the essence of the tradition. The content of Swamiji's lectures, on the other hand, is rooted in the tradition and places Vama Marga Tantra more accurately in context. Even when dealing with explicitly sexual matters, Swamiji explains the mystical purposes of Tantric sexuality with clarity and precision, and while his lectures are informed by his knowledge of Western psychology and physiology, as well as acupuncture and other Eastern disciplines, they are not focused on healing or "growth," be it sexual or emotional.

Thus, the Gnosticon lectures are of great historical importance in the development of Tantra in the West, and they helped shape what is known today as Neo-Tantra (a term originally coined by Avalon and his circle, more prominently used by Rajneesh to describe his approach, and now applied more generally to Westernized systems of practice that emphasize sexuality). While some traditionalists take a dim view of Neo-Tantra, it can, at its best, lead Westerners to approach sexuality with deeper awareness and a greater sense of reverence. The information that Swamiji shared in 1976, in the aftermath of the sexual revolution, is perhaps even more valuable today than it was thirty years ago, given the current climate of sexual repression in the United States. Beyond any historical value or cultural and political significance, the content of the lectures is often profound, and the techniques are extraordinary.

We knew Swamiji was reluctant to authorize the re-release of this information and its adaptation into book form, but we felt it was important to approach him about this project not only for its content and historical importance, but also because, at times, his work has been misrepresented, misunderstood, and appropriated without acknowledgement, and we wanted to set the record straight. We are deeply grateful that he encouraged us to use his material and allowed us the freedom to take liberties with it. We are also grateful for his willingness to provide additional information and elaboration whenever it was needed. Working on this book has afforded us an opportunity to absorb the teachings very deeply, and we trust that serious readers will have a similar experience if they study the material carefully.

We have done our best to retain as much of Swamiji's delightful and unconventional lecture style as possible while updating, clarifying, and elaborating when appropriate; as a result, certain points are repeated more frequently than one might expect in this format. While we have considered the sequence of chapters quite carefully, each topic can be studied independently, in whatever order seems appropriate to the individual reader. In some instances, we have relied on later versions of the lectures first given at Gnosticon; chapter 5 is based on a 1989 talk Llewellyn released on tape as *Sexual Tantra: Is It Possible?* The basic content of the chapters devoted to the Kama Marmas remains the same, but the discussion of each Marma point is considerably more detailed than in the original lecture. Out of respect for Dr. Swami Gitananda Giri Guru Maharaj, chapter 3 substitutes a discussion of the basic principles of Kriya Yoga, derived from some of Swami Anandakapila's more recent writings, for a description of the Hasta Mudras.

Readers who are familiar with Neo-Tantra may be surprised to discover that certain practices emphasized by many contemporary schools receive little or no attention in these pages. In 1976, Swamiji was largely unconcerned with male multiple orgasm or female ejaculation, and these topics are only mentioned in passing. Information about these techniques is widely available elsewhere. Both female ejaculation and male multiple or full-body orgasms are wonderful experiences and enjoyable—but not essential—parts of the sexual repertoire; however, they are not a core concern in traditional Tantric sexuality, nor does developing the capacity to experience them make one a Tantrika (Tantric practitioner). From the classical perspective, the G-spot is a trigger point for Swadisthana Chakra, nothing more. It is certainly not the key to sexual healing, nor is it anything new. It is discussed (though not under that name) both in Indian erotic literature such as the *Koka Shastra* and in the erotic novels of eighteenth-century Europe.

Some readers will undoubtedly note that this book is almost entirely heterosexual in focus. This is true of virtually all the available Tantric literature about sexuality; however, in the Tantric worldview, every human being is both male and female, regardless of external gender. Cultivating the capacity to imagine can enable any individual practitioner to transcend gender identity, however one defines it. For this reason, same-sex couples can employ any of the techniques we have described and create the necessary male-female polarities by means of visualization. Indeed, it is a very valuable experience for heterosexual couples to explore reversing genders by the same means.

While there have been some departures from the original tapes, we all feel that we are conveying the essential teachings Swamiji presented in 1976. The techniques are powerful, pleasurable, and effective. They should yield interesting results if you approach them with curiosity and an open mind. We wish you much delight as you put them into practice.

MARK A. MICHAELS
(SWAMI UMESHANAND SARASWATI)

one

Swami Anandakapila's Tantric Terminology

$\mathcal{I}$t is valuable to begin the study of Tantra by becoming acquainted with some technical terminology. Swamiji takes great pleasure in wordplay and has always had an interest in etymology. He discussed both of these subjects at some length in *Ecstasy Through Tantra,* and the material in this chapter supplements that discussion, providing an introduction to some key Tantric terms and philosophical concepts. Some of this terminology will today be familiar to many Western readers, but Swamiji's unique approach is likely to provide new insight, even into words that have become commonplace in the years since Gnosticon.

The sexual aspect of Tantra is a very serious matter, something extremely sensitive, and as you learn more, you may discover that just thinking about it can induce a very special kind of state. We are dealing with the most profound and sacred mystery, the essential activity of human life, both in terms of the survival of the species and in terms of its potential for connecting us with the transcendent. Tantrikas seek to experience the mystical while remaining firmly grounded in the physical world, and language is a very important part of this process.

There are a number of different ways to translate the Sanskrit roots of the word *Tantra*. To begin with, *Tantra* is composed of a prefix, *tanoi*, and a suffix, *trayati*.

Swamiji demonstrating Mantra Anesthesia at Gnosticon, 1976
Photo courtesy of Kailash Center for Personal Development, Inc.

Tanoi means "to expand"; *trayati* is often translated as "tool" or, even better, "instrument" and is probably the root of the English word *trowel*. In its purest sense, *trayati* actually means "to liberate" or "to burst free." So, *tanoi* and *trayati* combine to form *Tantra*, that which expands the mind-body complex and leads to the ultimate experience of liberation—liberation from the small stuff.

There are two distinct paths in Tantra. Swamiji was privileged to study both of them in India. One of these paths is known as the right-hand path, called *Dakshina Marga*. The other path is known as the left-hand path, or *Vama Marga*. *Dakshina* means "right," and *vama* means "left." *Marga* means "path." You may hear some variations in pronunciation, such as *Vam Marg* and *Dakshin Marg*, since the final "a" sound of the original Sanskrit is dropped in modern Hindi. Swamiji was trained by Hindi speakers and tends to use the Hindi pronunciation, but the meaning of the words is the same. For the purposes of this book, we have substituted the classical Sanskrit for Swamiji's Hindi pronunciations.

To the ancient Hindu mind, the terms *Vama Marga* and *Dakshina Marga* had very special meanings. If you are an old-school Theosophist, "left-hand path" refers to "black magic" (whatever that means) and is something quite dreadful. Conversely, "right-hand path" has implications of righteousness. It is important to discard these prejudices and understand that in the context of Hindu Tantra, Vama Marga and Dakshina Marga have few such connotations.

In English, as in most European languages, *right* has come to mean something very different from *left*. There is a long history behind this. In Latin, *dexter* means "right." A person is gifted with manual dexterity. A person is dexterous. And in French, which is derived from Latin, the word for *right* is *droit*, from which we get the English *adroit*. If someone is very manually dexterous, you might have the right to say that person is adroit. Most of us are right-handed, and by implication, right-handed people are adroit and dexterous while left-handed people are not.

Even more importantly, in both the Romance and Germanic languages, the word *right* has come to be associated with all sorts of good things: a good person displays moral rectitude; if I am right, I am correct; I have certain inalienable rights; "the Lord . . . leads me on the path of righteousness." In our culture, things that are right are morally correct. Thus, the right-hand path is the morally correct and socially acceptable path. This connotation is embedded in our language, and therefore in our culture, and consequently in the mind of every Western individual.

Now consider the left. In French, the word is *gauche*. That means "clumsy," and if we say someone is very clumsy or inept, that person is gauche. In Latin, the word is *sinister*; so, a left-handed Yogi, like Swamiji, may appear to be a sinister person, and that is a pretty odious implication. In our culture, we have really gotten tied up with ideas about right hand and left hand, and these associations go very deep.

The Theosophists did not have it entirely wrong, since there are many taboos associated with the left hand in Indian culture too. These mainly have to do with hygiene rather than morality or abstract notions of good and evil. Some of the linguistic distinctions between right and left also exist in the Sanskrit *dakshina* and *vama*, but *vama* has many more positive connotations. Indeed, it appears to have been the same word as *vaamaa*, which means "lovely, dear, pleasant, fair, agreeable, beautiful, splendid, valuable." This word can also refer to the female breast. Thus, while following the left-hand path does carry an implication of freeing oneself from conventional behavior and social norms, the negative implications that many in the West (and modern India) ascribe to it are exaggerated.

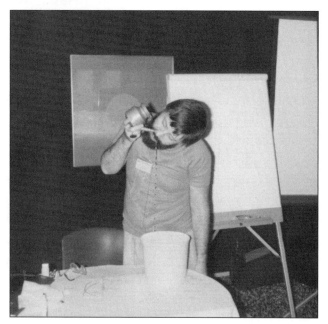

Swamiji demonstrating Siddha
Neti at Gnosticon, 1976

Photos courtesy of Kailash Center for
Personal Development, Inc.

There are more important and deeper meanings in the Sanskrit terminology. Dakshina Marga refers to the internal rotation of sexual forces between the mind and body. This produces a union between the male and female (or *Shiva* and *Shakti*) elements within a single individual. The Saraswati Order focuses on Dakshina Marga practices, moreso in the years since Swamiji was initiated. Swamiji's personal interest and our own, however, is in Vama Marga Tantra.

And what is Vama Marga Tantra, the left-hand path? It is the rotation of the conscious sexual forces between two individuals. That is the only difference. Dakshina Marga is do-it-yourself, and Vama Marga is practiced with a partner. But in both cases, it is a rotation of consciousness. That rotation can only be accomplished by means of the most powerful form of energy readily available in the human body, and that is sexual energy. In the most profound moments, the sexual energy in one way or another transforms into emotion.

Now, to go deeper still into meaning, the Sanskrit root *vam* means "left." It has come through into English; it is the root of the words *vomit* and *vomitous*. It has come to mean excretion, because somehow in our language, we always seem to put the most odious emphasis on things. Excretion is bodily waste, something your body has to throw off, and in our culture, we learn to feel disgusted by excretion. *Vam* in Sanskrit doesn't actually refer to excretion; it refers to secretion. And there is a big difference between an excretion and a secretion. The secret of Vama Marga or left-hand Tantra is the secret of the use of the secretions secreted in the secret places, the cavities of the body. And this is the secret, inner meaning of the term *Vama Marga*.

Let us consider the worship of the *lingam* and the *yoni*. *Lingam* means "penis" and, in addition, "a mark, spot, sign, emblem, or characteristic." It can also mean, quite simply, "the image of God." Thus, the term *lingam* can be understood as referring to the fundamental sign of existence. In cultures around the world, a very simple phallus often represents that sign of existence. *Yoni* means "the female vulva, genitalia, and womb." It can also mean, among other things, "home, place of birth, source, origin, spring, or fountain." *Yoni*, then, is the source from which all existence springs.

In temples all over India, you will encounter veneration of the male phallus and the female vulva. Lord Shiva is the patron deity of the Yogis; he is represented by the lingam. This Shiva Lingam is embedded in the circular, feminine yoni, representing

Domestic Shiva Lingam Puja

An early European representation of a domestic Shiva Lingam Puja from Moor's Hindu Pantheon, *1810. Note the lingam in the yoni base at the left of the illustration. This image is also significant for its depiction of a woman conducting a ritual, something that would have shocked nineteenth-century Europeans. The central role of women in ritual is characteristic of the Tantric tradition.*

the divine feminine. This is an object of veneration, not unlike the Christian cross, which is in fact a lingam without a yoni, since the only acceptable Christian worship of the divine feminine is the worship of the Virgin Mary.

In Hindu worship, the lingam is embedded in the yoni, just as a maypole is embedded in the earth; perhaps that is where that custom originated. In any case, the symbology is exactly the same: the phallic symbol inserted in Mother Earth. In India, the lingam is worshiped by dousing it in *ghee*, or clarified butter. This oil is massaged into the lingam and allowed to drip down into the yoni, and that is the fundamental act of *puja*, or worship.

It is quite stunning when you think about it. Many modern Hindus are rather pious and puritanical, a legacy of British rule and the Victorian era. Yet, they see nothing obscene or distasteful at all in this form of ritual. This is a very serious act of sexual worship, performed daily by and for millions of people.

Much as dancing around the maypole has persisted in the West, another symbolic Vama Marga tradition of worshiping the lingam and the yoni has persisted. Its deeper meaning has been obscured and forgotten, but it is still a very common practice. Whether it is a direct connection or merely an expression of a much deeper transcultural symbology is not for us to say, but even today, many in the West (particularly in the United States) are unknowingly practicing Vama Marga Tantra and are wearing its symbol on the left hand.

Mudra is the science of gesture and sign language; there are additional meanings to the word, but they need not concern us at the moment. In mudra, each finger has a particular significance, and the thumb always represents either man or God—*Brahman*, the absolute out of which all was created. The next fingers represent the holy trinity, which you find in many religions. In the Hindu tradition, the trinity is made up of Brahma, Vishnu, and Shiva. The fourth finger represents Shiva, and since the lingam is his symbol, mudra recognizes the fourth finger as the phallic finger.

The simplest symbol for the yoni is the circle or ring, and the wedding ring is worn on the fourth finger of the left hand, the lingam finger. Wearing a wedding ring on the fourth finger is a profoundly symbolic act. It represents the eternal union of the universe, between active and passive, between mind and body, between man and woman eternally—that lingam uniting with that yoni.

Here's the symbolic secret: If you are wearing a wedding ring and you hold your hand upright, according to mudra, you have the yoni and the lingam in what we call *vipariti*, or the female superior position. And in traditional Vama Marga ritual, the only way a lingam is inserted into a yoni is in the female superior position. That is very significant, because it is always the case in the Hindu Tantric tradition that woman is the embodiment of Shakti, the embodiment of essence, purity, divinity, the energetic principle, Goddess incarnate.

Now we will go to the core meaning of this Vama Marga, this left-hand path, this science of secretions, this worship of sexual energy. When we look at the two roots, *tanoi* and *trayati,* "expand" and "liberate," what happens? Suppose that, for the word *expand*, which is one of the root meanings of the prefix *tan*, we substitute the English word *tumescence*, which is the state *sahaja*, that natural state in which man and woman become focused in on their inner being. It begins with the swelling of the genitals, the swelling of the breasts, the engorging with blood, and the focusing of the mind inward. That is expanding, swelling, tumescence.

Then *trayati*, "liberation": it is that event that produces the bursting of the ego, the exploding forth beyond the bounds of self; that particular event we call orgasm starts the detumescence and, in that moment, liberation. And right there you have Tantra: tumescence and detumescence, the beginning and end of the sexual response cycle. That is the whole story of Vama Marga; it is the essential *Yoga*, or union.

two

Yantras: Secret Tantric Symbols

Swamiji wrote his first book, *Psychosomatic Yoga,* in the early 1960s. *Psychoso-matic Yoga* is long out of print, but it has been radically revised and enlarged and is now available as *A Chakra & Kundalini Workbook.* The Gnosticon lecture on which this chapter is based is an introduction to *Chakra Dharana,* a practice he de-scribed in considerably more detail and with a somewhat different emphasis on pages 89–113 of *A Chakra & Kundalini Workbook.* Swamiji claims that he wrote *Psychosomatic Yoga* when he was a young man who knew nothing. The fact is that he knew a great deal more about Tantra and Yoga than most Westerners did at the time. More importantly, he had already encountered some of the great Indian teach-ers of that era. He describes sitting with these teachers until other students "went to sleep," at which point the teachers often said something of value. Aleister Crowley wrote that the essence of Yoga could be expressed in four simple instructions: "Sit still. Stop thinking. Shut up. Get out!"[1] Crowley notwithstanding, Swamiji knew when not to "get out," although even as a young man, he had certainly mastered many techniques for doing so.

In the original *Psychosomatic Yoga,* there is a little diagram called "Chakra Tattwas Yantra." This diagram and the accompanying description provided the

---

1 Aleister Crowley, *Eight Lectures on Yoga* (Dallas: Sangreal Foundation, 1972), 32. Crowley's brief treatise is es-sential reading for any serious Western student of Yoga and Tantra.

key to meditating on the classical yantra diagrams, and their publication may have marked the first time the method was revealed in print in the West. Earlier books generally did not include independent diagrams of the yantras themselves and only depicted them in the context of the more complex and more familiar *mandalas*.

This system of meditation is a way to integrate yourself with the chakras, a way to play an internal mind game and thereby reprogram yourself. Working with the yantras is a very effective technique that can build a foundation for more advanced Tantric practice, whether Vama Marga or Dakshina Marga. One of the more important and complex inner Tantric rituals is known as *Tattwa Shuddhi*, or purification of the elements, and while it is far beyond the scope of this book to provide instruction in Tattwa Shuddhi, something that requires personal initiation, the method described in this chapter is a very effective way of beginning to work with the elements.

Let us begin with etymology and take a look at the word *yantra*. The prefix *yan* means "to conceive." *Tra* comes from *trayati* and means "to liberate" and also "tool," just as it does in the word *Tantra*. So, a *yantra* is a geometrical diagram, a picture form that can be conceived in the mind. In the simplest terms, it is a tool for conception in the mind. When used properly, that tool of conception or visualization or imagination helps you obtain mental liberation. There is a specific yantra for each chakra, and these yantras are two-dimensional representations of three-dimensional figures.

Knowledge about the chakras has passed from the East to the West, so by now, some concept of the chakra system is familiar to many Westerners. Many changes have been made over the years; much has been lost in translation, and much has been distorted. Theosophy has influenced the occult traditions of both the West and India, and the Theosophical version of the chakra system has been widely circulated, even though it barely resembles the classical Hindu system, which itself has a number of variants. Other concepts have emerged from an array of sources, including everything from Reiki to trance channelers. As a result, the traditional colors and shapes that are most commonly associated with the chakras are unfamiliar to most Westerners, and we have even encountered students who insist we must be wrong when we teach the traditional system.

Nevertheless, the classical system retains its power because it tends to work transculturally. You look at a red triangle, and that evokes fire, passion, burning up. You look at a blue hexagram, which is the primary symbol for Anahata (heart) Chakra, and that represents integration, union, mind with body, male with female. In other words, it is universal, essentially an archetype. Regardless of your background, the traditional symbols and associated colors are likely to have an effect on many levels of consciousness. For this reason, and because of its classical roots, we prefer the system described in the *Shatchakra Nirupana* (widely available in English as Arthur Avalon's *The Serpent Power*).

The symbol for Muladhara Chakra is a yellow or golden cube. Naturally, in a two-dimensional representation, that cube becomes a square. If you concentrate on a big yellow square, the symbol of the earth element, you can transform it into three dimensions—a cube—in the inner world of imagination. This practice of concentration helps you get in contact with solidarity, cohesiveness, or "getting it together," which are qualities of earth. This inner symbolic association is used for the purpose of inner and outer transformation. It is accomplished through the classical Tantric practice of *trataka*, literally "to look without blinking"—fixing the gaze on the object of contemplation (in this case the yantra), maintaining the gaze until an afterimage forms, and then meditating on the afterimage.

The system Swamiji developed in collaboration with Carl Llewellyn Weschcke, who designed the original graphics, included a center dot of white or black in the yantra. When performing trataka on the yantra, you fix your eyes on that point. It is called a *bindu*, a fixation point. This addition was the first original breakthrough in fifty years in Western occultism or Eastern occultism. While many classical yantras include a bindu at the center, these have symbolic meaning—the bindu represents the starting point of all existence—and are not designed to facilitate the formation of an afterimage.

Prior to Gnosticon, it was common practice to use a yellow geometric figure for trataka on Muladhara Chakra. Gazing on the figure, using the method we have just described, produced an afterimage in the complementary color, blue. This was true for all of the yantras: you always ended up with the opposite color when you stared at the diagram, closed your eyes, and tried to meditate on the afterimage. No one had conceived, literally yantrically, of using the complementary colors.

In the early 1970s, Swamiji and Carl Llewellyn Weschcke had a breakthrough, thanks to Swamiji's knowledge of physiology. The concept was Swamiji's, and the production was Carl's. Instead of a yellow yantra, they used a blue yantra. The design took over a year to develop and refine; they began by working with slides and then reduced the complementary-color yantras to a set of cards.[2] (The original cards are re-produced in this book as the color plates following page 26 so that you can do the exercises as originally designed. An improved formulation is available in *A Chakra & Kundalini Workbook,* which also includes additional information about the prac-tice of trataka, particularly on pages 110–111.) To the best of our knowledge, this method of working with the yantras is totally original. Since Gnosticon, other West-ern schools have borrowed it.

There are many ways to use this symbol system; some of the classical methods are described in *A Chakra & Kundalini Workbook.* As a general rule, classical meth-ods work upward from Muladhara Chakra, and we encourage you to begin this way, spending at least one day on each chakra. Once you have mastered this approach, you can also use the system to work on yourself for certain personality characteris-tics as your own circumstances demand. The basic technique is the same for each chakra, and it will provide you with a simple means for implanting the characteris-tics of the appropriate chakra in your consciousness.

For example, you can start with the symbol for Muladhara Chakra, represented on the card by a blue square. Gaze at the image for a minimum of thirty seconds, keeping your focus on the dot, or bindu, at the center, until the image is burned onto the back of your eyeballs and you see a white aura around the yantra. Close your eyes, and you will see the afterimage as a yellow square. Again, it symbolizes solidarity or cohesiveness. So, if you want to inject these qualities into your con-sciousness, you can concentrate on Muladhara Chakra in this way. It will help you connect with the earth element.

Swadhisthana Chakra is located between the hipbones. The yantra is a silver crescent; its element is water, and in Tantra the qualities of water are seen as femi-nine. Working with it can help develop adaptability and fluidity—think of the way water adapts to a container.

If you want to build your passion and power, you can work with Manipura (solar plexus) Yantra, a downward-pointing red triangle, and learn to play with psy-chic fire. You may have heard that Yogis do miracles. Actually, there are no miracles at all; it is all psychophysiology, breaking down mental barriers, causing changes to

---

2 To replicate the experience of working with the original cards, which were considerably larger than these plates, you can make enlarged color copies, preferably on photo-quality paper.

occur in conformity with the will, whether those changes are external or internal. That is genuine magic, and Manipura Chakra is frequently the source of that power.

From passion comes compassion. Tantrikas believe that if you are dead below the navel, you will never be alive. Some people have the misguided belief that you should just concentrate on the upper three chakras. They think that being "spiritual" requires disconnecting from and denying the realm of the physical. But we are born with physical bodies, and it is foolhardy to deny it. The way to activate the upper chakras is to make sure the lower ones are fully energized and use the heart as a gateway to the divine. If you want to feel loving and compassionate, concentrate on Anahata Yantra, a blue hexagram; the heart center has air as its element, and it is the balance point between the physical and spiritual realms.

Focusing on the diagram for Vishuddhi (throat) Chakra, a deep violet oval or Shiva Lingam, moves you into a more refined state. Its element is ether or space. Accordingly, we are moving beyond the physical and into a more abstract and spiritual dimension. Traditionally in the East, concentration on Vishuddhi Chakra makes one extremely receptive.

Once we reach the sixth and seventh chakras, we have left the realm of the physical elements entirely. The technique described above is designed to assist you in embodying the characteristics of these physical chakras. It does not apply to working with Ajna (third eye) and Sahasrara (crown) Chakras; techniques for working with these chakras are more advanced and are best undertaken systematically. Swamiji describes several methods for working with the upper chakras in *A Chakra & Kundalini Workbook*.

Returning to the practice of trataka and the physiology that makes Swamiji's method work, there is a chemical called rhodopsin, or visual purple, in the back of the eyeball. If you fix your gaze at something for an extended period and inhibit the blink reflex, you fatigue the eye. This fatigue causes pigmental burnout in the cones and changes the chemistry so that you start to see the afterimage in the opposite color.

It is very helpful to be in a relaxed state when working with the yantras. Swamiji was probably the first Westerner—and perhaps the first person—to identify relaxation as a variable that enhances the length of time you will retain the afterimage. The more you relax, mentally and emotionally, the longer the afterimage will persist.

While this seems self-evident today, this fact had not previously been recognized by cognitive and visual psychologists.

To reiterate, the yantra diagrams are designed for use at home, and they will begin to generate the effect after approximately thirty seconds of trataka. This is all the time that is needed to induce the eyes to release the necessary chemicals. Focusing on the bindu point accelerates and intensifies the pigmental burnout and produces a more distinct afterimage. You can usually recognize that the afterimage has begun to form when you see a white aura around the bindu and yantra. This is the signal to close your eyes.

To delve into the yantras more deeply, it is important to understand their tattwic dimension. The Sanskrit word *tat* is the root of the English *that*, implying "that which is." *Tattwa* is derived from *tat* and literally means "quality or element." The yantras are tattwic yantras, meaning they are diagrams that express the conception of the element that is the quality of the chakra. This expression resides in both the color and the shape.

Some modern approaches to working with the chakras have treated them in psychological terms, for example, linking Muladhara Chakra with "survival issues." Swamiji's method is very different. He is suggesting that the yantras are a kind of template and that by internalizing the tattwic yantras, you are also internalizing their tattwic qualities. At the same time, you are awakening these qualities, which are part of your makeup as a human being. This process enhances your ability to embody the particular tattwic aspects on which you are working. Unlike the psychotherapeutic model, which attempts to address perceived deficiencies or to make diagnoses based on the chakra system, we are describing a conscious effort to strengthen yourself by connecting more fully with characteristics and elemental energies that already exist within you.

As you practice trataka on any tattwic yantra, one of two things will happen. Some people find that after trataka, they can lean forward and palm the eyelids, without pressing on the eyeball, and an afterimage will appear inside the head—in what is called *chidakasha* in Sanskrit, the visual field behind the frontal bone, or the mental screen behind the eyes. If you find the image floating there, just allow your mind to enjoy it. This is the simplest way to implant the image—and thereby the tattwa—in your consciousness, and the only effort involved is trataka and watching the afterimage.

Other people find that when they palm after focusing on these diagrams, they don't see the afterimage, and chidakasha is completely black. In that case, keep your eyes closed but take your hands away so that some light filters in through the closed eyelids. Ninety percent of the time, the afterimage will emerge for you.

The basic palming method works as follows: While you are practicing trataka, start rubbing your hands together to generate some heat. The sensation of heat encourages the mind to relax. Then close your eyes, see the image flash, and place your palms over your closed eyes. When you palm, lean forward gently. It is important to remain comfortable. If the afterimage does not appear, take your hands away so that the light filtering through can produce the pattern. When the image begins to fade, you may find that if you blink your eyes, it will return for a split second with every blink. (For a more detailed discussion of the tattwas and the palming technique, see Swamiji's *Magical Tattwa Cards*.)

So, there are four levels on which to experiment. The first level is to see if you can produce an afterimage with the eyes palmed, in total blackness. Experiment two is to take the hands away and produce the image with the light filtering through the closed eyelids. Experiment three is to notice when the image fades and see if you can bring it back by blinking. This is the simplest way to internalize the tattwic images, and it is very important for directly experiencing and integrating the chakras into your own system.

The next level, experiment four, is to keep your eyes open and see if you can project the tattwic image into someone else, sharing the qualities with a partner. Just face your partner, try to implant the image, and observe what you experience. You can do this simultaneously or take turns; it can be a very useful technique for couples in the context of Vama Marga practice.

There are a number of other techniques you can explore if you want to start working at a more advanced level. One approach is simply to do trataka on the yantra, watch the afterimage, and try to hold it for as long as possible. Once it fades, try to recreate it on the inner plane of imagination. Another method is to visualize the yellow square in chidakasha, and as you watch the yellow square, simultaneously take it down to the physical location of Muladhara Chakra, which is halfway between the anus and the genitals, and then transform it into a three-dimensional gold cube.

Once you can do this, you have managed to split the mind in two ways. You see the yellow square in chidakasha, but by a magical act of creation you also see a yellow cube in Muladhara Chakra. This process activates the chakra and constitutes the conscious linking of the tattwic yantra with the physical location of the chakra. You can employ the same technique in working with each of the chakras.

Next, you can practice with your eyes open, much as you would if you were working with a partner. As you visualize the diagram floating in front of you, you simultaneously internalize it and recreate it in three dimensions inside the appropriate part of the body. Many spiritual systems emphasize practices that require closing the eyes. Working with the eyes open is characteristic of Tantric Kriya Yoga, and developing the capacity to enter altered states without retreating entirely from the external world can lead to some extraordinary experiences.

We have provided you with a few basic methods for working with the tattwic diagrams. In his more recent work, Swamiji has elaborated on and refined these basic techniques, but even today this method of working with the chakras is the foundation of much of his teaching. The people who attended Gnosticon had the privilege of learning the technique from Swamiji when he first made it public. They directly experienced the first original innovation made in the field in fifty years.

three

Kriya Yoga and Tantra: Energy and Consciousness

In Tantra and Yoga, we generally direct the flow of energy upward through the body, and this upward movement of energy is deeply connected with the concept of the tattwas and with an inner, alchemical process of purification. In Hatha Yoga, purification is generally accomplished by working from the outside in, through a rigorous practice of physical discipline. Tantric methods tend to be more direct and internal, and this is part of the reason many of them have been kept secret; this holds true for both Vama Marga and Dakshina Marga techniques.

Many people think the term *mudra* refers only to hand gestures, but *mudra* actually has a broader definition. Most simply, *mudra* means "a gesture (using any part of the body) that creates a psychophysical change." In the first part of the Gnosticon lecture this chapter is based on, Swamiji focused on hand mudras, specifically on a set of hand mudras, or *Tattwa Mudras*, taught by Dr. Swami Gitananda Giri Guru Maharaj.

Hand mudras are used in many Hindu and Buddhist rituals and often have a profound spiritual and psychic significance. Other mudras are employed by Yogis, not only for symbolic and mystical purposes, but also to regulate the flow of *prana*, or vital energy. This vital energy is most directly experienced through working with the breath, and few people know that mudras can be employed to modify the flow of the breath.

These *Hasta Mudras* or Tattwa Mudras, as taught by Dr. Swami Gitananda Giri Guru Maharaj, are a simple yet profound way of using the hands consciously to direct the breath and thus the flow of energy in the body. Altering the flow of energy can also alter mood, so one way to deepen your understanding of mudra—in its broadest conceptual sense—is to associate it mentally with the English word *mood*.

Simple hand gestures can alter the flow of breath because the position of the hands tends to affect the pelvic girdle and shoulder girdle; this short-circuits the nervous system so that the breath flows spontaneously to different locations. As most practitioners of Yoga are aware, there are three basic types of breathing: lower breathing, which includes diaphragmatic breathing and abdominal breathing; mid-breathing or ribcage breathing, which relies on the intercostal muscles; and upper breathing, which is centered around the clavicle or collar bone. The "complete breath" includes all three of these breaths in one, from the bottom up. Most practitioners of Yoga, however, are not aware that the use of mudras makes it possible to regulate breathing almost effortlessly. At Swamiji's request and out of respect for Gitanandaji, who was unwilling to make this information available to the general public, we will not describe the Hasta Mudras in this chapter. Swamiji teaches the Hasta Mudras to advanced students in our online OM-Kara Kriya® course.

Swamiji's Gnosticon lecture on mudras and Kriya Yoga was important because it was one of the first instances in which Kriya Yoga practices were described to Western seekers in the context of a discussion of Vama Marga Tantra. Paramahansa Satyananda was the first master of Kriya Yoga to write extensively and in depth about Tantric sexuality in English. Two of his Western disciples, Swami Janakananda and Swamiji, elaborated on Satyananda's groundbreaking work, beginning in the 1970s, and the information they shared had a profound, and often unacknowledged, influence on many Western Neo-Tantric teachers and practitioners of sacred sexuality. Kriya, however, is not very well understood, and we felt that it would be valuable to include a more comprehensive discussion of Kriya based on Swamiji's more recent writings, as a preface to what he taught at Gnosticon.[1]

---

1 This section is based on articles by Swamiji that first appeared on the Yoga Magik website, www.yogamagik .com (no longer available online), and on a more recent article expanding on the Yoga Magik material: Swami Anandakapila Saraswati (Dr. Jonn Mumford), "Kriya Yoga: Internal Alchemy for the Soul," *JOY: Journal of Yoga* 3, no. 6 (2004), http://subscriber.journalofyoga.org/kriya.htm (subscription required). The Yoga Magik material is included by permission of the Kailash Center for Personal Development, Inc.

The word *Kriya* implies an active, direct approach to controlling physical and psychic energies—rousing into full manifestation that spiritual and bioenergetic force normally latent in the temple-tomb of the physical being. Swamiji coined the acronym CREA to describe the practice of Kriya Yoga and its results. Kriya Yoga is a system of C-reative R-elaxation and E-nergy A-ctualization.

The shortest Sanskrit definition of *Kriya Yoga* is "activity," and, therefore, Kriya Yoga implies a direct and active method for piercing the veil of *Maya* (illusion) in contradistinction to other, more passive meditation approaches. Kriya also implies doing, performing, effecting, action, and rite. "The Sanskrit root *Kr* means to do, act, see to, conduct (affairs), make, cause, contrive. Hence, a broader definition suggests that Kriya means movement, motion, agitation—one of the three characteristics of *drsya* (profound concentration producing a deep state of introspection), the other two being *parkas* (clarity, consciousness) and *sthiti* (preventing fluctuation of consciousness)—the functions of *sattva* (purity) and *tamas* (inertia) *gunas* (qualities) respectively."[2]

Kriya has become very popular with Westerners, largely due to the influence of Paramahansa Yogananda and his disciples, both in the Self-Realization Fellowship and independent of that organization; the dynamic interplay of breath, posture, and mental visualizations that characterize Kriya practices offer sufficient variety to engage our mental processes. This approach is very well suited to the intense activity and overwhelming stimulation that we experience in the modern world.

The methods of Kundalini Kriya Yoga are quite magical. While there are many different Kriya systems indigenous to India, we are aware of only three lineages that have gained any currency in the West; Swamiji has been initiated into two of these three traditions. But before we discuss the different forms of Kriya Yoga, it is important to explain that the term *Kriya* has a different but related definition within the more familiar context of Hatha Yoga.

The term *Kriya* is in fact an integral part of authentic Hatha Yoga, as opposed to the watered-down forms that are popularly taught in gyms and health clubs throughout the Western world. In this context, Kriya is specifically attached to very vigorous internal cleansing procedures, which are known as the *Shat Kriyas*, literally "six actions," also called *Ghatastha Yoga*. The word *Ghatastha* carries the implication

---

2 Swami Digambarji and Dr. Mahajot Sahai, *Yoga Kosa*, vol. 1 (Poona: Kaivalyadhama S.M.Y.M. Samiti Lonavla, dist. 1972), 46.

of a cooking pot, suggesting that just as cooking utensils must be scoured after use, so the human body must be strongly internally scoured.

These practices are remarkable; some are quite difficult and should not be attempted except under the direct supervision of a qualified teacher. Swamiji studied them intensively in the early 1960s under the renowned Shri Yogendra at the Bombay Yoga Institute. The Shat Kriyas systematically purify the body of *mala*, or toxins, from top to bottom. This aspect of Hatha Yoga is an example of the breathtaking anatomical and physiological knowledge possessed by the ancient Indians—a knowledge that almost defies imagination in light of the limited technology they had at their disposal.

The Shat Kriyas are:

1. *Trataka* (to gaze): A special method of cleansing the naso-lachrymal ducts and the anterior coat of the eyeballs utilizing the natural antibiotic properties of tears, which are triggered through special eye-fixation techniques.

2. *Kapalabhati* (skull glowing): A powerful pranayama series that purifies the upper and lower respiratory tract.

3. *Vamandhouti* (vomiting): A variety of stomach washes purifying the mucosal stomach lining and stimulating the liver and gall bladder.

4. *Neti* (probe or thread): A prescribed series of nasal douches and probes of the nasal passages with thread, primarily intended to stimulate the central nervous system and the autonomic nervous system.

5. *Nauli* (abdominal muscle): The voluntary isolation of the rectus abdominis muscles, producing powerful, negative suction in the large intestine and bladder, designed to activate the colon and small intestines, and a prerequisite to the actual liquid rinse of the bowel and bladder by aspiration.

6. *Basti* or *Vasti* (bladder): A douching of the bowel with water and medicated solutions by creating a semivacuum in the large intestine and sucking fluid through the rectum with the aid of a bamboo tube.

Basti is an excellent example of the advanced level reached by Indian experimental physiology when compared to the West. The technique was well known in India long before Boyle formulated his theories on gas pressure in the seventeenth cen-

Swamiji demonstrating Yugala Neti at Gnosticon, 1976

Yugala Neti is an advanced form of Sutra Neti in which a knotted cord is used to stimulate a psychic-neural center in the nasopharynx that includes the sphenopalatine ganglion and the upper cervical ganglion. This technique, which is virtually unknown in the West and is potentially dangerous, should not be attempted without personal supervision from a teacher who has mastered it. Photo courtesy of Kailash Center for Personal Development, Inc.

tury. It involves gaining control over the anal sphincters while performing Nauli, with the result that water may be aspirated up into the rectum and colon. This is often done by inserting a tube or reed into the anus while squatting over a pot of water. The negative suction created can be quite powerful. Again, this potential was unknown to Western physiology. A variation of the technique can be used to aspirate liquids of varying density into the bladder (see *Ecstasy Through Tantra*, pages 20–26).

This is an extremely brief overview of a highly evolved system that utilizes physiological principles unknown in the West for hundreds of years. Different traditions arrange the six practices in different categories and sequences. Some traditions list Neti under Kapalabhati, but the essential elements are the same. Ayurvedic medicine has equivalent practices administered to patients, called *Panchakarma*, or "five cleansing actions." The Shat Kriyas have their place in Tantric practice and are important in their own right, but they are not Kriya Yoga per se. Armed with this understanding, we can proceed to an examination of the spiritual implications of meditation practices that belong to the Kriya Yoga tradition.

Kriya Yoga appears to have first emerged in the West through the teachings of Yogananda, transmitted from Babaji's lineage through Lahiri Mahasay to Shri Yuktewswar and others. A number of teachers now teach versions of these methods, which can involve up to 144 techniques. Lahiri Mahasay was from Calcutta; Bengal has long been a hotbed of both Kriya Yoga and Tantra. These two traditions are very closely related, and while some strict Kriya Yogis might disagree, we would suggest that traditional Kriya Yoga is, at its core, a form of Dakshina Marga Tantra.

Although they also originated in Bengal, the unique Kriya techniques Swamiji currently teaches are only distantly related to the lineage of Shri Babaji and the various branches of that lineage that have become popular in the West. Through a lifetime of study and practice, Swamiji has developed an approach to Kriya Yoga, including OM-Kara Kriya®, that derives from the rich heritage of the late Yogamaharishi Dr. Swami Gitananda Giri Guru Maharaj (Tamil Nadu, South India) and Paramahansaji Swami Satyananda Saraswati, founder of the Bihar School of Yoga (North-East India).[3] While all systems of Kriya Yoga have similar cultural and theoretical underpinnings, each system is distinct.

In the 1950s, Dr. Swami Gitananda Giri Guru Maharaj initiated Swamiji into a series of Kriyas that are the basis for the OM-Kara Kriya® system. Under personal direction, these are safe and sure magical routes to interior consciousness and the experience of U3 (Ultimate Universal Unity) states. They do not require a mastery of Hatha Yoga and are not physically difficult.

In later years, Gitanandaji stopped teaching this system but released another set of Kriya techniques involving very vigorous Hatha Yoga postures to pump the *ojas* (psychic energy) up the spine. These are known as *Oli Mudras* (*Shakti Mudras*), and they can only be taught personally to students with a solid grounding in Hatha Yoga.

Swamiji mastered several variations of the first of these Oli Mudras. The entire set is still taught to advanced students at Ananda Ashram in Pondicherry, South India, and is a component of the Gitananda Yoga system that is taught worldwide. In contrast to the earlier system from which OM-Kara Kriya® is derived, the Oli Mudras are dynamic and highly physical.

Swamiji also studied Kriya Yoga with Paramahansaji Swami Satyananda Saraswati at the Bihar School of Yoga in 1973, the year he was initiated into the Saraswati Order. Satyananda's techniques, which are not Bengali in origin, are marvelous, unique, and unrelated to the other systems described above. In his younger days,

---

3 Dr. Swami Gitananda Giri Guru Maharaj's Guru, Srilla Sri Swami Kanakananda Giri Brighu, was famous in Bengal as "the Sleepless Saint." Yogananda described an encounter with him in chapter 13 of *Autobiography of a Yogi*. While Kanakananda was, for a time, a disciple of Lahiri Mahasay, he had a vast body of Tantric knowledge and was also initiated into other systems. The Kriyas that Swamiji teaches are not the ones taught by the Self-Realization Fellowship or other groups in the Lahiri/Babaji line.

Swamiji demonstrating Shirshasana

A young Swamiji performing a preliminary Shirshasana with a Padmasana lock (1970s). This is a variation of Sahajoli Mudra called Urdhva Padma Asana or Urdhva Ekakin-Shirsh Asana. Photo courtesy of Kailash Center for Personal Development, Inc.

Swamiji demonstrating Sahajoli Mudra

Sahajoli Mudra, part 1: Using the Manduka Mudra (frog posture) to exert tremendous pressure, moving the Shakti towards the head (1970s). Photo courtesy of Kailash Center for Personal Development, Inc.

Swamiji taught them in Australia and the United States (including at Gnosticon). The technique described in this chapter is based on Satyananda's system, and it is quite powerful in its own right.

Consciousness is a form of energy, and one aim of Kriya Yoga is to induce certain states of consciousness, including trance. The first step toward achieving trance consciousness occurs when the brain produces alpha and theta waves. This results in a sense of deep relaxation, and the relaxation precedes and creates the conditions for the emergence of trance consciousness.

There are two main methods of relaxing: passive and active. In the passive method, you rotate the consciousness through the body and cultivate a feeling of heaviness in your fingers, your arms, your legs, and so on. This is basically the model used in Yoga Nidra. (Yoga Nidra is discussed in depth in *A Chakra & Kundalini Workbook*, pages 173–186.)

The active method involves tension and release. This method is probably more familiar; it is widely used in Hatha Yoga classes and is known as *fractional relaxation* in Western psychotherapy. In the active method, you are guided to make a fist, tighten it, extend the tension up the arm, lift the arm, and let it go. As with passive relaxation, the active approach includes the entire body (see *A Chakra & Kundalini Workbook*, pages 15–23). Swamiji's *Mind Magic Kit* includes a guided fractional relaxation tape and discusses the technique in even greater detail.

There is a tendency among therapists and Yoga teachers to rely on only one system of relaxation. Everyone is unique, and neither system is universally effective. If you tell people, "Your arm is getting heavy," a certain percentage will be just obstinate enough to say, "Like hell. It is getting light. She doesn't know what she's talking about." Other people, when told to ball up their fists and then release, find it impossible to let go completely, and the inability to do so may produce even more tension. Because of this, anyone teaching relaxation should have some familiarity with both systems, and on an individual level, it is very important to discover which technique works best for you. This may vary depending on circumstances, and with experience you will be able to sense which method is better for you at any given time.

Relaxation is immensely important and valuable in its own right. In addition, it is a precondition for gaining access to trance consciousness (*trance* implies transcendence). When you enter trance consciousness, your body begins to produce nectar.

Examine the word *trance* and you will find that it is an anagram for *nectar*. Something happens to the biochemistry of the brain when it produces alpha and theta waves, and this change in brain chemistry is the very core of Kriya, or Creative Relaxation and Energy Actualization (CREA) in Western, scientific terms.

On a more esoteric level, the practice of Kriya Yoga involves building a Jacob's ladder to heaven or the divine *lokas* (planes). The passageway is within us, and only we can open it. The door handle is on the inside. Kriya utilizes a process of internal alchemy to cleanse and then reopen the secret (latent) tunnels between the pelvic and cranial cavities. When this connection is established, Shakti, or cosmic fire, wells up in the now unblocked channels to flood the brain with spiritual distillations. This is the essential aim of all Tantric practice.

One very simple Kriya with which you can start comes from the lineage of Swami Satyananda and the Bihar School of Yoga.[4] This practice employs two energy flows: *Arohan* (upward) and *Awarohan* (downward). For the upward flow, inhale from Muladhara Chakra up to the throat and then to the bindu point at the back of the head, slightly above the third eye. That is ascending. For the downward flow, Awarohan, the breath goes through the skull to the third eye (pineal gland) and then down the inside of the spine.

There are a number of accessories in this practice that intensify it. One of the accessories is *Shambavi Mudra*. Legend has it that Lord Shiva taught this technique to his spouse Parvati. The basic technique is simple: look ahead; look up; look in. In other words, show the whites of your eyes. Shambavi Mudra happens spontaneously during orgasm, and the capacity to show the whites of your eyes in this way is one of the basic tests for assessing hypnotizability. You may find it difficult and uncomfortable at first, but you will improve with practice.

More importantly, for our purposes, when you turn the eyes up and in and hold them there, you stretch the lateral muscles of the eyes, and this produces bursts of alpha waves in the brain. Once you learn to hold it for an extended period, Shambavi Mudra alone can induce trance consciousness.

---

4 Paul Skye (Swami Ajnananda Saraswati) astutely observed that this Kriya is actually a synthesis of Pawan Sanchalana Kriya (conducting the breath consciousness) and the related Nada Sanchalana Kriya (conducting the sonic consciousness). Swami Ajnananda went on to point out that "these things grow and develop through the articulation and experimentation of the best teachers of a lineage," a point too often forgotten by people seeking pure, unadulterated "ancient" teachings.

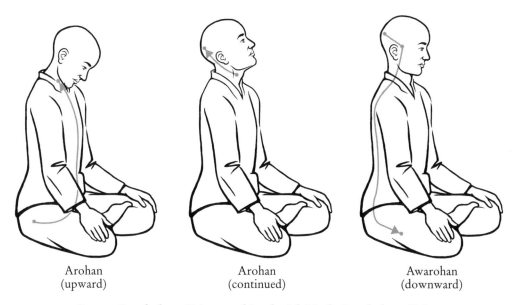

Arohan
(upward)

Arohan
(continued)

Awarohan
(downward)

Pawan Sanchalana Kriya combined with Nada Sanchalana Kriya

Shambavi Mudra

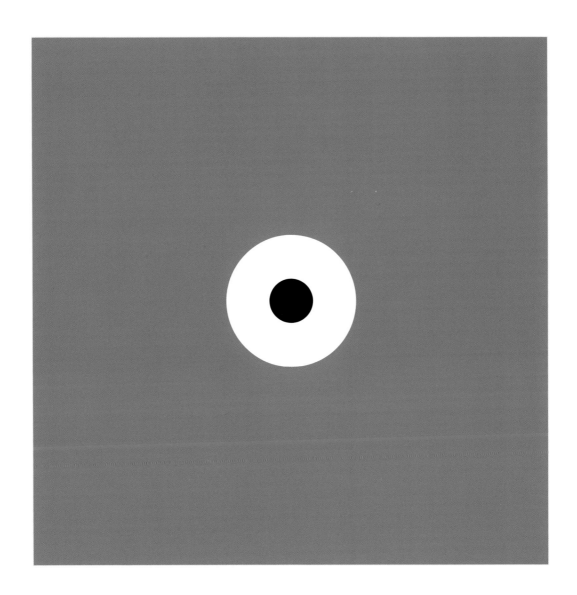

Original Gnosticon Tattwa Yantra Card: Muladhara

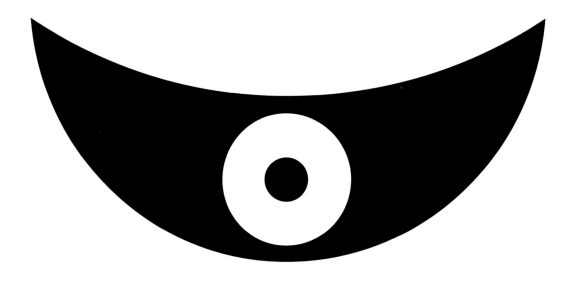

Original Gnosticon Tattwa Yantra Card: Swadhisthana

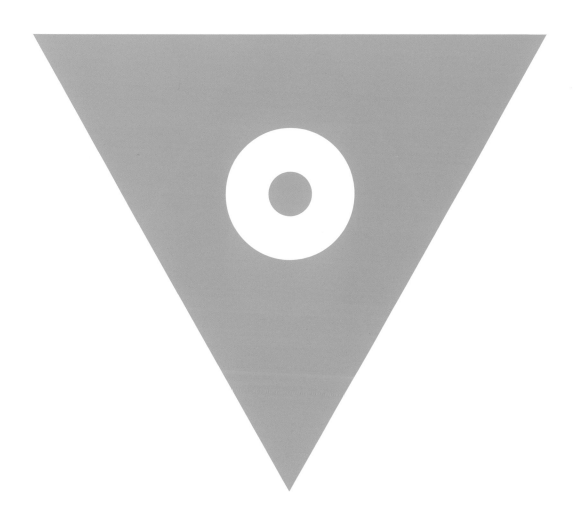

Original Gnosticon Tattwa Yantra Card: Manipura

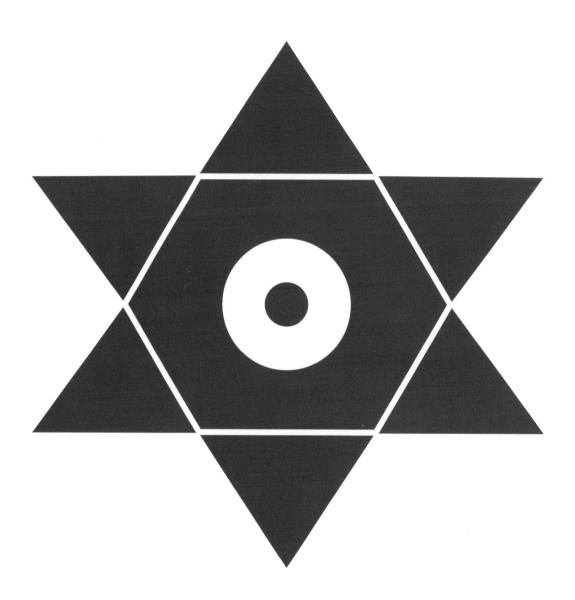

Original Gnosticon Tattwa Yantra Card: Anahata

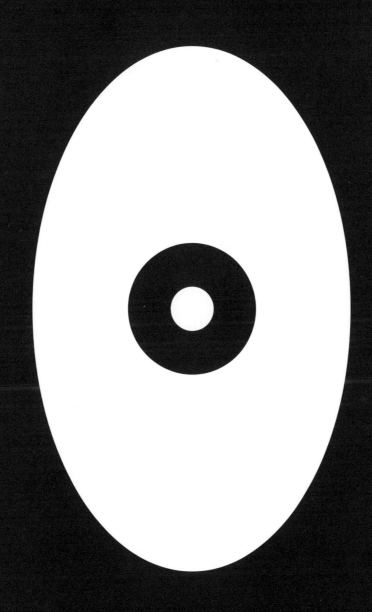

Original Gnosticon Tattwa Yantra Card: Vishuddhi

Tantrics have never been very particular about the means of inducing trance consciousness. Consider the *Nagas*, a particular Tantric sect. When *Naga Saddhus* (holy men) do their initial work, they smoke *bhang* (marijuana) very heavily, and they do their meditations under its influence. Many people are unaware that psychedelic drugs are quite traditional in the East. This has been well documented, for example in Agehananda Bharati's authoritative book *The Tantric Tradition*. But people are very moralistic, and many will deny it. If you go to India and you go along the banks of the Ganges, you will see hordes of these Saddhus smoking bhang, even though it is technically illegal in India just as it is in most of the Western world. If they like you, they will let you sit with them, and they will pass the pipe to you. This is a very special system and method for producing altered states of consciousness, but here we are concerned with creating altered states of consciousness using your own mind and body, without external supports.

Interestingly enough, the Naga Saddhus also call bhang *vijaya*, which means, roughly, "victorious"—the victorious smoke. The next accessory in our Kriya practice is the similarly named *Ujjaya Pranayama*, "the victorious breath." To perform Ujjaya Pranayama, you inhale through the nose, making a subtle sobbing sound. The best way to approach it is to think of imitating the sound of a snore, but with slightly less tension so that the sound is quite soft.

The third element is called *Akasha Mudra*. To perform Akasha Mudra, tilt the head back a little and inhale using Ujjaya Pranayama; this is all solid psychophysiology. There are receptors in the carotid artery known as baroreceptors. When you stretch your neck by tilting your head back and make a sobbing sound, you are affecting the baroreceptors. This drops the blood pressure and alters the consciousness. It is a very good thing to be able to alter your consciousness without any artificial assistance, the Saddhus notwithstanding.

The trick is to put these three elements together. It isn't easy, and if you are confused, don't worry about it. Confusion is a fact of life, and more importantly, confusion precedes fusion. You will get the hang of it with practice.

So breathe in, and as you breathe in, imagine you are sucking white energy up through your body to the throat. Once you have taken this energy up to the throat, tilt your head back into Akasha Mudra and add Shambavi Mudra—turn the eyes up and in. Take the breath up to bindu, using Ujjaya Pranayama, while repeating mentally, "Bindu, bindu, bindu." That is the point at the back of the skull, just above the

Akasha Mudra

third eye. As you start to exhale, imagine the white energy cascading down the spine and release Shambavi Mudra. At the same time, chant "OM" audibly. The white energy should flow down your spine, accompanied by the audible "OM" vibration. With a little practice, you will be able to send a shiver right down your back.

While both Pawan Sanchalana Kriya and Nada Sanchalana Kriya are Dakshina Marga practices, this technique can be employed in a Vama Marga context as well.

It is important to find a comfortable position. Do not hesitate to use a chair (placing a support under your feet) or sit with your back up against a wall. Westerners who have not trained extensively in Hatha Yoga often have difficulty sitting unsupported, and the most important thing is to find a comfortable way to keep your spine straight.

Here is the complete Kriya: Tilt your head down. Keep your eyes open and look vacantly at a spot about eighteen inches in front of you. Visualize a yellow cube between the anus and genitals and repeat "Muladhara" mentally. Now breathe in with Ujjaya Pranayama and suck the white energy up. Tilt the head back into Akasha Mudra. Turn the eyes up into Shambavi Mudra. Take a sniff of air, swallow (*Aprakasha Mudra*), and hold the breath while repeating "bindu" mentally. Move the energy from bindu to Ajna Chakra (third eye/pineal gland) and ejaculate the breath down the spine; let the white energy cascade down while chanting "OM." In the early stages, hold Shambavi Mudra as you chant "OM." This will accelerate the process of going into a trance state. Be sure to release it and lower your head when the energy reaches the throat.

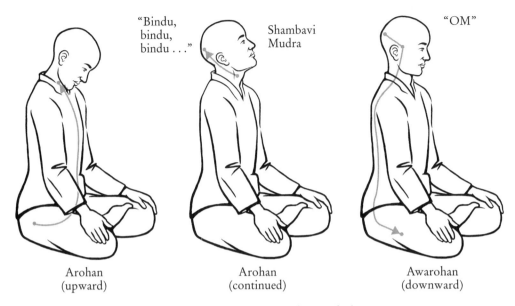

"Bindu, bindu, bindu . . ."   Shambavi Mudra   "OM"

Arohan   Arohan   Awarohan
(upward)   (continued)   (downward)

Complete Pawan Sanchalana/Nada Sanchalana Kriya

Upon completion, be sure your head is tilted down again and stare softly into space, eighteen inches in front of you. Breathe normally, and feel the mind empty for a few seconds. As you continue to gaze, close your eyes. Repeat this Kriya thirteen times. This is not easy. It will require study, practice, and determination to be able to complete thirteen rounds, but once you can, you may experience the essence of Yoga, the cessation of the fluctuations of the mindstuff.

Mastering Kriya takes extensive study and practice, but learning one simple technique can have a profound impact. The practice described here is but one of many ways of moving energy through the physical system. While it is relatively simple and can be done by a novice, it can be very powerful in its effects and psychic implications. Kriya techniques are traditionally passed from Guru to disciple, mouth to ear, in the context of a formal process of initiation, and written descriptions are usually modified so that the information does not go beyond the circle of initiates. Swamiji has kindly permitted us to include this Kriya just as he taught it at Gnosticon. While there can be no substitute for direct initiation, you can rest assured that the technique is complete and authentic, and if you practice it diligently, you are likely to have many interesting experiences.

four

Vama Marga Tantra

Tantra is a tactile path, whether it is Dakshina Marga, the right-hand path, or Vama Marga, the left-hand path. Either way, Tantra uses touch as the primary sensory avenue for the focusing of the mind. In the case of Vama Marga, we are dealing with the most exquisite and potent tactile sensation that the human being is capable of experiencing, and that is the sexual sensation. And when that sexual sensation expresses itself in orgasm, the bursting or climax, we achieve a state of Yoga, or union.

In the original Greek, *climax* refers to a staircase, a ladder to heaven. Heaven is a state of mind, and this universal esoteric truth exists across religions and cultures: "the kingdom of heaven lies within you" (Luke 17:21). The challenge lies in discovering how to have a direct experience of that state of mind, which can also be understood as a state of Yoga, or union, with the divine.

In the orgasmic state, Yoga happens naturally, automatically. In the *Yoga Sutras*, his famous, seminal text, Patanjali defined Yoga as "the cessation of the fluctuations of the mindstuff," and the fluctuations of the mind cease when orgasm occurs. That was a profound understanding of the ancient Tantrics. The Tantrics also understood, however, that the orgasmic moment itself was not the goal and that the process of climbing the ladder is perhaps even more important. In English usage, the original meaning of the word *climax* has been obscured, and we have tended to associate the word with a given moment, event, or brief period of time rather than with a process.

Western sexology can provide some valuable insights into that process. Masters and Johnson posited that the sexual response cycle has four phases: excitement, plateau, orgasmic peaking, and then resolution. The Tantric view is more nuanced, but it is important to have a basic understanding of the cycle as it is commonly understood in the West.[1]

The excitement phase manifests itself with erection in the male and lubrication in the female. This can occur quite rapidly in males but is often a more gradual process in females. Both erection and lubrication are caused by vasocongestion, a rush of blood to given areas—the genitals and breasts in both men and women. Thirty seconds into the excitement phase, both males and females can experience myotonia, which is muscle contraction. This is not conscious muscle contraction, but rather the beginning of a contracted muscular state.

The excitement phase can be initiated by *yantra-mandala* (erotic sight, vision, or image). It can be brought on by fantasy—pictures in the mind, imagination—or by direct stimulation of the erogenous zones, genitals, or spinal cord. In women, the mechanisms that bring about arousal are somewhat more varied than in men, probably due in part to cultural factors—some of which may have an inhibiting influence—but also due to biology. In many women, arousal can be produced by stimulation of the breasts; it can be produced by direct genital stimulation, although frequently only after stimulation of other erogenous zones. As with men, it can also be induced by yantra-mandala, or erotic fantasy. There is some evidence to suggest that women are less responsive to visual stimuli than men; however, recent research indicates that this difference results from societal factors, and some women may deny experiencing arousal in response to visual images even when physiological evidence of arousal exists.

Lubrication represents something very special, the inner essence of both Eastern and Western alchemical traditions. It is the first stage in the distillation of the true elixir of life, generated by a process of transudation (see chapter 15, "The Tantric Mass and the Secret of Amrita"). It is not formed by the uterus; women who have

---

1 In the years since Gnosticon, Western sexologists have developed a number of alternative models, some of which add desire as the first stage, and some of which attempt to fuse Eastern and Western views of sexuality. Rather than elaborate on these models, we have opted to retain Swamiji's original analysis. The Masters and Johnson model is still familiar in the popular imagination and remains useful both for the purposes of contrast and because the more recent Western efforts to understand the sexual response cycle represent, to a significant extent, elaborations on or responses to Masters and Johnson.

had a panhysterectomy (a total removal of the ovaries and uterus) can still produce copious vaginal lubrication and can also ejaculate. It is not produced by the Bartholin's glands; they produce only a few drops of fluid, but that is all.

During the plateau phase, there is an increase in the diameter of the glans (the head of the penis in the male) and a particular kind of secretion from the Cowper's glands (the male homologue of the Bartholin's glands). In both male and female, a sex flush begins to occur.

From the Tantric perspective, the classical texts mention two characteristics in describing the Kundalini experience: shaking, which is an expression of *Shakti* (energy), and heat. When you hear "shaking" in English, just think "Shakti." As for heat, the *Shatchakra Nirupana*, the classical Tantric text (rendered in English as *The Serpent Power* by Arthur Avalon), describes the production of heat that moves up the body from Muladhara Chakra at the base of the spine to Sahasrara Chakra at the crown.

When you consider these elements—the production of heat and shaking—the whole sexual response cycle is a paradigm of the Kundalini experience. We can state unequivocally that, in everyone who experiences orgasm, Kundalini is aroused and the chakras are open; similarly, the chakras are open and Kundalini is aroused in anyone who experiences a prolonged period of sexual excitement. It is a matter of degree. Many writers, teachers, and organizations have created an excessive interest in Kundalini and have encouraged much public anxiety over its purported dangers. In some instances, this mystification of Kundalini energy is well-meaning, if misguided, but in other cases, it has served as an effective means for would-be Gurus to exercise control over their disciples. Kundalini is a powerful force but not one to be feared.

During the plateau phase, the launching period for Kundalini energy, more physical changes take place. The respiration increases, the blood pressure goes up, and the heart races. This is when the gases are firing out, and the rocket is starting to shake, and it is getting ready to take off: that is what plateau is all about. Interestingly enough, the anus, the terminal end of the gastrointestinal tract, begins to tighten. If you have some knowledge of Yogic techniques, you may be familiar with *Mulabandha* and *Ashwini Mudra*. These practices are designed to activate Kundalini by deliberately locking or twitching the anus (see chapter 14, "Tantric Massage Magic").

The outer one-third of the vagina grips the penis (if vaginal intercourse is taking place), and the inner two-thirds balloons up during the plateau phase. In women who have had children, the womb, from which every one of us emerges, enlarges, sometimes doubling in size. As we start to ascend from the plateau phase into the orgasmic phase, there are a number of profound changes that take place; the whole psychophysiology of the body is affected. At the moment of orgasm, the male urethra contracts every four-fifths of a second, and along with it, the anus. Now, this is particularly interesting; the Tantric forms of Mulabandha and *Vajroli Mudra* involve voluntary twitching of the anus, urethra, and uterus. At orgasm, Vajroli Mudra and Mulabandha are automatically brought into play, and you get a two-way twitching back and forth between partners when orgasm is simultaneous.

In addition, there may be carpopedal spasm, in which both the hands and the feet convulse. Frequently, the back arches, and some people experience backache after a particularly intense sexual encounter. Respiration has tripled by the moment of orgasm, the pulse rate is doubled, and the blood pressure rises by a third. And in the female, during orgasm, the outer third of the vagina twitches approximately every four-fifths of a second, five to twelve times, depending on intensity, as do the uterus and the anus. The uterus contracts from above to below, exactly as it does in labor. That is one of the reasons that orgasms, by masturbation or other means, help to alleviate menstrual cramps: the uterus is squeezed from above to below, relieving the discomfort.

After ejaculation, the resolution phase in men usually includes detumescence, or loss of erection; this period of detumescence may be relatively brief in younger men but grows longer with age. Tumescence, or swelling, the *tanoi* (expansion) phase, extends up to the orgasmic peak. Then, during the resolution phase, the detumescence sets in very rapidly in men and more slowly or not at all in women. Detumescence is accompanied by a feeling of relief and relaxation. The same feeling of relief occurs with a sneeze. Consider that the sneeze is a very relieving event. If you were to go around interfering with people's sneezes, you would get into real trouble. The same principle applies; if you start interfering with people's orgasms, they won't appreciate it either.

This overview represents a basic, standard Western psychophysiological viewpoint, although we have alluded to parallels in the Tantric understanding. While these parallels are significant, it is even more important to examine the differences.

People in our society have tended to think of orgasm as the goal, the "big O" in the sky. Unfortunately, the very important work of sex researchers, such as Masters and Johnson, and those who have focused on teaching women how to experience orgasm has played into this tendency. These pioneers in the field of human sexuality have made very valuable contributions, but in many instances, their emphasis on orgasm reflects the goal orientation that characterizes Western society as a whole. This is a somewhat limited understanding of human sexual potential.

So, our cultural orientation has encouraged most of us to go straight after the orgasm, an orgasm that often amounts to a genital sneeze. The sexually liberated among us tend to think we should have as many of these as possible as often as possible and as quickly as possible. That is the common attitude. We are not saying this is good or bad, but we would like to suggest that there are other possibilities.

In the years since this material was first presented, there has been an explosion of interest in Tantra, particularly its sexual aspects, and far more information on the subject has become available to Western seekers. This trend is largely positive and reflects a significant shift away from the emphasis on the genital sneeze, and it incorporates the understanding that men can separate the orgasmic experience from physical ejaculation. Nevertheless, much of the so-called Tantric literature remains focused on orgasms, whether or not they include ejaculation, and many in the general public seem to believe that practicing Tantra is a kind of "sexual Olympics" that is all about having bigger, better, and longer orgasms.

Humanistic psychology helped shape a different kind of attitude that emerged in the 1960s and '70s, and in marriage counseling, therapists began to emphasize the resolution phase. Essentially, the idea was to tell people, "Don't worry about orgasm. The important thing about your sexual life is that during the resolution phase, your defenses are down, and this is the time for open communication. This is the time to start talking, to get close, to share." The humanistic idea is that the important phase is the resolution phase. So, over the last thirty or forty years, the prevailing Western view has been that the orgasmic and resolution phases are most important.

During the 1960s, a few Western researchers, most notably R. E. L. Masters (not to be confused with William H. Masters of Masters and Johnson) and A. M. Ludwig, did emphasize the arousal phase. Masters and Ludwig were also researchers of psychedelics, and both made reference to possibilities of inducing altered states of

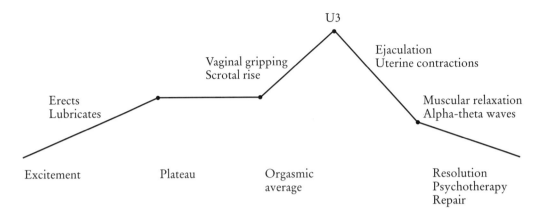

The Western sexual response cycle

A graphic representation of the Western sexual response cycle from Swamiji's original lecture notes. U3 experiences do not necessarily occur in the context of conventional Western sexual activity. Courtesy of Kailash Center for Personal Development, Inc.

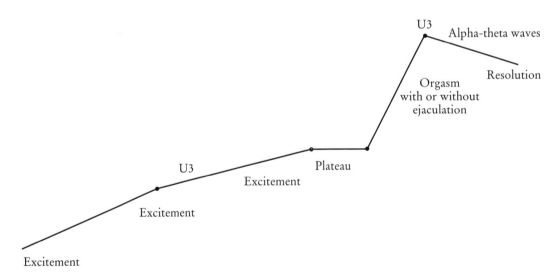

The Tantric sexual response cycle

Note that in the Tantric sexual response cycle, the U3 experience may commence during the excitement phase and persist through plateau and orgasm. This is a result of prolonging arousal.

consciousness—similar to states induced by psychedelic drugs—by means of prolonged arousal. This way of thinking about the excitement phase was informed by some knowledge of the Tantric tradition, at least in the case of Masters, but these ideas never gained much currency in the mainstream.

Now, what about the Eastern approach? Vama Marga says that the emphasis can very profitably be placed not on orgasm and not on resolution, but on the excitement phase. So, in contrast to the Western cycle, the Eastern model takes the excitement phase and prolongs it, prolongs it, prolongs it, and prolongs it. This protracted excitement phase is followed by a short plateau period, a sharp orgasm, and then a very slow resolution. The graphic depictions of the two models on the facing page reveal how profoundly different they are.

That sharp orgasm is the experience of Ultimate Universal Unity, or U3; the U3 state can also be experienced prior to orgasm, even during the excitement phase, when that phase has been sufficiently prolonged and a high level of arousal has been reached. Women generally have easier access to *Samadhi* (U3) experiences before and during orgasm, and whether your perspective is Eastern or Western, women are superior psychophysiological sexual organisms. The are capable of going higher and further faster and of losing the ego and transcending themselves more easily in the sexual experience. This has always been recognized in the hidden culture of the East, in the Vama Marga tradition.

This recognition of female superiority explains why most of the instructions in Vama Marga writings are for men and why the texts say very little about women. Some have suggested that these writings are sexist, but this is not the case. In traditional Vama Marga, it is well known that women are multiorgasmic, and provided they are pleasured and worshiped in certain ways, they can reach very high states effortlessly. Most of the focus is on men because men simply don't have the same orgasmic potential as women. Men must learn how to prolong the excitement phase, how to hold back, how to experience orgasmic sensations without ejaculating, and so on.

This greater orgasmic potential translates into a more powerful innate spiritual orientation in women. Many women have been cut off from this capacity for cultural reasons and have to learn how to activate it. Even so, most of the spiritual energy wave that is carried throughout the world is carried by women, because, by and large, women are innately more sensitive. The Kundalini force is naturally more aroused in them, and they are naturally more inward. In the West, we have a cliché about trusting a "woman's intuition." Of course, *intuition* means "teaching within." And the very genital structure of a woman is inward, just as the flow of Kundalini is inward, so naturally that power rises within her.

The stereotype about men is that they are more logical, very practical, and not very intuitive; male genital structure is a physical reflection of this stereotype. Most men naturally project outward and have to learn very carefully and meticulously how to go inward, experiencing and embracing those feminine aspects within themselves. This can be quite challenging for many men, since it undercuts deeply held cultural prejudices about what it means to be male.

Every one of us is both male and female; we all contain elements of Shiva and Shakti. Kundalini, which is portrayed as a feminine force, is active in all of us, in varying degrees. It is important to bear this in mind when talking about innately masculine or feminine traits. Engaging and harmonizing our inner masculine and feminine characteristics is a necessary component of any Tantric practice. That is why Dakshina Marga practitioners can rotate the energies inside their own bodies without relying on a partner.

In Vama Marga Tantra, the emphasis is placed on prolonging the excitement phase for both men and women. There are profound advantages to this shift in emphasis. The benefits can be explained in either Eastern or Western terms, and they are benefits in and of themselves. While prolonging the excitement phase may intensify orgasm, the Tantric understanding is that the path is the goal.

So, what is the advantage of paying attention to the excitement phase, of paying attention to the means rather than to the end? Or, better yet, forgetting the end entirely? The classical texts say that we possess not only a physical body—the texts call this *Annamaya Kosha*, which literally means "that body which depends on food for its subsistence"—but beyond that gross food body lie four other sheaths. We call this the doctrine of *Pancha Koshas*, or "five bodies." We say that humans are multidimensional creatures with not one body but five bodies: *Anandamaya Kosha, Vijnanamaya Kosha, Manomaya Kosha,* and *Pranamaya Kosha,* in addition to the physical body.

These are subtle bodies that feed on subtle energies. And just as the physical body has a network of nerves, so the psychic body has a network of tubes or channels that we call *nadis.* The word *nadi* means "to flow." And these nadis carry psy-

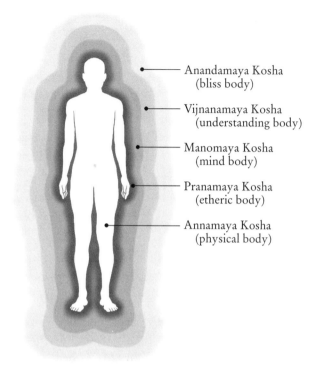

Anandamaya Kosha
(bliss body)

Vijnanamaya Kosha
(understanding body)

Manomaya Kosha
(mind body)

Pranamaya Kosha
(etheric body)

Annamaya Kosha
(physical body)

The Pancha Koshas

chic energies—prana if you wish, *chi* in Chinese, *ki* in Japanese, bioenergy, subtle energy, *orgone* if you are a Reichian. The terminology and mapping systems may be different, but the energy is the same.

When two people work together consciously to prolong the excitement phase, they cause the prana—the chi, the ki, whatever you want to call it—to flow through the psychic nadis. As that energy circulates again and again and again, a repair process can take place on multiple levels—psychological, emotional, and mental. That is the esoteric meaning of *maithuna*, or "Tantric union." It is a re-pair process. But before there can be a re-pairing process, there must have been a "de-pairing," or splitting. It takes two to make one, and when two make one, this is *yug*, Yoga, or union. The more the excitement phase is prolonged, the more profound the re-pair. At its best, this is an effortless, natural process.

During the excitement phase, a form of psychophysiological nourishment occurs for both men and women. This psychophysiological nourishment is a product of glandular secretions. The more the excitement phase is prolonged, the more the glands secrete. A very simple example of this is in women. Under certain circumstances, when the breasts are stimulated, the reflex goes straight to the posterior pituitary gland, which then releases a hormone that flows through the bloodstream down to the uterus, causing a uterine contraction. That is why many women can have orgasms from breast stimulation alone. Women are thrice blessed because they can also have Ultimate Universal Unity (U3) experiences from sexual contact and even from childbirth. The ability to experience orgasm during childbirth is a function of the ability to relax. This is uncommon in our society, in part because we have lost the capacity to relax and in part because anesthetics are so widely used. Nevertheless, all three things—breast feeding, sexual contact, and childbirth—can trigger U3 experiences.

Similarily in men, the pituitary and pineal glands release certain subtle hormones. Many argue that there are biochemical substances the Tantrics have known about for centuries, whether intuitively or by introspection, that have not yet been identified by Western science. From the Western perspective, the prolonging of arousal and the release of these various hormones and endorphins into the system produce an altered state of consciousness that can persist for some time, even after orgasm takes place. Leaving aside any mystical or esoteric considerations, it appears that prolonging arousal produces a very powerful and healthy natural high that can be beneficial for relieving anxiety and improving mood.

Significant problems can arise when we discuss prolonging the excitement phase. Many recent books on Tantric and Taoist sexual practices have tended to exacerbate these problems. Men are prone to worry, and sexual anxiety can be acute and debilitating. Unfortunately, there is widespread anxiety about ejaculation in both Eastern and Western cultures.

In Ayurvedic medicine, for instance, it is said that for every drop of semen, forty drops of blood are required. Semen is deemed to be distilled blood or cerebrospinal fluid, and there is a belief that when a man loses his semen, *shukra* or *bindu*, he loses his energy, his vitality. Taoist texts and Chinese sex manuals are filled with similar ideas; of course, many of these sex manuals were written for men who had harems and who were obliged to perform sexually with numerous partners, so there was a very practical need for them to control ejaculation.

Similar superstitions have generated their share of fear about ejaculation in the West as well. A hundred years ago, masturbation was commonly believed to cause insanity, blindness, and all manner of ills, and many doctors shared this belief; even today, Judith Reisman, a leading proponent of "abstinence only" education in the United States, claims that Alfred Kinsey, the founder of modern sexology, died of "brutal, repetitive self-abuse."[2] The fears need not be of such an extreme nature. A man may find, for instance, that he has a sexual experience in which he ejaculates and feels tired afterward. He hits the resolution phase; neurologically, his brain has been firing alpha and theta waves. In resolution, he goes into delta, or sleep. And he thinks, "Oh my God, that proves it. I have lost my vital energy. I have exhausted myself. I can't keep my eyes open."

There are a few things to say on this subject. The first is: we are simply not used to being relaxed, and there is nothing wrong with relaxation; indeed, we need more of it in this society. The second is that ejaculation is a form of surrender, while retaining semen can become a way of maintaining distance and control, which is not appropriate in the context of Vama Marga practice. Some texts, including the *Brhadaranyaka Upanishad*, the *Yoni Tantra*, and some *Tamil Siddha* scriptures, state that semen is an essential substance in ritual sexuality. Other texts may emphasize retention, but it is important to understand that there is an outer teaching that the actual loss of semen will devitalize you and an inner teaching that when you work with prolonging arousal and rotating the energies, releasing semen will not devitalize you, even though it contains vital chemicals. Also bear in mind that nothing is ever said about female orgasm or ejaculation in this context.

The key to this is attitude, at least according to our tradition; you are free to disagree with this—and many do—but we feel it is a very mentally healthy and reasonable way of approaching the issue. In sum, he who thinks that he will lose his energy every time he loses his semen will lose his energy; indeed, he will be devitalized. He

---

2 Daniel Radosh, "The Culture Wars: Why Know?" *The New Yorker*, December 6, 2004, http://www.newyorker .com/talk/content/?041206ta_talk_radosh. According to Radosh, Reisman also believes that "The Nazi Party and the Holocaust itself . . . were largely the creation of 'the German homosexual movement.'" Despite her extreme views, Reisman has long been admired by social conservatives, has acted as a consultant for the Department of Health and Human Services, and received over $700,000 from the Reagan administration to conduct research on pornography.

who thinks he will be regenerated every time he shares his semen will be regenerated; indeed, he is going to be regenerated. In life, we generally get what we think.

The inner essence of the teaching is that the vital force lies not in the gross semen, the fluid ejaculate; it lies in a subtle energy that we call *ojas*, meaning "strength or power." It is all attitude. The whole thing is imagination, hypnosis if you wish. As Einstein so famously observed, "Imagination is more important than knowledge."

So, in our tradition, what do men do? We visualize that we are sucking the semen up the spinal column, or up certain psychic channels. It is not the actual semen we are sucking up; it is the pranic energy, ojas, in the semen. Once you have brought the ojas to the head and you release the physical ejaculate, it doesn't matter—simply doesn't matter. Again, it is all about attitude; if you feel that you have brought the energy into the brain, sure enough, you will have that energy. And if you have had no feelings one way or the other, for God's sake do not let this book screw you up and put ideas into your head.

From the Tantric perspective, prolonging the excitement phase has a profound meaning and an impact on every aspect of the human mind-body-spirit complex. Western mass culture tends to be orgasm-oriented, and some therapeutic models are more resolution-oriented, because immediately after orgasm, people are hyper-suggestible and defenses are down. During all phases of lovemaking, it is important to be kind and to avoid saying anything destructive or hurtful, but this is particularly important during the resolution phase. In Vama Marga Tantra, we say: focus on the excitement phase, and you are likely to discover new sexual dimensions in yourself and in your partner.

five

Tantric Sexuality: Is It Possible?

*I*n later chapters, we will examine a number of specific techniques for exploration within the context of Tantric sexuality, but before we move into the realm of practice, it is important to examine the entire question of Tantric sexuality from a more theoretical and philosophical perspective. Tantra is a paradoxical path in many ways, and at the highest levels, it forces us to move beyond logical thinking and binary oppositions into the realm of analogical thinking and the understanding that most perceived antitheses are, at some level, "both-and" situations.

Unlike Swamiji, who was a teenage Yogi, we came to Tantra in our adult years, with virtually no background in Yoga. We were drawn, quite frankly, by an interest in Tantric sexuality. Like many Westerners, our initial interest in Tantra was stimulated by the recognition that we had seen glimmers of the transcendent in our sexual experiences and the realization that we hungered for more in this realm. Westerners tend to imagine that Tantra is a sexual Yoga (in the watered-down Western understanding of that term), merely an array of sexual techniques that will please partners and produce Olympian orgasms. Alternatively, they may believe that Tantra is a healing modality, a form of couples therapy, a series of practices for enhancing intimacy, a way of loving consciously in a pair-bonded relationship. Tantra can encompass all of these things, but none of them define it entirely or come close to doing it justice.

Westerners (and today this term includes virtually anyone who owns a television, regardless of national origin) who wish to pursue Tantra as a spiritual path face an even more profound paradox.[1] Tantra emerged in a cultural environment that is vastly different from our own—perhaps not as different, however, as some would suggest, since East and West have met repeatedly since the time of Alexander the Great, and English, German, the Romance languages, and Sanskrit are all related (in contrast to Chinese, Japanese, or Tibetan), so there are certainly very deep commonalities. Nevertheless, it is important to recognize the gap and to understand that actions mean different things in different contexts, and that much gets lost in translation. If we can recognize this challenge and bear it in mind, if we can be aware of the vast cultural chasm and understand that Tantra is not an easy New Age panacea, that it is not about love or sex or healing as these terms are commonly understood, that it is not natural, that it is not simple—with that understanding, it may become possible to taste just a little of the nectar that the Tantrikas of old described as the honey one licked from the razor's edge.

This awareness is at the core of the teaching Swamiji delivered in this 1989 lecture. Some may see it as a retreat from the material he presented at Gnosticon, and it is fair to say that today Swamiji is less sanguine about the ability of Westerners to practice authentic Tantra than he was more than a quarter century ago. At the same time, the issues he raised in this lecture are worthy of consideration by anyone with a serious interest in Tantra, and a careful reading may lead some to understand that attempting to practice Tantra—including sexual Tantra—may be extraordinarily difficult but that it has the potential to be profoundly rewarding.

Swamiji began with a simple, direct question: "Tantric sexuality: is it possible?" He concluded that it is possible but highly improbable; we prefer to say it is possible but very difficult. All forms of Yoga, or union, are difficult and even unnatural. As Swamiji has often pointed out, this form of Yoga is perhaps the most difficult of all.

---

1 The impact of television on non-Western cultures is starkly illustrated by a study conducted in a rural community in western Fiji during the 1990s, when television first became widely available. Prior to the introduction of television in 1995, only 3 percent of adolescent girls in the region reported having vomited to control weight. By 1998, 15 percent reported having done so. Other indicators of eating disorders also increased dramatically. Becker, A. E., R. A. Burwell, S. E. Gilman, D. B. Herzog, and P. Hamburg, "Eating Behaviors and Attitudes following Prolonged Television Exposure among Ethnic Fijian Adolescent Girls," *The British Journal of Psychiatry* 180: 509–514. Becker has continued her research and has published additional articles on this subject. This is only one study among many that demonstrate the culturally transformational power of television.

Westerners generally think that Tantra means sex, and that is a misunderstanding. What is unusual about Tantra as a spiritual path is that it includes human sexuality as one method for altering consciousness and achieving mystical experience. But in the Tantric scriptures, the passages devoted to sexuality, while important, are relatively few in number, and many Tantric practitioners—perhaps even a majority—view these passages as purely metaphorical.

Human sexuality is high-octane fuel. It has explosive, indeed incendiary, potential. Sexuality is something that most humans handle very poorly, and Anglo-Saxon culture is particularly maladroit when it comes to sexual matters; these problems are deeply embedded in the English language and the system that emerged out of English common law, so as English becomes the *lingua franca* of the entire world, some of these issues will find their way into societies that are not historically Anglo-Saxon. The society of the United States, for example, is by no means purely Anglo-Saxon, but attitudes toward gender relations are strongly influenced by both Anglo-Saxon antecedents and the structure of the English language. This structure informs and infects our attitudes toward sexuality in many ways, most of them unconscious.

On the surface, modern couples are often faced with problems of flagging sexual interest, and people tend to address this problem using one of two methods. The first response is to seek a quick fix for the sexual "flat-tire syndrome." This can inspire a quest for erotic and exotic sexual techniques, some of which appear in this book. Techniques and novel sexual experiences have their value, but they generally do not address the core issues, and the search for novelty or technical mastery often ends in disappointment.

When disappointment sets in, people often turn to our Western Yoga—psychotherapy—and seek to improve communication skills or "work on their relationship" in counseling of some form. Couples therapy is quite likely to fail and is often more useful in ending a relationship gracefully than in salvaging it.

This is not to suggest that sexual techniques, communication skills, and couples therapy have no value. They all have their place and can be quite effective in improving relationships, particularly relationships that are already relatively healthy and well established. These methods, however, do not get to some of the deeper roots of the problem.

There are a number of fallacious ideas about human relationships that are widely held in Anglo-Saxon society and in much of the Western world. We are socialized to believe that love, sex, and marriage form a triad that evolves automatically and effortlessly, just the way a rose blossoms. Most people are consciously aware that life simply does not work that way, but the cultural mythos is so powerful that we tend to expect it will. Notwithstanding the sexual revolution of the '60s and '70s, most people cling to the belief that the Western model of marriage is either an ideal to strive for or an expression of the natural order of things; embedded in this belief is the idea that nonmarital sex of any kind is at best inferior and at worst immoral. These beliefs are cultural constructs that are fundamentally at odds with human biology.

On the average, the most passionate sexuality between two people has a lifespan of no more than eighteen months; the same applies to one form of emotional intensity. At the end of this eighteen-month period, bonding relationships between people often grow out of the prior sexual intensity and infatuation. This phenomenon can be explained by what is known as the Solomon-Siegel model, named for the team of Canadian psychologists who devised the hypothesis. According to Solomon and Siegel, intense sexual attraction produces certain amphetamine-like chemicals in the brain. As pair bonding begins, the brain produces opiate-like substances that supplant the more stimulating hormones. Another way of understanding this paradox is to recognize the distinction between being in love and loving (Thomas Lewis, Fari Amini, and Richard Lannon's important book, *A General Theory of Love*, discusses this in detail) and to realize that most humans crave both of these experiences.

It is also important to recognize that every culture has had different values and perspectives with regard to love, sex, and marriage and that no one model is either more natural or morally superior to any other. In many polygamous societies, marriages are focused on male sexual pleasure and procreation. In Ladakh, a Tibetan Buddhist region of North India that has a harsh climate and scarce resources, polyandry is widely practiced, with one woman frequently marrying two brothers. In many Christian cultures, the "Madonna-whore" syndrome leads men to seek sexual gratification outside of marriage, with mistresses and prostitutes, because they cannot see their wives as sexual beings; for such men, sex with someone you love is only for procreation, and to have sex with a woman for pleasure alone is to defile her. In traditional Hindu society, marriage is neither for love nor for sex. It is a socioeconomic arrangement that is undertaken after consulting priests and astrologers. It is hoped that love and sexuality will develop in time.

These are but a few examples of the vast array of social and sexual arrangements that exist around the world, and in most societies, cultural practices are elevated to the level of moral and religious obligation. The ties between religious ideology and beliefs about sexual morality are perhaps strongest in Judaism, Islam, and Christianity, all of which embrace a patriarchal notion of the deity that is reflected in the social organization of sexuality. In Western cultures, the Christian view of women and sexuality retains enormous power even as the influence of religion on civil society has waned. In the West, women have long been objectified, and despite the efforts of the feminist movement, this objectification of women persists. If anything, it has been intensified by a mass-marketing culture that is increasingly focused on objectifying both women and men.

As Tantric practitioners, we embrace the feminist ideal. True feminism frees both men and women in its ultimate call, but we must examine and accept the realities of the society in which we live, and the reality is that, at some level of consciousness, all Western men view women as objects. Recognizing this and consciously struggling to combat it within themselves is one of the most effective ways for men to work against this current and thereby experience some of the promise of Tantric sexuality.

The objectification of women is far more pervasive and complex than it might first appear, although it is not necessarily synonymous with misogyny or contempt for women, which are prevalent enough in their own right. It can encompass the view that women are valuable objects just as easily as it can the view that women are objects of contempt. The roots of this idea are very deep, dating back at least to the composition of *The Book of Exodus*; the Tenth Commandment forbids covetousness, and "thy neighbor's wife" follows "thy neighbor's house" among the pieces of property not to be coveted. The view of women as property is also deeply embedded in our language. "He possessed her" is a euphemism for sexual intercourse that has existed in our Anglo-Saxon literary tradition for centuries. At English common law, women remained little more than property and had virtually no independent rights—including rights of ownership—until very recently.

So, in our culture, men often view women as valuable objects to be possessed. There are certain qualities that men tend to want in any valuable object. They want it to be new, unused, and beautiful—and therefore capable of increasing their own status or worth in the eyes of other men who desire it also. They generally want the object to be useful. To understand how this manifests itself in interpersonal relationships, replace the adjective "new" with "young" and "unused" with "virgin." For "beautiful," add "desired by others," because men often seek attractive partners to bolster sagging self-esteem and diminishing virility, hence the odious but descriptive term "trophy wife." Replace "useful" with "catering," because many men still expect women to play a servile role and cater instantly to their every need.

The list of ways in which women are dehumanized is long, and indeed volumes have been written on the subject. The objectification and dehumanization of women pervades popular culture, still manifests itself in the legal arena, and persists in the medical profession and the way pregnancy and childbirth are managed. Despite all the advances that have taken place due to the efforts of those in the feminist movement, unconscious attitudes shaped by long-standing traditions, some of them thousands of years old, cannot be altered in a few decades.

Although the institutions of the Western world are built upon and reinforce male power, the current structure of gender relations also dehumanizes men. Feminism in its highest form liberates and gives equality to both men and women. From the male perspective, if women are objects to be possessed, as a house and a car are to be possessed, men become little more than money-making machines fixated on wealth, power, prestige, and status. Once a man possesses his valuable object, he becomes obsessed with the possibility that someone will take it away—the biblical injunction against covetousness notwithstanding—even though the initial motive for obtaining it was, in part, to arouse desire and envy in other men. Thus, men end up being possessed by their possessions.

Men are often further dehumanized once the initial physical passion has begun to fade; at this stage, the relationship between a man and a woman often changes to that of child and mother, to a relationship based on dependency and a kind of infantilization, so that what began as catering becomes control. This transformation can be understood as expressing a fundamental alchemical and hermetic principle: whatever is strong in one polarity must eventually reverse to the other polarity. So, the master ends up being the slave, and the slave ultimately becomes the master. The hunter is captured by the game.

The truth, from the Tantric perspective, is that women carry the power; they carry the Shakti. It is not far-fetched to suggest that the entire history of gender relations in the West is merely an attempt by men to deny this basic fact and to deprive women of their innate power, a power that strikes fear into the hearts of most men.

In order to control this fear, men find themselves in a position where they have to maintain the pretense of strength, rationality, and unemotionality. Eventually, many men crack and even die under the strain of what society expects from them. Anatomically, in terms of muscle mass, men are the strong ones, but do not be deceived: women are the tougher, more resilient ones—both physically and emotionally.

Now, this is a rather grim view of gender roles. It is not comprehensive, nor is it universally true, but it remains a powerful and perhaps even dominant paradigm in Western society. Women, of course, are not objects. Women are sentient, sensitive human beings; men are also sentient, sensitive human beings. But the whole Anglo-Saxon cultural thrust dehumanizes women in social and sexual relationships, because an object is not a human, is not sentient, has no feelings. On a superficial level, men benefit from the dehumanization of women, but they pay a heavy price and are themselves dehumanized in the process.

The Tantric approach demands that we recognize these facts and that all of us, men and women, work to overcome these unconscious tendencies within ourselves. In Tantra, consciousness and awareness are crucial, and much of the work of the Tantric practitioner lies in finding ways to break free from cultural conditioning, habitual behavior, and unexamined taboos. In ancient India, this may have entailed engaging in sexual relations across caste lines or with a stranger; in the modern, Western world, the challenge is far more internal, since the taboos are, for the most part, far subtler. Thus, in today's world, the twin realms of relationship and sexuality, and the nexus between them, may be the most fertile territory for living life in accordance with Tantric principles.

Now, let us return to the specific question of whether Tantric sexuality is possible. In order to understand Tantric sexuality, we must begin by defining a couple of terms: *Shiva* and *Shakti*. Shiva represents the manifestation of the masculine principle. Shakti represents the manifestation of the feminine principle. Tantric sexuality involves the re-enactment on a personal level of that creative process which is constantly taking place on a cosmic level. This is the interplay between Shiva and Shakti. Shiva is consciousness; Shakti is power as manifest in matter. Each of us humans is a microcosmic embodiment of these cosmic qualities; each of us is divine.

We can also say that every human is androgynous and that we all contain both Shakti and Shiva, regardless of biological gender. Consciousness (Shiva) without power (Shakti) is impotent, but if consciousness without power is impotent, power

Yab Yum—the quintessential Tantric sexual posture

without consciousness is blind—unfocused and unproductive. Power needs direction, but if you have direction without power, nothing happens. On a cosmic level, Tantra conceives male and female as the crystallization, the material manifestation of polar opposites; this manifestation is an embodiment of the eternal process of creation that is the universe, or what some might refer to as God.

In terms of traditional Tantric sexual practice, there are four distinguishing features:

1. Absolute, unconditional equality or parity must exist between the participants.

2. Sexual intercourse is conducted in a female superior position, usually the classical *Yab Yum* posture.

3. Tantric sexuality is goalless.

4. The purpose of Tantric sexual activity is to produce altered states of consciousness.

In thinking about parity and equality between the partners, it is worth noting that some Tantric texts specify that practitioners should engage in sexual activity with a person other than a spouse. This is because it is extremely difficult to arrive at true parity or equality with a long-term partner, and also because it is far more challenging to embrace completely the belief that one's partner is an embodiment of the divine. It may be easier to achieve parity with a stranger, because there is no emotional investment, but this parity is somewhat artificial. We take no moral position with regard to monogamy; it is suitable for some people and not for others. Whether you are monogamous or not, there is great value in striving for the more hard-won parity that can be experienced in the context of a committed relationship, with all its complexities. The effort to achieve parity and equality and to approach your partner with an attitude of reverence and worship is perhaps the most challenging and rewarding aspect of striving to live the Yoga of relationship.

The traditional Tantric scriptures specify that Tantric sexual positions are female superior positions. In Yab Yum, the partners have symbolically left the earth and have polarized themselves to it at right angles; this means that the spine is erect and the hips are free to move in a way that is uniquely human. The partners are in physical alignment on a vertical rather than horizontal axis. Seated on the earth, they draw its force upward toward the sky, through Sahasrara Chakra, into the cosmos, firing toward the stars, uniting together with the earth and the heavens.

Tantric sexuality is not orgasm-oriented, though orgasm may take place. It emphasizes and prolongs the excitement phase. When excitement is prolonged, the other three phases of that four-beat rhythm—plateau, orgasm, and resolution—are much more profound and occur automatically. The reason for emphasizing the excitement phase is intimately related to the last fundamental characteristic of Tantric sexual practice: the production of altered states of consciousness.

Conventional sex can be for procreation; it can be an expression of love; it can be for simple pleasure; it can be recreational; it can be used to relieve anxiety. All of these aspects of sex can be quite wonderful, and we do not wish to minimize their importance and value. We firmly believe that leading a balanced and enjoyable sex life is a critical part of being a healthy, happy, well-adjusted human being. The classical approach to Tantric sex, however, requires a very different attitude and a commitment from both partners to approach it as a tool for consciousness expansion and a means to experiencing transcendence. The end result can be quite satisfying, but it differs from the satisfaction one experiences in conventional intercourse; the critical difference lies in the intention.

So, is Tantric sexuality possible? We repeat that it is possible but difficult. The difficulty lies in the nature of human relationships and the burden of a culture that requires us to dehumanize one another. In these conditions, we face a paradox—a profound paradox.

Relationships are the crux of the matter. They bring us face to face with our karmic patterns in all their intensity and difficulty. Despite this difficulty, most of us return to relationships again and again and again. Contrary to popular belief, celibacy is probably easier—not necessarily satisfying, but easier. The greatest challenge a human being can face is that of actually evolving through involvement in a relationship. Relationships are extraordinarily complex and challenging, and one always has the option to decide whether or not it is worth it. By committing and recommitting ourselves to relationships, by maintaining an attitude of reverence toward our partners, by striving for parity, equality, and kindness, we are practicing a form of Tantric *sadhana* (spiritual practice) of the highest order, for we are finding divinity in the most familiar and yet the most challenging of places.

six

Practical Sex Magic

Swamiji first delivered this lecture on Masturbation Magic at Gnosticon in 1976, but we are relying on a version recorded in 1989 and released by Llewellyn as a tape entitled *Autoerotic Mysticism*. Ironically, the subject matter was probably less controversial in the 1970s than it was in 1989 or than it is today. As Swamiji makes clear, self-pleasuring is an enormously powerful tool for transformation; it is safe and beneficial in many ways. From this perspective, it is tragic that in twenty-first-century America, masturbation is still considered an abomination in some quarters. Radio preachers continue to denounce it as deleterious to physical, mental, and spiritual health, and in 1994, the surgeon general of the United States, M. Joycelyn Elders, was forced from office in large part because she advocated masturbation as a tool for combating teen pregnancy and the spread of sexually transmitted disease.

The subject of masturbation has a long history of being taboo in both the East and the West. In the Western world, masturbation was commonly called "self-abuse" and has often been blamed for a variety of mental and physical ailments. In the nineteenth and early twentieth centuries, various devices were designed and sold to prevent adolescent boys and girls from pleasuring themselves. Jokes about hairy palms have persisted among young people to this day, and the more conservative branches of psychoanalysis have tended to view both male and female adult masturbation as infantile at best and pathological at worst. Freud's own writing is replete with condemnations of masturbation as a cause of various psychological ailments.

By the 1980s, a widely held Eastern taboo about masturbation began to take hold in Western occult and New Age circles, encouraged by the popularity of books on Taoist sexual philosophy and techniques, but also, in all probability, due to preexisting anxieties about the practice that are deeply embedded in Western culture. There have even been attempts to justify this superstition scientifically by claiming that the zinc lost through ejaculating semen depletes the body of this essential nutrient. This is not unlike the common Indian superstition that one drop of semen is composed of forty drops of blood, so that if you are a man, you are literally squirting your life away with every ejaculation.

Physiologically, this is absurd. Swamiji and his students used a calculator and a biochemical table to determine that a man would have to be on a distilled-water fast for ten days and ejaculate five hundred times during that period before he could deplete his body of zinc. Even the most virile sexual superman probably could not manage fifty ejaculations per day for ten days. We would take this a step further and contend that while non-ejaculation can be a very useful practice in certain specific contexts, excessive suppression of the ejaculatory response is both physically and psychically counterproductive. There is danger in dogma of any kind. Each human body is unique, and any serious practitioner of Vama Marga Tantra must discover his or her own personal truth.

In light of all this controversy, it may come as no surprise that the word *masturbation* is derived from a Latin root that means, literally, "to stir up." And what does masturbation stir up, besides controversy? Quite simply, it stirs up sexual energy, in psychophysiological terms, and psychic energy, in occult and esoteric terms.

The truth is that if masturbation could have been patented, prescribed, and peddled, it would have made someone a billionaire. Here is something that is environmentally friendly, safe, inexpensive, and, if you will forgive the pun, ready at hand for producing both psychic and psychological relief and changes. Swamiji applies the term *Masturbation Magic* to a method we humans can use to reprogram ourselves, to adjust our attitudes according to the circumstances of our lives. The key to doing this is practice. As human beings, we have a self-erasure device: if we are not constantly affirming what we want, if we do not have goals that are constantly being set and reset, we fall back into habitual behavior and old patterns. There are many methods for combating this tendency, and it has been one of the main occupations of occultists, of esoteric students, and of those with an interest in the inner life to explore these methods. We are suggesting that conscious masturbation is one of the fastest and most effective ways to reprogram your attitudes and bring about changes in your external environment.

To a significant extent, the most pleasurable aspects of human sexual activity arise during an excitement phase that is characterized by various forms of mutual masturbation. In the early years of the 1970s, a new word came into vogue: *foreplay*, a convenient euphemism for what is, in essence, mutual masturbation. In the '70s, it became fashionable for men to receive training in foreplay so that a woman could enjoy her moment of climactic liberation. In Swamiji's experience, this had a big effect on sexuality. In the early '70s, he found that most of the people he counseled for sexual problems were women; by the late '80s, the majority were men. In our experience over the first few years of the '00s, each gender has its share of what could be termed "sexual problems," and the biggest problem we encounter among couples is difficulty being kind to one another; some of the material in this chapter should help illuminate just how serious a problem this lack of kindness can be. Although it is not intrinsically a sexual problem, it has a profound impact in the realm of sexuality.

The meaning of "sexual problem" itself merits some examination. We suggest that a sexual problem begins when you define yourself as having one, unless the behavior involved is compulsive and harmful or involves nonconsensual activity (in which case the term "sexual problem" is, if anything, too mild).

Human sexuality generally and masturbation in particular are part of an occult psychic tradition, both Eastern and Western. Masturbation Magic is based on something recognized in the East for thousands of years, long before 1976, when research by Masters and Johnson suggested that masturbation is likely to produce the most intense orgasmic experience. It is important to understand that this research in no way suggests that a partner is superfluous, because the most intense orgasm may not be the most satisfying one; we would not presume to suggest any hierarchy of orgasmic experience. Indeed, we encourage our students to appreciate the array of orgasmic possibilities that exist and to refine their awareness and enjoyment of each experience in its own right. Thus, the essential principles of Masturbation Magic can be applied to any sexual encounter.

These essential principles of Masturbation Magic can be articulated in a few brief statements:

1. The key to the entire process is the degree of excitement (and/or the orgasmic pitch), not the method of attaining it. In other words, it doesn't matter how you masturbate; instead, you must discover what does that magic internal trick for you, what will build up the greatest amount of excitement or the most intense orgasm. (It is important to note that Masturbation Magic can work quite successfully even without orgasm, provided you build up enough excitement.) You arrive at the method empirically by exploring what really arouses you, what enables you to turn your nervous system on so completely that you lose self-consciousness. This applies to both solo masturbation and mutual masturbation (or foreplay), and it works with or without a partner.

2. Use any fantasy that gets you very excited. It is imperative to feel free in the mind to pick the fantasy that will do the trick for you. It might be a rather common fantasy or something quite bizarre; it doesn't matter. People's descriptions of their favorite erotic fantasies make utterly fascinating reading and have been the subject of more than one bestseller. Despite the success of these books, there is still a lot of superstition about fantasy. Contrary to popular belief, whatever goes on in the mind as an erotic fantasy is fine, provided it is not accompanied by a compulsive urge to act it out (particularly if that urge involves violence, children, or nonconsensual behavior). At a physiological level, the brain does not discriminate; whatever works, it accepts. There is no such thing as a bad thought or a bad imagination, but there are certainly harmful actions.

3. The essence of sex magic is that when you are highly aroused, you become hyper-suggestible. Suggestibility is crucial. Suggestibility is a state in which the noncritical acceptance of ideas becomes possible. In a normal state, for example, if you are feeling unwell or upset and somebody tells you that you are really feeling great, the left hemisphere says, "I don't feel that way, and that statement is nonsense." If you are in a meditative state, a hypnotic state, or a state of sexual excitement and you are given the message that you feel great, you are quite likely to accept it and feel great, particularly if the suggestion is made when you are sexually aroused. When you are in such a highly receptive state, the suggestion is taken deep into the mind and can extend into all areas of life.

4. When you are in a high state of sexual excitement, huge quantities of energy are released in the body. If you are an occultist, you can extend this to include the energy field outside the body. If you are a psychophysiologist, the indicia of energy released are dramatic: rising blood pressure, tripling of respiration, quadrupling of heart rate in some cases, and distinct alterations of brainwave patterns, accompanied by a surge in hormonal secretions. Regardless of your perspective, the excitement phase, particularly in the context of masturbation, represents a significant energetic phenomenon.

Taking points 3 and 4 together reveals that as you become sexually excited, you become hyper-suggestible, and at the same time, huge quantities of energy become available. This combination of energy and hyper-suggestibility represents a unique opportunity for self-programming and for altering those things in life that you may wish to alter.

This is because the left brain is literally knocked out. It is an all-or-nothing phenomenon. When you are deeply into the excitement phase and are highly aroused, thinking, analyzing, and rationalizing become nearly impossible, particularly for men. As a general rule, the female brain is better at multitasking, so, for example, men tend to become less verbal during lovemaking. For some women, this capacity for multitasking can interfere with the early stages of arousal, but once a high state of arousal is reached, both men and women will experience hyper-suggestibility.

The secret of hyper-suggestibility has been known for many centuries by the Tantrics, but it is still little known in the West. Dr. William Sargant is one of the few contemporary Western psychiatrists to have discovered this secret, something he articulated in his books *Battle for the Mind* and *The Mind Possessed*. Sargant argued that when we are sexually excited, we stop reasoning and rationalizing and are suggestible to the point that the mind becomes like a sponge that absorbs whatever message it receives. Ironically, sexual problems often begin as a result of this increased receptivity. So, we have a double-edged sword; heightened arousal can be used to program us either positively or negatively.

So-called sexual problems can develop between partners when one says something derogatory to the other at a critical moment, when both are in a state of excitement and defenses are down. People are absolutely hyper-suggestible in the late stages of the excitement phase and all subsequent phases of the sexual response cycle. At such times, each partner is likely to take on the other's attitudes, ingest them, and adopt them, usually quite unconsciously. For this reason, it is particularly important to communicate gently and kindly during states of arousal, since unkind words about a partner's appearance, lovemaking skills, or anything else will go straight in, are likely to influence future behavior and self-esteem, and can severely damage any relationship.

To reiterate, from about the midpoint of the excitement phase through the resolution phase, people are hyper-suggestible. There is little resistance to environmental stimuli. In addition, there is a vast amount of energy released during this period. This produces a closed circuit, a biofeedback loop: the more excited you get, the more hyper-suggestible you become; the more hyper-suggestible you become, the more excited you get; and the more excited you get, the more energy you generate. This produces a classical magical, occult, esoteric situation, a perfect swirl, a vortex of energy, and that is what sex magic is about; that is what Masturbation Magic is about. Within this vortex, reprogramming yourself becomes possible.

Sex magic can be defined as the art and science of utilizing sexual excitement to bring about changes in conformity with the will. In 1976, when Swamiji first lectured on Masturbation Magic in the United States, a rather crude idea on this subject was quite popular. At that time, magical practice often involved a group sitting in a circle, getting into a state of sexual excitement. One person would sit in the center of that circle and act as a focusing lens. The participants would work on a group project, such as healing somebody, and while the participants were becoming sexually excited, the person in the center would focus on a healing transmission, as would each couple in the circle. Swamiji argued that from a magical viewpoint, this approach was a terrible waste of time. In fact, he called it "hogwash," because the participants were being asked to do two things that are mutually exclusive—an approach that is virtually impossible. You cannot sustain focus on a project and at the same time let go, give in, and surrender to an altered flow of sensual sensation.

Sex magic and Masturbation Magic require you to know when and how to imagine or visualize a project. Suppose, for example, that you want to be promoted to a managerial position; the idea is to visualize yourself sitting at that desk, actually doing those managerial tasks. The original theory, popular during the 1970s, suggested that you should focus on being in that managerial chair throughout the whole course of lovemaking, sexual excitement, or autoeroticism. Frankly, it is difficult to imagine two more diametrically opposed sensations, unless you have a very unusual fetish and find visualizing yourself in a managerial chair sexually exciting.

Swamiji's system of sex magic or Masturbation Magic does not require you to do the impossible or eroticize the mundane; the overtly magical component should take no more than five to ten seconds, and the entire process involves a few simple steps:

1. Build excitement. Extend the excitement phase of your lovemaking or your masturbation, and let the excitement build and build and build. During this stage, you do not think about your project, your desire for change in your life, or your self-affirmation. Rather, you focus on masturbating, including an erotic fantasy that will accelerate and heighten your arousal. Keep your attention on the fantasy and the arousal. This is designed to quiet the left hemisphere, the thinking, rational part of the brain.

2. Begin to visualize when you reach the brink of orgasm. When you have reached your maximum state of sexual excitement, when you have reached the preorgasmic stage or the point of no return, when you are just about to go over the edge into orgasm (for a man this may include orgasm with or without ejaculation), you flash the visual image of whatever you desire. The visual image is important because the mind responds more strongly to images than to words, and most occultists would hold that the same applies to effecting changes in the physical environment.

   There is a specific technique for flashing the image, and this is a crucial component of the practice; you flash the image just as you go into the orgasmic experience and perhaps for a second or two after. The best way to flash the image is to imagine a colored slide as big as a football field, in three dimensions out in front of you, and you just flash it on and off like a neon sign—that image of what you desire in your life. Making that image flash on and off is a subtle little trick that adds a subliminal element to the process. It helps implant the message at a deeper level and facilitates breaking through to the unconscious.

   From an occult, magical perspective, you are actually moving energy from inside the mind-body complex to the external environment. The same principle applies to using concentration to affect the throw of dice; however, Masturbation Magic moves more energy than simple concentration. From a purely Western, psychological viewpoint, what you are doing is reprogramming your attitudes, so if you are after that managerial position, your attitude toward getting it, your desire, your goal-seeking ability, and your adaptability are increased. This internal change will influence the person who can offer you that position. It doesn't matter which way you choose to look at it; this is a very powerful technique.

3. Regulate the breath immediately before and during orgasm. Breath control at the climactic moment is another secret of Tantra and Yoga. Tradition holds that regulating the breath is an effective technique for enabling the mind to focus itself fully on a limited area, such as a project or a meditative experience. The key lies in holding the breath at the moment when the prana has been built up to the highest possible level. In a sexual context, this adds to the surplus of energy already in the body from the sexual excitement. So, in the practice of Masturbation Magic, as you approach the climactic moment, you take a deep breath in and swallow. This is called Aprakasha Mudra (see chapter 3), and it helps lock the air within the lungs. Swallowing should enable you to hold your breath for the duration of the orgasm and for a few seconds after, as you begin the descent from orgasm into the resolution phase. If you experience discomfort with this element of the practice, then discard it, but be sure to employ other conscious breathing techniques in its place.

To recapitulate, this is a method, a technique, that goes in steps. Step one, get excited; enjoy that excitement phase, and let the left brain be flooded out of its rational mode with sensual sensations. Step two, visualize your project only as you reach the preclimactic phase, and then hold and flash the visualization outside of you in three dimensions and on a massive scale; keep flashing throughout the orgasm and for a couple of seconds afterward. Step three, just before you begin to orgasm, take a deep breath and swallow to lock in the breath; hold the breath through the orgasm.

So, we are dealing with a very concrete method. It has been known in the East, in Tantra. It has not been recognized within the general context of Western culture and has been kept hidden and secret for the most part. It can be applied in many areas of magical or Yogic endeavor, including Enochian magic, ceremonial magic, and the Golden Dawn. In those five or ten seconds, any ritual can be done in the mind. It is a way to contact your inner jinni or genie that has its genesis in the genitals. All these words are related, and in this method, in this technique of Masturbation Magic and in sex magic generally, the genitals make the genius. And out of that genius come the jinn or genies who produce the results for you.

seven

Keys to Autoerotic Mysticism

Now that we have provided a basic overview of a practical form of sex magic that can be undertaken in the context of both self-pleasuring and partnered sexual activity, we feel it is important to delve into the topic of masturbation in somewhat more detail and to examine the ways in which masturbation can serve as a tool for self-transformation with more specificity. When Swamiji gave his original 1976 lecture on Masturbation Magic, others—particularly feminists—were doing their own original work on the subject, albeit from a rather different perspective. Betty Dodson is perhaps the best known of these sexual pioneers. Dodson first came to prominence in the early '70s, and her first book, *Liberating Masturbation: A Meditation on Self-Love* (later reissued in expanded form as *Sex for One: The Joy of Self-loving*), appeared in 1974. At Gnosticon, Swamiji discussed a February 1976 *Penthouse Forum* interview with Dodson at length, and the points raised at that time remain as important today as they were more than a quarter century ago. In the interview, Dodson advocated "joy-full masturbation which is indulging self-love without guilt or hang-ups. As a result I have full capacity orgasm available to me anytime I want it, and this lightens the romantic burden."[1] Dodson's observations

---

1 Sheila Weller, "Inside Betty Dodson," *Penthouse Forum: The International Journal of Human Relations* 5, no. 5 (1976): 41. The interview makes clear that Dodson was deeply interested in Eastern disciplines at the time but had only made the connection between masturbation and spiritual practice in the previous year. Today, Dodson remains a passionate masturbation advocate but takes a rather dim view of Tantra, at least in its Western manifestation.

highlight the fact that Masturbation Magic is partner-independent; it is self-sustained sexual magic.

Dodson went on to describe hours-long masturbatory sessions as a form of meditation and to point out that her masturbatory practice did nothing to interfere with her ability to be orgasmic with lovers. This remains a particularly significant observation because there is an attitude in our society that masturbation is a solitary activity that interferes with relating to others. Even today, it is not uncommon for people in monogamous relationships to view a partner's masturbation as detrimental, as somehow disloyal; some even see it as an act that borders on infidelity. It is a mistake to view human sexuality as a zero-sum game; in fact, masturbation is not only a form of training for interacting with partners, it is an essential human behavior, and, except in extreme instances of compulsive activity, it is not a practice that detracts from a healthy relationship with a partner. Of course, if a man is masturbating to the point of ejaculation too frequently, it will limit his ability to function with his partner; women, on the other hand, can have a virtually limitless orgasmic capacity.

It is a fundamental psychological and physiological fact that the female is a superior psychosexual apparatus. This is simply the truth. Swamiji has long contended that the female design is nature's master plan on planet Earth. Any man who doubts this needs only to ask himself why he has nipples. In the original master design, we are all created female until about the eighth fetal week. It is only then that differentiation begins to take place; this fact might also lead us to conclude that men and women are more alike than we usually acknowledge, and indeed, it is the Tantric understanding that each of us contains both Shiva and Shakti and that male and female are not as different as we might imagine. Due to cultural taboos, however, women are frequently cut off from their sexual power, and masturbation can be an essential tool for enabling women to explore, awaken, and embrace their sexuality.

This was, perhaps, Betty Dodson's most important discovery. It helped to liberate a generation of women and has produced a sex-positive subculture that celebrates masturbation as a practice. In the broader culture and among men, however, masturbation remains taboo and tends to be looked upon as shameful and immature, still a kind of secret vice.

Dodson described her use of masturbation as a meditative practice, as a path to "self-knowledge, cleansing, and regeneration," and also as a "healing process," an effective tool for problem solving. That is an absolutely succinct description of Masturbation Magic from a totally independent source; Dodson took up transcendental meditation after writing *Liberating Masturbation* and had no prior experience with meditative practice and no apparent knowledge of the Golden Dawn, Crowley, or Eastern Tantra. But Dodson intuited something profound when she realized she could use masturbation as a tool for self-healing. Consider those times when you feel just a little off-color, slightly ill, out of sync, or unwell without being able to identify the source of the angst. Employing Masturbation Magic at those times is a very effective way to recharge and regenerate the psychic and physical aspects of the human organism.

One approach is to follow the steps described in chapter 6: become sexually excited, and at the preclimactic moment, take a deep breath. The visualization in this context is specifically aimed at healing and energizing, so as you reach the brink of orgasm, you visualize a white energy burst from head to toe and from toe to head, and you flash that energy burst several times, into the climax and immediately thereafter. By bathing your entire body in this burst of energy, you are implanting a powerful message of energizing and healing into your whole mind-body complex.

As Dodson indicated, the practice of masturbation can also be used as a tool for problem solving. Some problems can be solved by reason alone, but others resist the rational approach and require work at deeper levels. These more complex and vexing issues often have to be worked out in the unconscious. This requires you to stop thinking about the problem rationally and to stop the conscious mind. The way to accomplish this is by getting *involved* to *evolve* and thereby *resolve* the problem by filling the conscious mind with sensations of sexual excitement. High states of sexual arousal have the effect of stilling the mind and taking attention away from the problem. Needless to say, the problem is not forgotten, but it has been shifted into the unconscious, and that's where such things are solved. And the word *solve* is related to the word *dissolve*, and when the mind focuses on pure sensual sensation to experience a climactic moment, it is as if our problems are dissolved; out of this dissolution, the solution can emerge. Dodson described this as getting into her body to clear her mind, and that is about the simplest and most direct way of explaining another way that Masturbation Magic works.

It is also possible to define Masturbation Magic as a form of reprogramming. Although Masturbation Magic can be considered a form of sex magic, the principles have much in common with those of behavioral psychology. Unlike analytic therapy, which is problem-oriented, behavioral psychology is solution-oriented. Behavioral psychologists are generally uninterested in the roots of psychological problems, because they contend many problems can be resolved by treating the symptoms and the circumstances.

Masturbation Magic works from the same basic premise. For example, one method for improving self-confidence employs deep relaxation, or perhaps hypnosis, accompanied by visualizations and affirmations; these might include images of the subject acting in a confident fashion and more general affirmations aimed at bolstering self-esteem. Masturbation Magic can be used in a similar fashion to enhance self-confidence, but it is simpler and more direct. What you do is produce a vision of yourself acting and feeling confident in a five- or ten-second scenario, and then you use the process described in chapter 6. Allow your brain to be flooded with sexual excitement. As you approach the climactic phase, take a deep breath and hold it. Then flash an enormous picture of yourself acting with total confidence, and you have Masturbation Magic working as a form of behavioral psychology. This approach can be applied to any aspect of your life or behavior that you would like to change. Unlike visiting a therapist or purchasing self-hypnosis tapes, this method costs nothing, and it affords you the opportunity to use pleasure as a vehicle for self-transformation.

No discussion of masturbation would be complete without mentioning the vibrator. Betty Dodson and other sex-positive feminist pioneers of the 1970s embraced vibrators as one of the most important tools for female sexual empowerment. While there was nothing particularly new about vibrators—indeed, we have a hand-cranked model dating to the turn of the twentieth century in our personal collection—Dodson and her colleagues made it acceptable to discuss their use openly and explicitly, at least among some groups. The quality and variety of sex toys currently available far surpasses the standard of 1976 or 1989, when Swamiji delivered his updated lecture on Masturbation Magic. As we have already discussed, the general American attitude about masturbation is perhaps more negative than it was in the 1970s, and despite the plethora of sex toys now available, hostility toward their use comes from many quarters. A recent federal court decision upheld an Alabama law banning their sale, and the United States Supreme Court declined to hear an appeal of the Eleventh Circuit Court of Appeals decision.[2] We have heard vibrators denounced by some Neo-Tantric practitioners who contend that they are addictive and desensitizing.

This Neo-Tantric attitude is probably based on a somewhat misguided belief that "natural" experiences are superior to those achieved by artificial means. While there is some merit to this point of view, it is at odds with the Tantric approach, which is fundamentally a pragmatic one. A more expansive view of sexual enhancers—from vibrators to Viagra—would treat these as useful tools, provided they are used with discrimination and awareness. The potential problems lie not in the items themselves but in the ways in which they are used.

Vibrators can be used by both women and men to increase arousal and inten- sify the orgasmic experience. A vibrator as a masturbation device increases sexual excitement for Masturbation Magic, sex magic, or any form of self-pleasuring; it is important to note that vibrators can also be used with a partner. Conventional in- tercourse is not the most efficient way for women to reach orgasm, and for some women, the use of a vibrator can be essential in this context. As Dodson and oth- ers have shown, the vibrator is often the key to teaching women how to climax.

The trick is to get the right kind of vibrator. Dodson has long advocated the Hitachi Magic Wand, and Swamiji suggested an Australian model called the Pifco. These are massage aids that produce a very strong, controllable vibration. For this reason, these products are very helpful for women who are just beginning to de velop their orgasmic capacity. Today, there are many different high-quality prod- ucts to choose from on the Internet or in upscale sex boutiques; these are a far cry from the shoddy merchandise found in the sex shops of yesteryear.

It is important to say a few words about orgasm; many in the Western world have gotten the idea that the essence of Tantra is the quest for bigger and better or- gasms. While we certainly believe that orgasms are wonderful, humans are unique

---

2 *Williams v. Attorney General of Ala.* 378 F.3d 1232 (11th Cir. 2004). Cert. Denied sub nom. *Williams v. King*, 125 S. Ct. 1335, 73 USLW 3485, 73 USLW 3495 (U.S. Feb 22, 2005) (NO. 04-849). Fortunately, the statute and decision have limited practical effect, since they apply to in-state sales only and do not restrict Internet and mail-order purchases. Nevertheless, the reasoning on which the decision is based has chilling implications for the future of sexual freedom in the United States. Similar laws are on the books in Mississippi, Georgia, Louisiana, and Texas, and shortly before publication, a misdemeanor prosecution for selling sex toys was pend- ing in Mississippi.

and individual, and there is enormous potential for harm in becoming overly focused on orgasm, whether in regard to quantity, quality, or way of reaching it. Ultimately, Tantra is not about goal orientation, it is about the experience along the way.

Some women have difficulty experiencing orgasm with a partner but orgasm with ease when they masturbate. Others do not masturbate or cannot experience orgasm in masturbation. In many cases, anorgasmic women can learn to experience orgasm by masturbating; once this is accomplished, they may find it possible to orgasm with a partner. Actually, the importance of orgasm is overstated, and it is not essential for anyone to orgasm with a partner. Remember that a sexual problem exists only if you are concerned about it—only then. Orgasm is not everything. Individual happiness is far more important, so again we have to be very careful in making judgments about what constitutes a sexual problem or what is "normal." It is a sexual problem when you are actually dissatisfied, not when somebody else complains.

In any event, the vibrator is a very useful tool for exploring and expanding sexual response. For women, it is a superb tool for producing intense sensations, leading to multiple orgasms for some. One reason the vibrator is so effective is that it produces a physical response, sometimes including an orgasm, before you have time to think. Thinking during lovemaking leads to self-consciousness. Self-conscious rumination inhibits orgasmic response, but the stimulation a vibrator provides can produce such rapid and intense arousal that there is no time to set up defenses or blocks. In other words, it breaks through defenses faster than you can erect them, no pun intended. Since women tend to become aroused more slowly than men, we often suggest that women "prime the pump" by masturbating either manually or with a vibrator prior to a sexual encounter, or even before going on a date. This can be a wonderful time to work with Masturbation Magic.

Using a vibrator to engender or increase your orgasmic potential is truly a form of Yoga. A vibrator can produce a sensation faster than you can block it with worry or tension. In the *Yoga Sutras*, Patanjali wrote, "Yoga is the cessation of the fluctuations of the mindstuff." Every intercourse, every maithuna, and every act of masturbation has the potential to be an act of Yoga, or union, provided there is a cessation of the fluctuations of the mind. Fluctuations of the mind include thought, reason, anxiety, and mental chatter. These are the things that inhibit the orgasmic response, and intense arousal can clear them all away.

There has been much discussion about women, but it is not as well known that vibrators are equally effective for men. If a man is experiencing problems with erection that are not organic in nature, for instance, if he is feeling fatigued or under a lot of stress and is not responding as he usually does, he can use a vibrator. The easiest way to use it is to enclose the penis within the fist and place the vibrator on the outside, so that the vibration goes through the hand and into the penis. This will often produce an erection and lead to orgasm. Couples too can heighten their sexual experiences by using a vibrator with each other to produce very powerful sensations. Thus, for both men and women, individually or in couples, the vibrator can serve as a powerful adjunct to Masturbation Magic and as a tool for sexual exploration in general.

If you want to get even more out of self-pleasuring—and therefore more out of Masturbation Magic, sex magic with a partner, or sex with a partner in general—you can use conscious masturbation as a technique for enhancing your sexual flexibility. One method is to experiment with different positions. Most people have one preferred position in which they masturbate; frequently, this is lying down. If you vary your masturbation experiments so that you learn to masturbate and climax sitting up, with one leg up on a chair, standing, or lying face-down as opposed to face-up, you can create new dimensions for yourself. So, when you masturbate, change your method. After you have begun to experiment with new methods, you may wish to explore new fantasies, as this too is likely to increase the range of your sexual response.

A vibrator becomes a very valuable adjunct in this context; it can help you start retraining yourself with new fantasies and new positions, which helps you to make yourself more flexible and open sexually. And this is something to consider very seriously. Masturbation Magic affords you an opportunity to bring about internal changes in yourself and external changes in terms of how you react to and interact with the environment.

Masturbation Magic is the essence of the most powerful human relationship possible: your own relationship with your inner world. Ultimately, all orgasms take place in the head, in the cranial cavity. This practice is more than simple self-pleasuring; it is an opportunity for self-exploration in safety and in comfort.

We human beings are responsible for our own pleasure and our own self-development. Ultimately, that is all we have in life. It is also a truism in human sexuality that we are responsible for our own orgasms. Embracing this doctrine of sexual magic leads to the understanding that in the climactic moment, that moment of no-thought that is orgasm, lies more than simple pleasure. That moment is literally the path to self-development by way of a self-engendered, mystical experience.

Approaching autoeroticism as an opportunity for mystical experiences is a powerful way to explore and balance our internal polarities at the deepest level, and this is the essence of the Tantric approach. All men have an inner feminine aspect, just as all women have an inner masculine aspect. Most people are afraid to embrace and explore these inner realms. Masturbation Magic gives a man an opportunity to explore his feminine aspect, just as it gives a woman an opportunity to explore her masculine aspect, in safety and in security.

In Western occult psychology, the conscious mind—whether we are biologically male or female—represents the masculine, active principle, and the unconscious mind represents the feminine, receptive aspect of our being. In Hindu Tantra, the masculine, Shiva principle is pure, inert consciousness, and the female principle is energy, or Shakti. There are polarities within polarities, masculinities within femininities and vice versa. But on a very profound level, Masturbation Magic allows an occult interplay to occur in such a way that the things in the active, conscious masculine mind can be readily ejaculated into the feminine unconscious to grow into a flower of self-development.

Masturbation Magic is a dynamic method of becoming the actor in life rather than the reactor, and the total essence lies in following the steps we detailed in chapter 6:

1. Focus on an erotic fantasy during the excitement phase.

2. As you approach climax, flash the three-dimensional colored vision we have described, the vision of that which you wish to bring about.

3. Inhale deeply, swallow, and hold the breath while climaxing and for a few seconds thereafter.

Thus, Masturbation Magic represents a powerful dynamic secret of Eastern Tantra and the Western sexual magic tradition. Literally, as with everything in life, it is in your hands.

eight

The Tantric Theory of Perfume Magic

Perfume Magic is a dramatic and exotic topic; in the simplest terms, it is nothing more than the art of leading someone around by the nose. This is more than mere aromatherapy, however. Magic is the art and science of causing changes to occur in conformity with the will; these changes can be either external or internal. Both external and internal changes can be effected using perfume once you have developed some basic skills.

The association between Tantra and magic is strong, but this association is not very well understood. Many Westerners tend to hold an exalted view of Eastern spirituality while disdaining magic as somehow unspiritual. The Tantric tradition certainly has a sublime dimension, but it also encompasses cruder forms of village magic—among them *Vashikaran Tantra*, techniques for bringing others under your control. The *Saradatilaka Tantra*, an extensive Tantric text not of the Vama Marga tradition, includes both instructions for spiritual liberation and spells for killing enemies, curing diseases, treating snakebite, acquiring wealth, having children, and attracting lovers.

In examining the Tantric aspect of perfume, we hope to place it in a cultural context that is suitable for Westerners but remains true to the essence of the tradition. "Tantric aspect" has a slightly different meaning in the context of Perfume Magic, a meaning related to the tradition of Vashikaran Tantra. In plain English, becoming adept in this art will enable you to grab someone by the nose and lead the person straight to bed. That is the essence of Perfume Magic.

The sense of smell, which is our primordial sense, is directly related to Ajna and Muladhara Chakras. That is the underlying premise of aromatherapy, and perfumes have many therapeutic applications that go far beyond aromatherapy as it is popularly understood and practiced. Scents can be used very effectively in psychotherapy. This approach originated in France, and Swamiji was the first Australian to employ it systematically. This form of aromatherapy unplugs the conscious mind and instantly connects a patient with the unconscious memory reservoir, frequently with fascinating and profound results. Certain scents can evoke powerful memories that often include a strong visual component.

Olfaction is also the quickest, most direct sensory avenue for awakening the genital center. When a person is exposed to particular categories of odors that are pleasing, the genital center awakens. The scent may not directly produce arousal, but it primes the psychic and physical pump, creating the conditions in which arousal can occur.

In order to understand how this works, we need to understand some basic anatomy and physiology. Consider the brain. Symbolically speaking, the brain is the embryonic spiritual person, and in occult anatomy, it is said that there is a cerebral master served by twelve disciples—the twelve nerves that come off the base of the brain, the medulla, and the brain stem. The first and foremost of the cerebral master's disciples is the olfactory nerve, cranial nerve one. At the end of the olfactory nerve are the olfactory bulb and tract. These sit between your eyes in the ceiling of your nose, and they penetrate deep into the limbic system of the brain, where most instinctive drives are generated. The ecstasy centers, the sexual response centers, the behavioral centers, and the emotional modification centers are located there. The olfactory nerve shoots straight through to the most primal part of our brain.

The olfactory nerve penetrates a bony plate and extends down into a postage-stamp-sized opening right at the top of your nose. This is stunning. First of all, this bony plate is almost tissue-thin; the cribriform (which means "like a sieve") plate is penetrated by actual holes. The end of the olfactory nerve is the only part of the human nervous system that is directly exposed to the environment.

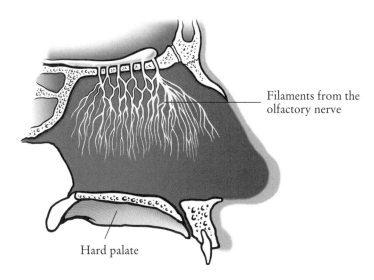

Filaments from the
olfactory nerve

Hard palate

The olfactory dendrites

The nerves hang down. You have heard the phrase "hanging loose." Well, the olfactory nerves are actually hanging loose; the filaments dangle. They don't literally dangle like the strands at the end of a mop. There is a mucus membrane that holds the filaments in place and protects them to some degree, but only to some degree; this mucus membrane is quite thin and permeable.

In the early 1970s, there was a big scare in Sydney. People were not chlorinating their swimming pools, and consequently, children were showing up in hospitals with something called amoebic meningitis. The amoeba that causes this form of meningitis lives in inadequately chlorinated swimming pools (and also in hot springs, since it can tolerate high temperatures). Australian kids were doing what kids will do—jumping into swimming pools. And, of course, if you don't hold your nose when you jump in the water, the water can be forced in. When amoebae were present, they would get driven up through the pores of the cribriform plate, right through to the meninges and the brain, and then start to reproduce, causing cerebral meningitis and inflaming the outer layer of the brain. There is no other place in the body and no other circumstance in which you will find such direct exposure and such nakedness.

Now consider another example. The G-spot in the mouth is up along the uvular ridge, approximately two-thirds of the way between the back of the teeth and the

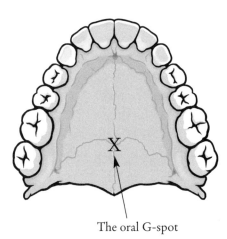

The oral G-spot

The oral G-spot is located toward the back of the hard palate

point at which the soft and hard palates meet. The brain sits right over the cribriform plate, and there are holes through it; this is where the dendrites hang down, directly above the oral G-spot. These nerves produce various kinds of problems in certain circumstances. We are all aware that viruses exist on the borderline between life and nonlife, and we all know that viruses can be so potent that we get the word *virulent* from the same root. Viruses are much smaller than other microorganisms, and they consist basically of a protein wrapping and a nucleus of DNA or RNA. Consequently, viruses are absolute vampires. They penetrate through a cell wall and ultimately take the cell over.

You may be wondering what this has to do with Perfume Magic. There is a subcategory of virus called a neurotropic virus—*neuro* meaning "nerves" and *tropic* meaning "to change." These viruses favor neural tissue. The polio virus is one example, and another is the influenza group of viruses. The word *influenza* is related to the concept of the "evil eye." It comes from the Italian for *influence*, and that is how they explained the illness in the sixteenth century: it was believed to be the result of the evil eye, so if you fell ill, a witch or black magician must have looked at you.

You catch influenza through exposure to someone who is infected. A person sneezes and throws out a fifteen-foot vapor cloud, and you go and inhale it. Or, you touch the person and then rub your eyes or pick your nose. Then the virus works its way up until it finds one of those dangling dendrites hanging. It latches on, starts climbing up, and begins to multiply. This is an example of how viruses can get at the only exposed part of the nervous system.

There is a way to inoculate yourself against influenza for the rest of your life, but this inoculation has a very serious side effect. You could perform a variation on a classical Yogic technique known as *Sutra Neti* (see chapter 3) by tying a knot in a wax cord and then ripping the cord through your nose, tearing out all the filaments. And you would never get influenza again. Unfortunately, you would never smell anything again either, and your sense of taste would be severely impaired. So, don't try this at home.

To reiterate, this olfactory sense is the most primal evolutionary sense. In more primitive vertebrates, taste and smell are combined. Unlike the many sensations of the skin, unlike the eyes and unlike the ears, the tracts from the olfactory nerves by-pass a relay station called the thalamus in the brain, so the sense of smell is unmediated by cognitive processes and goes straight back into the limbic system. That is why a smell will evoke a memory more quickly than an image, a sound, or anything else. Physiologically, smell hits us on the most primitive, unconscious level, often in ways that we can't begin to understand.

A classic story concerns a patient of Freud's who came to him as a middle-aged man. Freud's patient had a unique and disturbing experience: he had suddenly fallen in love with his wife's maid, who happened to be a walking, talking dragon. And there was no logical reason for him to fall for her. She was not attractive; on the surface, there was nothing in particular that would lead to understanding why this had happened. After about the fourth analytic session, he had a flash of insight, and they discovered the reason. The maid was wearing the same perfume that the man's mother wore when he was about five. He had fallen in love with the smell. Now, can you imagine that, saying, "Darling, it is your smell that I love, not you"? But it is often truer than we suspect. Each of us has an individual and very powerful odor print. The power that odor print has in our erotic lives is something we seldom recognize; it frequently affects us beneath the level of conscious awareness.

Cultivation of olfactory sensitivity leads to ESP—extra-sensual perception—and that extra-sensual perception leads to extra-sexual perception, and extra-sexual perception ultimately leads to extra-sensory perception. So, we have three kinds of ESP.

This relationship between sexuality and the nose is widely recognized in both East and West. In Tantra, we state unequivocally that the nose is the psychic genitalia. The nose is to the astral, mental, and spiritual bodies as the genitals are to the physical body. Thus, the psychosexual gateway to the subtle bodies is through the nose.

This relationship between the nose and sexuality is recognized in many cultures and is expressed in a wide variety of ways. For example, in Papua New Guinea, where Swamiji lived for a time, some tribal groups make a mask whose nose is elongated down to the genitals; the nose is explicitly and physically represented as linked to the genitals. This is a characteristic of an ancient culture that is about as remote as possible from the West, and yet it graphically represents an understanding of the linkage between sexuality and smell.

This primal awareness that exists around the world is embedded in a physiological fact. The lining of the nose is similar to nipple and genital tissue. There are only three parts of the body that contain erectile tissue: the genitals, the breasts, and the nose. The tissue of the nose is erectile tissue, and that means that under excitement and in certain other circumstances, those tissues will engorge and triple their thickness. During the excitement phase, the nasal mucosa thicken. In fact, one might say that sinusitis is caused by sexual frustration. Now, this is an oversimplification; nothing absolutely causes anything. But in some cases, constant sexual frustration, without any relief, can lead the nasal mucosa to engorge and trap sinus secretions in the cavities. There have been many instances in which sinusitis symptoms have been relieved by orgasm.

So, this tissue inside the nose is capable of swelling and contracting in a very definite way. And the nasal mucosa are not only made of erectile tissue, they are directly linked to sexual function. In ovariectomy, when the ovaries are totally taken out, or castration, the absence of normal circulating sexual hormones will start to shrink the nasal mucosa, and eventually they will atrophy, dry out, and become extremely thin. Sexual hormones, including estrogen, can be used to return nasal mucosa to their normal state.

During pregnancy, many women experience nosebleeds or nasal congestion. This too reveals the direct correlation between the nostrils and the uterus. The lining of the uterus is called the endometrium. During pregnancy, as this lining thickens, the tissue in the nose tends to thicken, leading to nasal congestion. Similarly, at puberty, prior to menarche, some girls experience what is known as vicarious menstruation—in other words, a nosebleed.

The connection between the nose and genitals is not limited to the similarity in tissue. The olfactory nerve itself is also intimately connected with the gonads, and the production of sexual hormones affects the sense of smell. Women often observe that their sensitivity to odors varies over the course of the menstrual cycle. Some women become more sensitive to odors at ovulation; others experience this sensitivity just before menstruation. As a general rule, females have greater sensitivity to odors than males under almost all circumstances.

The final implication of the Tantric perspective on the nose has to do with prana and the fact that the nose is the only freely exposed part of the nervous system, with the dendrites literally dangling. In Yoga, there is a strong emphasis on breathing through the nose, and some Yogic doctrines hold that breathing through the nose extracts the prana, or chi, or subtle, psychic energy. One of the easiest ways to experience this is to go down to the seaside on a particularly clear, fresh day and take a deliberate breath through the mouth and then take a deliberate breath through the nose. You are likely to notice a difference in the feeling inside you when breathing in that fresh air through your nose. You have taken in an equal amount of oxygen in each case, but you should be able to observe a subtle (or perhaps not so subtle) effect on the nervous system.

So, the sense of smell has a profound impact on human functioning on many levels. Physiologically, the nasal opening is a very vulnerable spot, and aromatic inputs affect us at the most primal levels. Psychically, the olfactory organs are directly connected with our basic drives and with Muladhara Chakra, so that scents evoke primal memories and stimulate the sexual response in realms untapped by the conscious mind. Armed with this knowledge, the Tantric practitioner can use an array of scents to work magic on others as well as on him- or herself, even when the targets of this magic have full knowledge that it is being employed. The next chapter will address specific ways to make use of this powerful magic.

nine

Perfume Magic in Practice

$\mathcal{I}$n this chapter, you will learn some terrible things, some things that may incense you—but in a good way. *Terrible* can mean "inspiring awe," and *incense* comes from the same Latin root as *incendiary*, "to kindle or to set on fire." When we become very angry, we are positively incensed. So, the word *incense* is an allegory for a change or an altered state of consciousness, the fire of transformation. For this reason, incense should be lit every time you meditate. If you make a practice of lighting incense every time you meditate, you will create an unconscious stimulus for yourself and produce a Pavlovian response. Before long, you will have conditioned yourself so completely that you will be halfway into a meditative state the moment you catch the scent of the incense.

You should be very careful about the quality of the incense you buy. The odor should be light, since it will impregnate all the hangings and the carpet. There is a potent Indian incense that, among many other things, has the very traditional cow dung and urine in it; these substances are considered sacred in India. But it is so potent that if you burn it regularly for a few months, the odor will completely permeate the room (and perhaps the adjoining rooms as well) and will be virtually impossible to eliminate.

Swamiji has a cautionary story about incense from his early years in Sydney. At the time, he had an apartment in Kings Cross; it was an interesting place in an interesting part of Sydney. He held some of his classes in the apartment, and he used

80   Chapter Nine

to burn this incense. When he moved out, he and his students couldn't get the place clean and couldn't get rid of the odor. The landlord was an archbishop, and he accused Swamiji of running a black magic cult, which was no small matter in Sydney at that time.

You also have to be careful because many cheaper incenses use artificial ingredients, and not just for the scent. Some use diesel oil as the glue to hold the sandalwood together. If you light it, you can smell the diesel. So, we recommend you use high-quality sandalwood (*chandan*) incense from India; *sambrani*, which is popular in South India, is wonderful too, but it is much smokier and more potent. The Rosicrucians use rose, and this is another good selection.

There is a correct etiquette to using incense in the Hindu and Tantric traditions, and many people are unaware of this. The most important thing to understand is that once the stick is lit, you never blow it out. When you create fire, you create Lord Agni, and this is a symbol of transmutation. Agni is the master alchemist. He takes the body at cremation and transmutes it to a higher level. The flame is sacred, and it is disrespectful to blow upon a flame. This is more than just blind obedience to ritual; it has a deeper, psychic meaning. One euphemism for dying is to say, "So-and-so has expired." The expired breath is dead breath. It is full of carbon dioxide. Never insult Lord Agni by actually blowing upon the flame; respect the flame that stands for transformation and the light of consciousness. Always wave the end out. And, if you want to get rid of the glowing end, you snuff it out. The same goes for candles: you should snuff them, clap them, or wave them out.

Let us turn to perfume. Women through the ages have learned to be clever and skillful in the use of perfumes, but in Western society, it is only recently that some men have begun to develop any knowledge of perfume. *Perfume* is derived from the Latin word *per*, meaning "through" (as in *permeate*), and *fume*, meaning "smoke."

Originally, perfume was composed of powdered incense, and its object was to send a message to the gods. Contacting the gods through smoke or scent is a practice that exists in spiritual traditions the world over. In Tantra, we ourselves are God, and when we use perfume, we are sending a message to ourselves, to the higher self, and to others. The application of perfume enables your physical body to send a message to the subtle bodies of another person through the nose. The scent you wear touches the unconscious mind of anyone who is within olfactory range. Not only does your personal use of perfume affect those around you, it also affects your own mental state. So, when you wear perfume, you trigger your unconscious and generate a mild altered state of consciousness in yourself.

Beware of synthetic oils. Just as with incense, they may contain very unpleasant ingredients, so you must have confidence in the source. In some instances, synthetic products can be perfectly all right. The problem is not that synthetic oils are not "natural" but that synthetic oils are often more allergenic.

Swamiji has a wonderful gift for laughing at himself and seeing the humor in his own foibles. He tells of returning from India after being initiated by Paramahansa Satyananda. On his return, he brought quite a few *tulsi* (basil) *malas* (strings of beads) back to initiate his own students in Kriya. Tulsi is sacred to Lord Vishnu and is reputed to lower the blood pressure and produce a state of equilibrium. He soaked the malas in sandalwood oil (which has other effects) to supplement the benefits of the tulsi. He distributed the malas to his students at the initiation, and he gave himself one. Within three days, he developed an allergic reaction because the sandalwood oil he used was synthetic. It took months for that reaction to go away, and one of his students also developed it. There were no hard feelings, but this anecdote illustrates the perils of using synthetic oils.

Although natural essential oils are preferable and less allergenic, there are no guarantees. If you are concerned about developing an allergy and you want to be careful, dab a bit of the oil on the crease inside your elbow and leave it there for twenty-four hours. If you do not get a rash, you probably will not have a reaction.

From a Tantric viewpoint, Perfume Magic revolves around primal olfactory stimuli, and the most primal olfactory stimuli are all related to modifications to and amplifications of the basic sexual odors of the body. Fifty percent of what people call the aura is olfactory awareness—subliminal olfactory awareness. Each of us emits an olfactory field, which others are constantly sniffing. Most of us never even realize it, but these olfactory cues have a powerful influence on how others perceive us. The cues emanate from certain scent glands and the secretions from under the arms and in the groin. The Tantrika, unlike the average person, makes conscious and intentional use of these cues.[1]

---

1 Swamiji recently observed that "contemporary research indicates vanilla (for women) scent has an aphrodisiac effect upon men, as does lavender. This has resulted in an upsurge in available vanilla perfumes and colognes. Unani (traditional Arabic indigenous medicine) teaches that sandalwood attar is an anaphrodisiac; however, this is contradicted by the use of sandalwood as a base in many Western perfumes and colognes for men. The Unani

In the classical perfumer's manual, the essential scents include musk—a word derived from *mushka,* a Sanskrit word for "testicle"—and civet. In fact, musk comes from the glandular secretions of a male deer, and civet comes from the sexual part of the civet cat. The civet cat is a loveable animal, absolutely fair and impartial to every other living thing; it hisses at any creature it sees. Also valuable to the perfumer is castorium, which comes from the sexual organs of the beaver. Ambergris, a secretion of the sperm whale, is another important ingredient; ambergris is usually found floating in the ocean or washed up on the beach, so whales are generally not killed to obtain it.

If you were to do an analysis of one of your favorite commercial perfumes, you would find a base of one or more of these substances. If you are familiar with the traditional oils and understand their properties, you can learn to make them your own. This will enable you to take whatever perfume you like and make it uniquely yours. We will start with the traditional scents; these have withstood the test of time, and modern chemical analyses have validated the traditional understanding.

The first is musk. Musk works for both men and women, although it is somewhat more effective as a feminine scent. It is important to understand that no matter how a perfume may smell on its own, placing it on your skin will alter its odor. It mixes with the secretions from your skin, as well as with your aura, your overall energetic makeup. You will have to discover for yourself just how it works for you.

Sandalwood is recommended for men as a Tantric perfume. For meditation, it is equally good for men and women, but as a personal scent, it is more suitable for men because it has a molecular structure that is also found in male urine and semen. At a subliminal level, it mimics the odor of male urine and semen, and as you will discover, this mimicry is an essential component of its effectiveness.

Patchouli is another scent that is best used by women. Both patchouli and musk were very popular in the 1960s and early '70s, and many people dislike them because they were overused in those days. Today, patchouli is fairly exotic, and for younger people, it can be a very effective scent. For those who came of age when patchouli

---

and Tamil Siddha traditions agree that musk is a powerful enhancer of sexual mood for both men and women. Since I gave these lectures in 1976, the interest in what was formerly considered 'folklore' accelerated rapidly, and by the end of the twentieth century, this interest had generated extensive 'odor' research." Many references to this research are readily available online. (Personal communication, March 22, 2006.)

was in vogue, it can still be very effective because of the memories it evokes. Nevertheless, you don't have to like any particular scent, because, as we will explain, you can learn to take whatever you do like and make it uniquely yours.

Patchouli has a profound effect on many men because its aroma mimics vaginal secretions. Speaking of secretions, there is a *secret* to impart about *secretions*: the two words are closely related. The body's secretions—not *ex*cretions but *se*cretions—are wonderful tools, as long as there is no pathology present and as long as they are fresh. Perspiration, which we will talk about later, is a very powerful aphrodisiac perfume when used properly, but it must be fresh. Stale perspiration gives us the body odor that most people find repulsive. Isn't it amazing? Here we have something that is wonderfully stimulating when fresh, but once it is stale, it shuts off the sexual response completely. And all this happens through the olfactory system.

Our body odor actually changes due to sexual excitement, since it is based on our sexual secretions and perspiration. This has a number of implications. In the past, the powers of the nose and the sense of smell were recognized. Nowadays, we live in a civilized era, and the powers of the olfactory sense are mostly underappreciated. But even today, when you say someone "has a nose for this" or "has an instinct for that" or "can smell trouble," you are embracing this ancient wisdom and are talking about those extra-sensory perceptions that have devolved from extra-sexual perception and extra-sensual perception to the olfactory sense.

Georg Groddeck is almost a forgotten man today, but he deserves to be remembered. He was a genius who had a significant impact on Freud. His *Book of the It* gave Freud the term *id*. Groddeck believed that as civilization grew more stratified, it became necessary to control human sexuality to maintain the structure of society. He contended that one key way to control sexuality was to repress sensitivity to odor. Groddeck's insight about the sense of smell is important, whether or not you accept his broader thesis.

Of course, we know that dogs have an incredible extra-sensual perception that borders on the extra-sensory; it far exceeds our own capacities. Remember that the human olfactory epithelia—those little dendrites—are just the size of a postage stamp. Those same olfactory epithelia take up two-thirds of a dog's snout. Female dogs leave a urine trail containing a sexual hormone when they are in heat, and potential mates respond to the smell. Dogs can pick up something that is unique about any individual human too. That is, dogs can detect an individual odor print. Just as each of us has a unique fingerprint, so each of us has a unique odor print. And dogs can track us; if they have a piece of clothing or something to get the scent from, they will track us to the end of the world if necessary (but even dogs have trouble distinguishing between the odor prints of identical twins).

There are three important factors to bear in mind: First, it is quite clear that odor functions as a powerful sensory pathway unto itself. Second, our ability to perceive the world is determined to a large extent by our physiological limitations—this is the real meaning of *maya* (illusion). Third, despite our limitations, to the extent that we can learn to use our senses more fully, we can start to see beyond the veil, so to speak.

This is all leading somewhere very practical and scientific. A hormone is a bio-chemical message released into the bloodstream and taken to a target site in the body. For example, the adrenal glands sit on top of the kidneys—*suprarenals*, "above the renals," to be pedantic about it. The adrenals have a number of functions, the release of adrenaline the most familiar among them. So, if you shout, "Boo!" and frighten someone, adrenaline is released from a portion of the suprarenal glands. It flows through the bloodstream, dilates the pupils (improving vision), causes the heart to race, raises blood sugar, and induces a systemic alerting response. Adrenaline is the hormone. It is a chemical messenger that sends the alert, the flashing red light, the panic button.

That kind of chemical message is well understood in the scientific community and has been for years. More recently, scientists have started talking about a new kind of chemical message. Actually, the entomologists have been observing this in insects since Aristotle's time, although it was not until 1956 that a specific substance was identified in silkworm moths.

These chemical messages are called *pheromones*. Pheromones are airborne messages; hormones are carried through the bloodstream systemically, but pheromones are airborne olfactory messages. It is well known that the male in some species of moth can track the female moth for five miles, but it was not until the 1970s that anyone thought of examining whether something similar could exist in human beings. Now we know that we humans are constantly sending out pheromones, or olfactory signals, to each other.

Most of the early studies on pheromones used women as subjects. In the early 1970s, Professor Martha McClintock, formerly a professor at Harvard University and now at the University of Chicago, began a study with women living in a dormitory. McClintock found that after a period of time, women living closely together begin to experience synchronization of their menstrual cycles. McClintock theorized that when women begin to menstruate, they release a pheromone. She then went a step further. She decided to test the connection between length of menstrual cycles—whether it was a long duration or a short duration, such as a twenty-eight-day cycle or a thirty-eight-day cycle—and frequency of sexual intercourse with boyfriends (she had another, euphemistic term for it). She found that the more incidents of sexual intercourse, the shorter the menstrual cycles, so if you have someone whose normal cycle is twenty-eight days and she becomes very sexually active, her cycle might shorten to twenty-three or twenty-four days.[2]

McClintock concluded that the more sexually excited we become, the more we give off these pheromones, or subliminal olfactory cues. So you see, boy loves girl, boy makes effort to please girl, girl turns on, and that turns boy on even more. Boy turns on more, which pleases girl more. Girl turns on more, including menstruating more frequently as she gets more and more excited. You see the cycle of boy-turns-girl-on, girl-turns-boy-on, boy-turns-girl-on. You have this constant feedback system going on, and it is quite subtle and quite interesting.

Research on pheromones has continued gradually since McClintock did her pioneering work, and various commercial ventures offering pheromone-based perfumes have been set up, but it is probably best to use your very own pheromones. They are triggers for sexual responses in other people. Fresh perspiration is the most powerful. There's truth in the old story about the country bumpkin at the dance who changed his luck when he learned the trick of putting a handkerchief under his armpit, dancing with the ladies, and offering it to them to wipe their brows. Fresh perspiration has a strongly aphrodisiac effect.

---

2 McClintock was a scientific prodigy. Her first publication on the subject of pheromones appeared in *Nature* just two years after she graduated from Wellesley College, where she had conducted her research as an undergraduate. Martha K. McClintock, "Menstrual Synchrony and Suppression," *Nature* 229 (1971): 244–245. The article shocked the male-dominated scientific community. She has remained a major figure in this field of research, and in 1998, she published another groundbreaking article in *Nature*, showing that pheromones also play a role in regulating ovulation. Kathleen Stern and Martha K. McClintock, "Regulation of Ovulation by Human Pheromones," *Nature* 392 (1998): 177–179. Even more recently, McClintock conducted a study indicating that breast-feeding women and their infants produce a pheromone that increases sexual desire in other women. Martha K. McClintock, "Social Chemosignals from Breastfeeding Women Increase Sexual Motivation," *Hormones and Behavior* 46, no. 3 (2004): 362–370.

When Swamiji was very young—in his early teens—his father was an officer in the Canadian army. He was a senior officer, nearing retirement, and he had a batman. A batman is a soldier, in this case a corporal, who is assigned to look after an officer's personal needs. This batman used to look after Swamiji and give him all kinds of tips. The batman told Swamiji, "Look, you want a girlfriend. What you do is put a handkerchief under your testicles for a couple hours before the dance, and then take it out and put it in your pocket." Maybe it was a placebo, but Swamiji claims he believed in it, and it worked. To this day, he insists it did wonders for him.

Dr. Alex Comfort, who wrote *The Joy of Sex* and also was a Sanskrit scholar and translator, conducted scientific research on monkeys. In one experiment, he did panhysterectomies on female monkeys, meaning he removed the ovaries and the uterus; in monkeys, this type of surgery results in the utter absence of vaginal secretions. When Comfort introduced these neutered female monkeys to a group of sex-starved male monkeys, the male monkeys were more interested in each other.

After Comfort observed this for a while, he removed the female monkeys, smeared their fur with vaginal secretions from other female monkeys, and then returned them to the cage. Suddenly, the male monkeys went mad. They actually recorded a case of a male monkey attempting to mount a female monkey 213 times in an hour. Now that is what you call incendiary!

This is not to suggest that we humans have the same olfactory capacities as monkeys do, and the mating habits of monkeys are not identical to our own. Still, they are our close relatives, and the experiment has implications for us. So now we get down to the fundamental question: how do we grab them by the nose and lead them into bed?

Modern perfumes always have a sexual base of civet, musk, or castorium. You may have already guessed what transforms an ordinary perfume into your own personal Tantric sexual perfume. But it is not quite that simple; you must do several things in a specific order. Remember that the nature of sexual secretions and perspiration favors periods of sexual arousal, since that is when you emit the strongest psychic and olfactory signals. You can take any perfume that you like and potentiate it, Tantrically, so that it sends out your personal pheromone.

There are several steps to making your own potentiated perfume. Remember that sandalwood is optimal for men, but you are free to use your favorite scent. Vetiver, which Swamiji did not discuss in the original lectures, is another excellent choice for men and a personal favorite. It is made from kush-kush grass, which is sacred to Sri Ganesh. So, you take your favorite perfume and put your own semen into it, plus one drop of urine. Ejaculate and collect the semen first. You should urinate after ejaculating and collect the first third of the urine in a glass. Then take one drop of that urine and as much of the semen as you want and mix them with your perfume or oil. You have now Tantrically charged the oil and infused it with your pheromone. Note that this is done during and immediately after a period of sexual excitement.

The process is similar for women, but it is even more magical. If you are pre-menopausal, wait until your moon time arrives and use your menstrual blood—not a lot, just a couple of drops. You must bring yourself to orgasm while menstruating, while the anatomic reservoir has menstrual blood in it. The orgasm will charge the blood psychically and, in all likelihood, add to its pheromonal content. So, you take a few drops of your blood after orgasm and, just as with men, collect the first third of your urine in a glass. Then add the blood and one drop of the urine to your favorite perfume or cologne, preferably musk or patchouli. So, there it is: one drop of urine, a few drops of menstrual blood, all taken immediately after orgasm, and guess what? You have your own pheromone, your own personal Tantric scent. Post-menopausal women can use vaginal fluid or female ejaculate to good effect.

Most perfumes contain a preservative—sometimes natural and sometimes artificial—so the menstrual blood and the semen are not likely to spoil. If you are concerned about spoilage or want to be sure you are using a natural substance, you can add a tiny bit of balsam of Peru, and that will function as a natural preservative.

Once you have created your personal scent, the trick is to learn to use it correctly. In order to make your scent work for you, you need to know the perfume points. These perfume points lie at six pulse points and three perspiration points.

A pulse point is located where an artery is close to the surface of the body, and you should be able to locate each one by feeling the pulse. Remember to apply the perfume on both sides of the body. The psychology and physiology of this are wonderful, because by using the pulse and perspiration points, you are involving a feedback system. As you become more excited or sexually stimulated, the heart rate increases and the blood flows through the arteries more rapidly. Blood carries the infrared radiation that releases olfactory stimuli, or pheromones. This feedback system reinforces the effect of the scent.

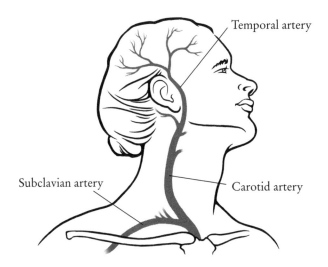

Pulse Points 1–3: The Temporal, Carotid, and Subclavian Arteries

The pulse points are as follows:

1. The Temporal Artery. This is located between the tragus and the jaw; the tragus is the little flap of cartilage that covers the ear opening. This is the proper place on the head to put your perfume. You don't dab it behind the ears; that is totally useless. The temporal artery is the first pulse point; if you kiss your partner, it will be closest to the nose, which will set hearts racing.

2. The Carotid Artery. Here's the reason that vampires are said to go for the neck. The carotid is located between the voice box and the adjacent muscle. If you feel around gently, just one finger at a time, you should be able find the pulse; the carotid is the third largest artery in the body.

3. The Subclavian Artery. This one is more difficult to find, but with patience, you should be able to locate it. Take your cologne and reach down inside your collarbone. If you don't feel a pulse, just press down a little. This is one of those places military trainees learn to stab with a knife or bayonet. All the pulse points are targets in the lethal martial arts, since the blood vessels are so close to the surface, but we are talking about love here. It is amazing that you can go to the same parts of the body for such different purposes.

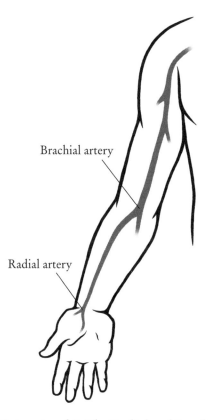

Pulse Points 4 and 5: The Radial and Brachial Arteries

4. The Radial Artery. This pulse point is located on the thumb side of the wrist. We should all know how to take our own pulse. Apply the perfume on that exact pulse point. Now imagine you are on a date and you are facing each other across the dinner table, and it is tantalizing. Maybe you are talking with your hands, or maybe she talks with hers, and you get a whiff of her perfume . . .

5. The Brachial Artery. This is the point on the inside of the arm at the elbow and below the biceps, on the little-finger side of the tendon that runs down the center—the point where the blood pressure is measured. So, if you ever get it into your head to seduce your doctor, you can rely on this point.

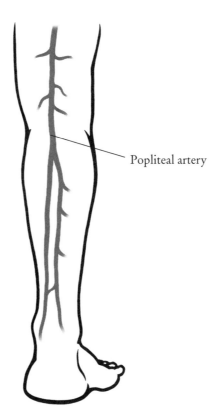

Popliteal artery

Pulse Point 6: The Popliteal Artery

6. The Popliteal Artery. This artery lies behind the knee. It is a little tricky to feel, but you need not locate it exactly. All that is necessary is to dab some perfume behind the knee. You should also note that it is an erogenic zone, as are all the other pulse points. The erogenic zones are discussed in more detail in chapters 10 through 13.

The Perspiration Points

For women, a key perspiration point is between the breasts, in the cleavage, where the body heat builds up. Of course, this is also the location of Anahata (heart) Chakra. As you get sexually excited, your heart rate increases and you generate more infrared light. This means you will start to perspire more. So, as your body heats, the perspi-

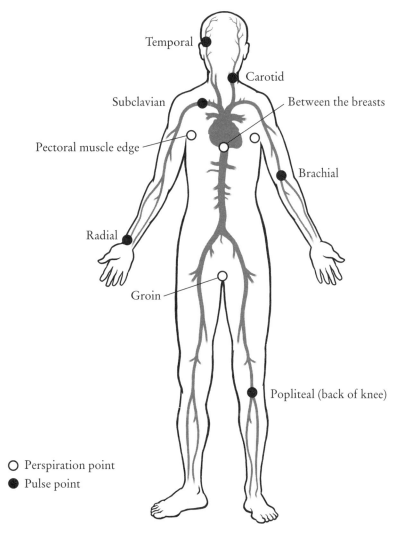

Map of the Perfume Magic pulse and perspiration points on the body

ration points will release more of the scent. Between the breasts is a particularly important point for women, and it is fine for men as well.

Equally important for men and women are the groin and under the arms—actually not right in the armpit, but toward the front, on the edge of the pectoral muscle. You don't want to interfere with the sweat glands. Always remember to make sure you do not have an allergic reaction, since the skin in the groin and armpits is very sensitive.

If you want a concrete demonstration of how the olfactory sense can touch the unconscious and evoke memories, here is something you can try at home. You will need to enlist a friend and have a blindfold handy, as well as a selection of different scents. You can use a tester for aromatherapy, select several essential oils, or choose a mix of fresh fruits, herbs, and spices. As a general rule, most of these scents will trigger a memory.

There are five steps:

1. Check the subject's nostrils and find out whether the left or right nostril is open or dominant.

2. Blindfold the subject, since that will intensify the focus.

3. Tell the subject to relax and observe anything that goes through the mind, without trying to identify the scent.

4. Place the source of the aroma under the subject's dominant nostril. This step is complete when the scent evokes an experience (often a visual experience) in the subject. Take a moment and allow the subject to experience any memories that the aroma evokes. Ask her to tell you what age she is in the memory and what she sees. Try a few different fragrances.

5. Reverse roles.

This simple experiment demonstrates the strong connection between the olfactory sense and the unconscious. Smell is the sensory avenue for Muladhara Chakra, so it is connected not only with the deepest reaches of memory but also with our most basic drives, including our sexuality. Although the olfactory sense is directly related to the earth element and those aspects of our makeup that some would describe as "gross," it also operates on the most subtle levels, and indeed on every level of our being.

Once you have mastered the basics of Perfume Magic, you will know how to strengthen your aura, how to lead people around by the nose, how to get them right between the eyes and drag them into bed or do whatever you want—and that knowledge should fill you with awe and wonder and get you all fired up.

ten

Overview of the Tantric
Erogenic Zones or Kama Marmas

In the years since Swamiji first discussed the Kama Marmas, other authors and teachers have borrowed some of this material, sometimes without acknowledging their debt to his pioneering work and usually without placing it in the proper context. To the best of our knowledge, the Gnosticon lectures were the first time this material was presented in a public forum in the West. Swamiji made an important contribution not only in bringing this classical South Indian material to the Western world, but also in synthesizing ancient teachings with modern understanding and presenting a system that is straightforward, logical, and easy to put into practice.

In order to make sure the information is made available in its entirety and is presented in the context of his other teachings on Tantra, he has been kind enough to supplement the original lectures with information that expands upon and explains the material more fully. Some of this additional material is derived from lectures given in Sydney, Australia, in the 1980s, and some of it comes from his personal archives and is being made public for the first time.[1]

---

1 This additional material includes Sanskrit terminology related to the Kama Marmas. Marma therapy, which is akin to acupressure, exists in both the Tamil Siddha and Ayurvedic traditions. Unlike the Ayurvedic Marmas, which are specific points, the Kama Marmas encompass entire zones surrounding the specific point. Some of the terms are identical to those applied to the Ayurvedic Marmas; others are unique to this system, which

Swamiji used the term *erogenic zones* to avoid confusion with erogenous zones, which were a popular topic in Western sexology during the 1970s. Although the Tantric erogenic zones would all qualify as erogenous zones, they have psychic and psychological implications in addition to physical importance, hence the need to highlight the distinction. As a prelude to an in-depth discussion of the erogenic zones, it is worth remembering that for thousands of years people in the East intimately understood the sexual response cycle that was first fully articulated in the West by Masters and Johnson in the 1960s. Because Eastern knowledge about sexuality was so sophisticated and was unconstrained by concepts of sin, it was possible to develop an art of sexual practice that far surpassed anything similar in the West. This body of knowledge, and the aesthetic it produced, led in turn to a very different orientation in terms of what is sought in the sexual experience.

As we explained in the chapter on Vama Marga Tantra, the Tantric approach to the four-phase cycle of excitement, plateau, climactic peaking, and resolution requires, first and foremost, a focus on the excitement phase. If the emphasis is placed upon the excitement phase, the human sexual experience can become goalless. If you remain focused on prolonging the excitement, it is possible to enter a state in which there is nothing to achieve, nothing to reach after, and nothing to accomplish. There is no masculinity to be demonstrated and no femininity to be demonstrated, and suddenly there is nothing to be proved or disproved. And that is a very interesting thought—one that Western psychologists would do well to integrate into their outlook.

In Western terms, we carry ourselves as whole beings into every sexual encounter—including our past experiences; our current mental, emotional, and physical states; and our hopes and expectations about the encounter itself. Carrying

---

Swamiji adapted from traditional sources. He has provided the following description of the origins of this system: While training with Paramahansa Satyananda at the Bihar School of Yoga in 1973, Swamiji was exposed to the teachings of Tamil Siddha practitioners. These teachings provided him with the concept of working with the Kama Marmas. Siddha is a South Indian system of indigenous Tamil medicine that can be traced to the eighth century CE, if not earlier, and traditionally is said to predate Ayurveda and Unani systems. The Siddha system of erogenic zones is based on the phases of the lunar cycle and follows a daily rotation in a woman's body, starting at the right big toe. Some elements of this system were popularized the *Ananga Ranga,* a fifteenth-century Indian sex manual. Swamiji worked for three years to translate this system and to develop classifications and groupings that would be most suitable for Westerners, while integrating the Indian approach to sexuality as enjoined in the classical love manuals and the Tantric texts. He first presented the results of this work at Gnosticon.

ourselves as whole beings encompasses the positive and the negative, the full range of human emotion and experience. Sexuality is extremely powerful and extremely fragile; every given moment in a sexual experience has no predictable outcome. Unconscious factors will always come into play, even among the most self-aware individuals.

This shows up externally in men more than in women. A man can have all sorts of unconscious processes going on internally, and at any given moment, these may affect his sexual function—something impossible to disguise, and the reasons sometimes impossible to identify. Virtually all sexually active men will experience impotence, loss of erection, or premature ejaculation at some point in their lives. There are many things that can trigger these incidents, but for our purposes, the most important contributing factor is goal orientation. If one approaches a sexual experience with expectations, this creates a condition in which there will be success or failure. The experience can then turn into a kind of test, and tests are often accompanied by debilitating performance anxiety.

From the Tantric viewpoint, one should emphasize the excitement phase. Implicit in this approach is the understanding that the excitement phase has its own ebb and flow, so for men, the external sign of arousal is not nearly so important. Whatever happens, each experience is unique and has its particular intrinsic value on its own terms and not as a mere prelude to a "main event." Thus, there is nothing to lose—no success, no failure, only the fullness of the experience itself. This concept is easy to understand intellectually, but it takes time to absorb it and live it, particularly in the West, where we are trained from an early age to be goal-oriented beings.

There is a strong relationship between language and sexual attitudes, and it is very interesting to consider the word *rapture* from this perspective, since it illustrates some of the complexities that are embedded in our cultural mores. *Rapture* can refer to "a blissful state of excitement," yet it is etymologically related to *rape*. Today, that word sends chills up everyone's spine, but in the fifteenth century, *rape* didn't mean what it means now. *Rape* originally meant "abduction" or "carrying away by force," and from *rape* came *rapt*, and from *rapt* came *rapture*. So, *rapture* implies being taken outside of one's normal state, being swept away or carried off, but in a very positive sense and by an altogether different kind of force. The indefinite prolonging of the excitement phase induces a state of rapture, a state in which only the present matters. Who can say what the outcome of a rapturous state will be? What do we say about people who are infatuated? They are *wrapped up* in each other, and *wrapped up* has the same meaning and the same sense of being enclosed, enfolded, and transported or carried off.

Being wrapped up in your partner is a specific psychic state that is characteristic of Tantric sexuality. That enwrapment or enfoldment comes from prolonging the excitement phase. The excitement phase is also the psychic phase, and truly experiencing it involves becoming aware of and immersed in a subtle energy that few in the West ever consider or even recognize.

Remember that in Vama Marga Tantra, we develop ESP, not extra-sensory perception but extra-sensual perception. Ideally, in Tantra, there is no such thing as genital excitement, although the familiar signs of genital arousal may of course be present. We Westerners are prone to think that sensual sensation is synonymous with sexual sensation, which is synonymous with genital sensation and genital sensation only. And we are likely to believe that this is the natural order of things and that the genitals are the proper place for sensual perception to be experienced.

In Tantra, we strive to turn the entire surface of the skin into a massive genital. That is one of the hidden meanings of the Sanskrit root *tanoi,* "to expand." The Tantric approach is to transform our consciousness and refine our awareness so that every square inch of the skin becomes an erogenous zone and the entire body one massive genital. To accomplish this, the Tantrics have developed a brilliant and very refined understanding of the erogenic zones. By using these zones consciously as a map for sensual stimulation, you can begin this process of transformation.

There are three categories of erogenic zone, and we can identify them as primary, secondary, and tertiary. These include, but are not limited to, the zones that are commonly identified as erogenous zones in Western sexology. Within these zones, there are specific trigger points, known as *Marma points*; these are similar conceptually to acupressure or acupuncture points, and in fact often correspond with specific points in the Chinese system.

Like the chakras, the Kama Marmas serve as a roadmap of the body and energetic system and are a very useful tool for exploring erotic experience and expanding your sensual perception. In fact, the location of the Kama Marmas, or erogenic zones, is directly related to the first five chakras and their respective sensory avenues, or *jnanindriyas* (knowing organs), and activity-output paths, or *karmindriyas* (action organs).

It is not necessary to have a comprehensive understanding of psychic anatomy to benefit from working with the Kama Marmas. Your own experience is more important than theoretical knowledge. Nevertheless, the chart below is worthy of contemplation and is based upon the allocations of the classical *Shatchakra Nirupana*, a book that any serious student of Tantra should peruse.

The first general principle in Tantric lovemaking is that stimulation should proceed downward toward the genitals, except in the case of the erogenic zones of the feet, legs, and thighs, from which the movement should flow upward toward the genitals. In a general sense, this is a more feminine approach to stimulation, moving from the periphery of the body to the center. The purpose is to get the pranic energy flowing toward the genitals without touching the genitals themselves until the energy is sufficiently directly engaged.

Chakra (psychic)	Jnanindriya (sensory/afferent)	Karmindriya (motor/efferent)
Muladhara (earth)	smell—nose	legs, feet—ambulating
Swadhisthana (water)	taste—tongue	hands—grasping
Manipura (fire)	sight—eyes	anus—expelling
Anahata (air)	touch—skin	genitals—secreting, procreating
Vishuddhi (space)	hearing—ears	throat, neck—speaking

Pranic energy is the subtle psychic energy that pervades the universe and exists within each of us; it is analogous to *chi* or *ki* in the Chinese and Japanese systems, and it runs along certain well-defined pathways. In the Hindu tradition, the central pathway is *Sushumna*, the central channel, and alongside and wrapped around Sushumna are the "stepsisters" *Ida* and *Pingala*. Most of that energy is running in Ida and Pingala, but some of it is always running in Sushumna. When we can stop all of the energy running in Ida and Pingala and get it to run up Sushumna, then we get ecstasy; we get rapturous, totally swept away from ourselves. By concentrating the energy in the genital region, we create the conditions in which we can begin to direct more and more of it into Sushumna and thereby create this ecstatic state.

These psychic tubes for the transfer of subtle energy have their anatomical counterparts. In this context, the word *psychic* refers to something that cannot be demonstrated anatomically but that can be directly experienced. You can develop your own

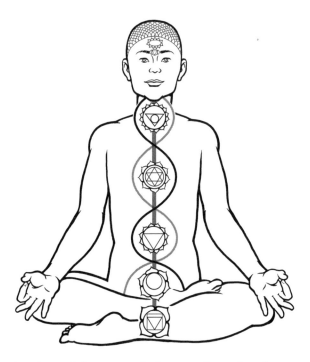

The classical depiction of Ida, Pingala, and Sushumna,
in which the channels meet and cross at the chakras, forming a caduceus

empirical evidence that the Sushumna channel carries a subtle energy. It is as real as the spinal cord. The only difference is that if you read about the spinal cord, you believe it. If you get into an argument about anatomy, you can (theoretically) go down and look at a cadaver and locate the spinal column. On the other hand, you can't touch a Sushumna, but you can discover what happens when you start playing with your own Sushumna.

To reiterate, we begin the process by concentrating energy in the genital region, thereby stimulating the movement of energy into Sushumna. Remember, there are very specific patterns that can be followed in the context of stimulating particular points and zones so as to maximize stimulation and arousal.

The terms *primary*, *secondary*, and *tertiary* do not refer to the order in which the zones should be stimulated, but rather to the general degree of sensitivity in the given zone, although this may vary from individual to individual. There are many details about specific points that are worthy of attention and understanding,

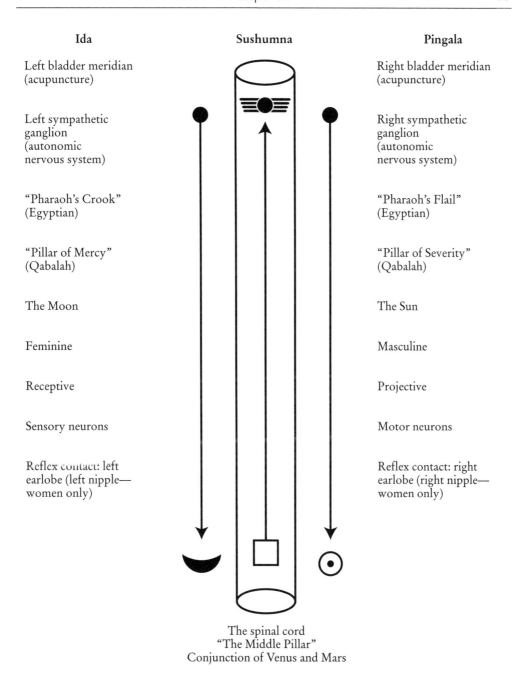

Ida   **Sushumna**   **Pingala**

Left bladder meridian   Right bladder meridian
(acupuncture)   (acupuncture)

Left sympathetic   Right sympathetic
ganglion   ganglion
(autonomic   (autonomic
nervous system)   nervous system)

"Pharaoh's Crook"   "Pharaoh's Flail"
(Egyptian)   (Egyptian)

"Pillar of Mercy"   "Pillar of Severity"
(Qabalah)   (Qabalah)

The Moon   The Sun

Feminine   Masculine

Receptive   Projective

Sensory neurons   Motor neurons

Reflex contact: left   Reflex contact: right
earlobe (left nipple—   earlobe (right nipple—
women only)   women only)

The spinal cord
"The Middle Pillar"
Conjunction of Venus and Mars

Ida, Pingala, and Sushumna represented as parallel channels

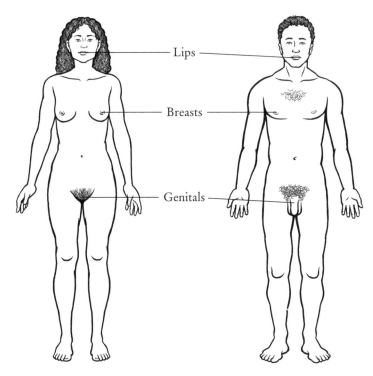

The Primary Erogenic Zones

but as an initial matter, it is necessary to establish the categories and have a preliminary knowledge of the classical sequence.

Primary zones include the lips (and, more generally, the mouth as a whole), the
breasts (particularly the nipples), and the genitals.

Secondary zones include the earlobe, the nape of the neck, the sacral-lumbar
junction, the gluteal fold, and the inside of the thigh.

Tertiary zones include the outside surface of the little finger, the center of the
palm, the navel, the anus, the anterior nares, the external auditory meatus, the sole
of the foot, the big toe, the thumb, and the back of the knee.

The traditional approach involves simulating (usually by kissing or licking) the
secondary zones first, then the primary zones (though not the genitals), then the
tertiary zones, and finally back to the primary zones (including the genitals). This is
a four-beat pattern, and there is certainly room for modification and expansion so
that, for example, you might work very gradually and not reach the genitals before

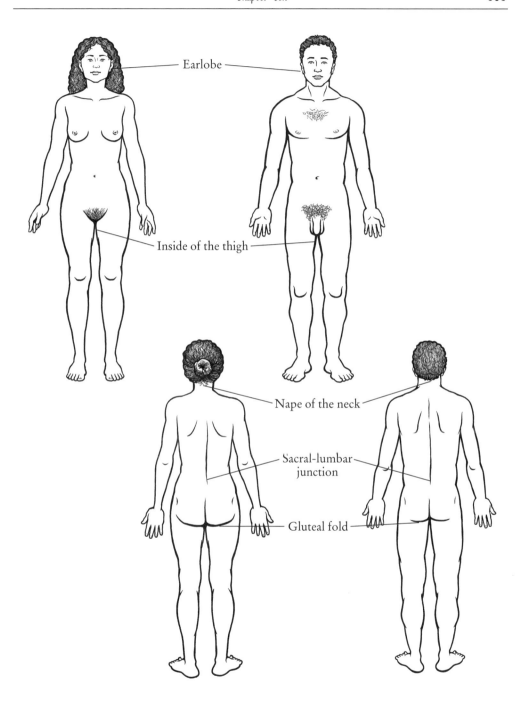

Earlobe

Inside of the thigh

Nape of the neck

Sacral-lumbar
junction

Gluteal fold

The Secondary Erogenic Zones

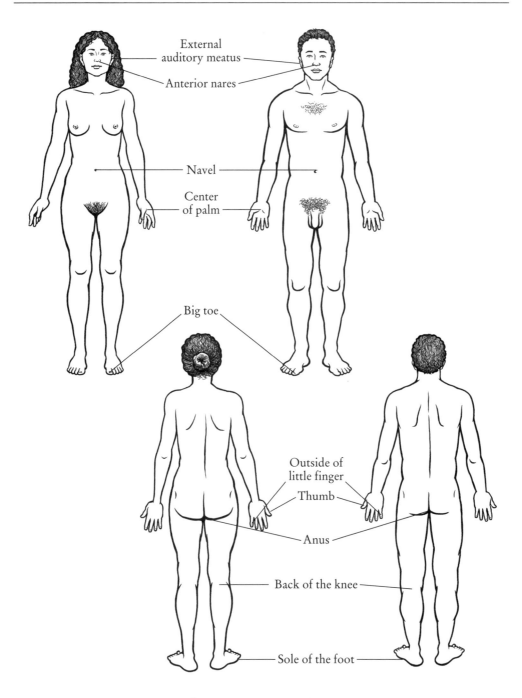

External
auditory meatus

Anterior nares

Navel

Center
of palm

Big toe

Outside of
little finger

Thumb

Anus

Back of the knee

Sole of the foot

The Tertiary Erogenic Zones

six or eight cycles of stimulation. Another traditional Tantric understanding recognizes that a woman's left side is more sensitive than her right and that, conversely, the right side of a man's body is more sensitive than his left.

Here is a simple cycle of stimulation following two rounds of the four-beat pattern just described:

1. Earlobe (secondary)

2. Mouth (primary)

3. Nape of the neck (tertiary)

4. Breasts (primary)

5. Sacral-lumbar junction (secondary)

6. Mouth (primary)

7. Navel (tertiary)

8. Genitals (primary)

Another, simpler way to work with the zones would be to stimulate each of the secondary zones very gently and then proceed to the primary zones, again stimulating them very gently, by kissing—lips, breasts, genitals. Then you move on to the tertiary zones, stimulating each one. And in this way the Tantra happens. Remember, *tanoi* means "to expand." And what has been expanded? Once you have started with the secondary zones, gone on to the primary zones, and then moved to the tertiary zones, you have expanded. The sensuality of the excitement phase has been established.

This is just an overview of the zones and how to work with them. This limited roadmap should provide you with some valuable tools for exploration; however, there is still far more to understand about the Kama Marmas, and the following chapters deal with some of these deeper elements from both esoteric and exoteric perspectives.

eleven

The Primary Erogenic Zones

To recapitulate, the primary erogenic zones include:

1. The Lips (and Mouth)

2. The Breasts

3. The Genitals

They are identified as primary zones because they are the most sensitive, most saturated with nerve endings, and most directly responsive to sexual stimulation—not because they are to be stimulated first. Many Western men have a tendency to go straight for the genitals, partly because of the way in which male arousal functions and partly as a result of the pervasive misleading information about sexuality that circulates in the popular media, not to mention what passes for erotic material in Western society.

In Tantra, we recognize the importance of the primary zones, and rather than rushing to them, we tend to save the best for last. A comprehensive discussion of the neurophysiology of the zones is beyond the scope of this book, and your own experience is, of course, paramount. Nevertheless, there are a number of important esoteric and exoteric factors concerning the zones that may be useful as you begin a conscious exploration.

Primary Erogenic Zone 1: The Lips (and Mouth)
(Oshthaadhara Marma)

To kiss someone on the lips is very intimate. Kissing crams two consciousnesses to-gether. If you are familiar with George Orwell's novel *1984*, you may remember that the authorities wanted to break the hero, Winston Smith, and brainwash him. In order to do so, they had to identify his phobia, and they learned he was afraid of rats. Now, it would have been awful to stick his hand or leg into the rat cage—but not awful enough, because it is possible to distance yourself from your limbs. The lips are far more vulnerable, not only because they are made of soft, sensitive tissue, but also because they are so close to the brain. So, in the novel, the torturers thrust the hero's head right into the rat cage, and this just snapped him, producing instant psychosis. Of course, *1984* is a novel, but Orwell had a profound understanding of human psychology. He knew that the lips are very close to the core of one's being.

At approximately eight weeks in the womb, a fetus's oral reflexes become evi-dent. By birth, these reflexes have developed into strong reactions. A prime reflex in the newborn infant is the "sucking reflex," which actually develops well before birth. (Ultrasonic uterine scanning frequently reveals the fetus sucking its thumb.) Just touching an infant's lips educes the sucking reflex, and merely stroking the in-fant's cheek produces the "rooting reflex," in which the baby turns its head toward the side that has been stroked. This rotation of the head is accompanied by sponta-neous oral sucking movements. These reflexes prepare the lips for maturation into a powerful erogenic zone and, more generally, instill the blueprint for oral sexuality throughout our lives.

Freud, of course, recognized the primal linkage between the mouth and sexual-ity; he asserted that during the oral stage of development, the mouth is the primary source of pleasurable sensation and that the relationship between infant's mouth and mother's breast is the first erotic experience. While some of Freud's views have fallen into disfavor in recent years, it is certainly true that infants will seek oral gratification even when they are not hungry.

To illustrate further just how intimate the mouth can be, consider the stereo-type that prostitutes will not kiss their customers on the mouth even though they engage in all sorts of other intimacies. Similarly, in this era of sexual openness, it is not uncommon for people to have intercourse on a completely casual basis. Shar-ing toothbrushes, however, is something that even long-term couples seldom do.

Primary Erogenic Zone 1: The Lips (and Mouth)

Long before Freud, the Tantrics understood the connection between the mouth and sexuality. In the classical Tantric chakra system elucidated in the *Shatchakra Nirupana*, taste is the sensory avenue for Swadhisthana Chakra, the sexual center, which regulates the fluids of the body, including both sexual fluids and saliva. The old occult aphorism "as above, so below" is certainly apt when considering the linkage between the mouth and the genitals.

The rule of "celestial correspondences" dictates that the lips represent a horizontal yoni, just as the eyes do. The skin underneath the eyes and the lips becomes red, swollen, and sensitive as sexual excitement builds to a crescendo culminating in orgasm.

"As above, so below" is a physiological fact as well as a psychological one; the tissue of the labia majora and minora become engorged, starting as bright red and spreading to a darker hue. This is the anthropological basis for the cosmetic use of lipstick and eye shadow. The lips are a mirror image of the vulva, and this erotic symbology of lips is echoed in the plastic surgeon's term for the ideal female upper lip: "Cupid's bow." Lipstick and eye shadow evoke the promise of the swollen and burgundy yoni in a state of arousal.

The profusion of sensitive tactile receptors in the lips is exceeded only by the concentration present in the clitoris. This sensitivity extends into the mucous membrane on the inside of the lips, and when you examine the sensory flow to the brain on a homunculus, the relationship between lips and genitals is quite vivid.

The lips, genitals, hands, and fingers occupy more receptors for sensory cues than do the entire trunk, arms, and legs. In addition, the genitals and toes share the same brain area. The significance of this fact will become apparent when we examine the tertiary zones.

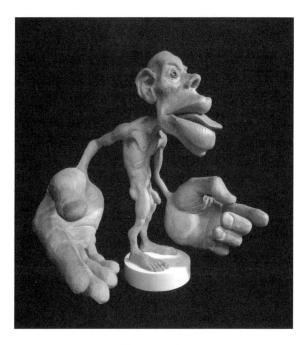

Homunculus

A way of depicting the relative sensitivity of body parts. The homunculus reveals what the body would look like if sensitivity determined size. Reproduced by permission of the Natural History Museum, London.

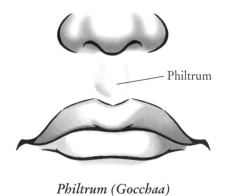

Philtrum (Gocchaa)

The upper lip in the female has a psychic tube, or nadi, known as *shanka nadi* in Tantric anatomy. Shanka nadi connects to the clitoris, and hence the male should suck the female's upper lip while she sucks his lower lip (*adharapaana*). This has deep psychic implications, including the exchange of pranically charged saliva between Shiva and Shakti. Each partner visualizes a psychic force being drawn into the body, nourishing every part.

An understanding of the erotic power dwelling in the upper lip is implicit in the term for the deep gutter running from the base of the nose to the margin of the mucosal membrane. This prominent indentation is called the *philtrum*, which means, literally, "love potion." This anatomical term reflects the medieval belief that the upper lip transmitted an aphrodisiac through kissing.

Primary Erogenic Zone 2: The Breasts (Kuchamukha Marma)

The breasts are extraordinarily important, situated as they are in the region of Anahata (heart) Chakra. The sensory outlets for Anahata are the nipples (functioning as subchakras) and all sensations of touch throughout the body. The Anahata Yantra, a six-pointed star, symbolizes the fusion of male and female energies, pair bonding, and sacred union.

The six-pointed star, or hexagram, graphically represents a very sophisticated physiological feedback loop between the nipples, the pituitary gland (associated with Ajna Chakra), and the genitals. When the two triangles are untangled and separated, they form the *Damaru*, or Shiva's drum, symbolizing the steady rhythm of the first sound imprinted upon us in the womb, the throbbing "lub dup" of the beating heart. It is significant to note that the alchemists of the Middle Ages used the hexagram as a symbol of powerful changes produced by the interaction of feminine water with masculine fire.

An equilateral triangle may be arranged apex up or apex down to clarify this relationship further. A triangle apex-down is the feminine fire triangle (Hindu) or water triangle (Western alchemy). A triangle apex-up is the masculine water triangle (Hindu) or fire triangle (Western alchemy).

In general, women are more responsive to stimulation of the breasts than men. While individuals vary and some women do not like having their breasts touched at all, many women can reach orgasm through nipple stimulation alone; it is not

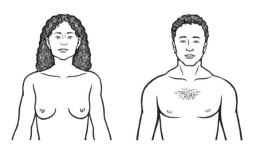

Primary Erogenic Zone 2: The Breasts

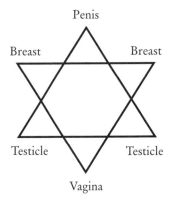

Anahata Yantra

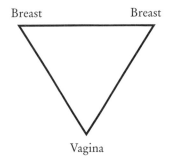

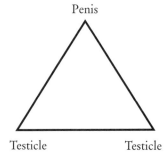

Triangle, apex down (Shakti Yantra)   *Triangle, apex up (Shiva Yantra)*

uncommon for mothers to experience orgasm while nursing, and this capacity may be nature's way of reinforcing infant-mother bonding.

Leonardo da Vinci was the first Westerner (at least the first Western male) to observe and describe a direct link between the breasts and the uterus, recognizing that nipple stimulation can trigger uterine contractions. Da Vinci actually drew a diagram depicting what he believed to be a nerve that ran from the nipples to the uterus. Today, we know that da Vinci was mistaken and that the system is more complex than he imagined. He was a man of his time and had virtually no knowledge of glandular and hormonal systems. He could not have known that nipple stimulation can trigger a response in the posterior pituitary gland, something discovered centuries later.

Stimulation of the sensitive area around the nipple affects a nerve that in turn sends an impulse to the pituitary to release the hormone oxytocin (popularly called the "bonding" or "cuddle" hormone). Oxytocin is then pumped through the body by the heart, producing alterations of brain chemistry in both sexes and uterine contractions in women.

The ancient Indians did recognize the connection between the breasts and the pituitary, although not in accordance with the mechanistic, Western model. In the classical view, Ajna Chakra (and therefore the pituitary) and Muladhara Chakra are directly linked; hence, the aftermath of orgasm is often accompanied by psychedelic visions. If an individual's nipples are sensitive, stimulation will induce Ajna, Anahata, Swadhisthana, and Muladhara Chakras to open. Also, be aware that stimulating the left nipple awakens Ida and stimulating the right awakens Pingala. Thus, just working with this pair of reflex points has a variety of impacts on both physical and psychic levels.

As we have indicated, the Tantric understanding is represented graphically by a downward-pointing triangle with its apex at the yoni, surmounted by an upward-pointing triangle with its apex at Ajna. This ancient Tantric imagery also represents both the ascent and descent of Kundalini, played out in the microcosm of the body.

Even in societies where the female breast is customarily bared, its erotic power does not necessarily go unrecognized. Indian culture is but one example of this phenomenon; it was not uncommon for village women in South India to go barebreasted until a couple of generations ago, but one needs only a few glimpses of South Indian sculpture to see that the erotic power of the breast is fully appreciated in that society. From this perspective, it is easy to understand why the image of the breast is so fetishized in Western men's magazines.

Remember that the nipples are important for both women and men. In our embryonic origins—before differentiation takes place at around the sixth or seventh week of pregnancy—we are all female. Men generally have lost nipple sensitivity, but many can redevelop it. Learning to relax is one key to reawakening this sensitivity. Regardless of subjective experience, during orgasm, a man's nipples will go erect. The nipples of some pubescent boys become sore enough that wearing a shirt can cause discomfort, which demonstrates the profusion of nerve endings in the male nipple. Thus, the physiological apparatus for sexual response is clearly present in men. For many adults, activating it can present a challenge.

There are two techniques that are usually pleasing to both men and women. Most people will respond to gentle stroking with moist fingers, moving inward from the areola to the nipple, provided that the hands are wet with saliva. Gently rotating a wet palm on the entire nipple area is another generally effective technique. These methods can be very helpful in cultivating sensitivity and increasing the capacity for experiencing pleasure. Sucking the nipples is probably the best-known method and perhaps the most effective, provided the area is first awakened with caresses.

Nipples represent the most primitive of sexual archetypes; the white milk of the breast awakens unconscious breast-feeding memories while simultaneously mimicking the whiteness of semen being released from the lingam. Breast milk is often ejected the same way that spontaneous ejaculation of semen may occur, and many lactating women report that a child's cry will elicit this response.

One interpretation of Hindu temple architecture holds that it is replete with sexual and body imagery. The nipple is represented by the *Shikhara*, or peak, of the temple tower (*Vimana*) over the main cubicle (*Garbha Griha*), or "womb room," where the temple deity is permanently installed and worshiped.

Indeed, there is a widely held anthropological concept that all temples, churches, cathedrals, and mosques are symbolic representations of the human reproductive system. It is also worth noting that another theory suggests the design of pottery across cultures reflects an externalization of primordial, archetypal breast-feeding memories.

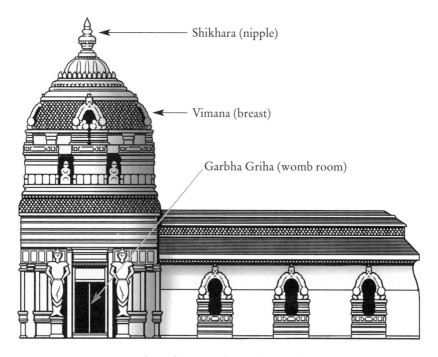

Shikhara (nipple)

Vimana (breast)

Garbha Griha (womb room)

Plan of a typical Hindu temple

The nipples tend to become tumescent in meditation and dreaming, as we enter theta states or REM sleep. This is yet another indication of their importance in psychic anatomy. As a final point, you should understand that the nipples are not only receptors of psychic energy, they are also radiators of psychic energy, although this is something you will have to experience for yourself. Here is one way to do so: when stimulating your partner's nipples, visualize sucking in a white or golden stream of energy, which is drawn through the top of your partner's head and down into the breast and then into your psychic body, bathing you both in celestial energy. This is a powerful meditation that evokes the deepest and most primal imagery, transforming physical nurturing into a psychic phenomenon and building a powerful energetic bond between you.

Primary Erogenic Zone 3: The Genitals (Vyajjana Marma)

Let's think about language when we consider the genitals, but not the vulgar terms that are so widely and negatively used in the West. This is a realm of beauty and mystery. Everyone is sensible enough to know that the rule is "be gentle with the genitals." But the Tantric understanding—which at this level has much in common with anthropological theory—holds that the gateway to life is a temple. That gateway consists of the labia majora and the labia minora, which together make up the vulva. The word *vulva* is Latin; it is derived from Sanskrit, and it shares the root of the English word *involve*—the manifestation of the life force into material form. And out of that *inv*olvement comes *ev*olvement. So, we can say that the vulva is the gateway to life, and it is also the gateway to spiritual transcendence.

Nothing on God's green earth is so difficult as a relationship. And it is truly through a relationship that we all evolve. We *ev*olve to the degree that we are *inv*olved. And from the Tantric perspective, the yoni, the vulva, is a most sacred map. It is the focal point of that sexual transmutation in which one is ever drawn to the source of being in the vulva, as an act of involvement that can lead to evolvement.

There is a most beautiful soft pad of fat just over the female pubic bone, where the yoni begins, and it is still called by its Latin name, the *mons veneris*, or "mountain of Venus," for the goddess of love. There is a deeper implication hidden here. From *Venus*, we get the word *venereal*. Unfortunately, most of us associate the word *venereal* with disease, but it means, literally, "pertaining to love." In its original sense, *venereal* also related to the concept of worthiness, or "worth-ship," of the yoni and the lingam, the reproductive system. Like the Tantrics, the Romans understood the connection between sex and sacredness and worshiped the lingam and the yoni, and these Latin terms remain in our language even though their original meanings have very nearly been lost.

So, we use that root, *vener*, if we think highly of somebody. If we speak of a respected teacher, we might say that she is venerable, that she is worthy, indeed that she is worthy of veneration. These words come from the same root. At the deepest level of meaning, the actions of the genitals—venereal activity—and the genitals themselves are objects worthy of worship. And in Old English, *worship* was spelled as *weorthscipe*, or "worth-ship." Each of us has to decide what is worthy of worship in our own lives, but as our language reveals, these Tantric concepts of wor-

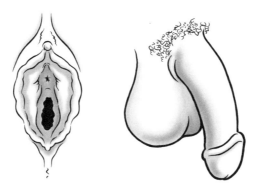

Primary Erogenic Zone 3: The Genitals

shiping the venereal—the lingam and the yoni—are part of our human heritage. It is just that in Tantra this way of worshiping was never suppressed.

It is also worth recalling the fact that the word *genital* has the same etymological root as *genius*, among a number of other words, including *genesis*, or "beginning," and *progenitor*, or "ancestor." The psychic states that can arise from careful lovemaking can lead us to the fullest expression of our human potential, our inner genius. From this perspective, we are all potential geniuses.

In Tantra, the genitals are worshiped, and in classical left-hand rituals, they are anointed and offerings are made to them. It is important not to confuse worship with stimulation in this context, although the stimulation should be done with an attitude of worship. The ritualistic veneration of the lingam and yoni may precede the act of maithuna, or sexual union, but in maithuna itself, the genitals are the last of the zones to be stimulated, and intercourse takes place only after considerable energy has been concentrated in the genital region.

In South India, the full Shiva Lingam Tantric Puja involves a complex ritual to produce *Panch Amrit*, equivalent to the Communion wine of the Catholic Mass. The Vama Marga Tantric interpretation of the symbolism is just one perspective, one that Brahminic Hindus are likely to reject. Other interpretations are equally valid.

First, the lingam is washed with water, symbolic of the pure midstream urine, or *amaroli*. Then, a ripe, peeled banana is crushed over the head of the lingam. This is homeopathic magic; the shape of the banana enshrines the virile power of the penis.

Next, the lingam is bathed with milk (the color of semen), and then honey is massaged over the top of Shiva's member and allowed to drip down into the yoni base; honey incarnates the sweetness and viscosity of healthy semen. The last ablution consists of washing the lingam with coconut milk, the equivalent of nutrients contained in prostate fluid and glucose-rich vaginal secretions.

The entire ceremony can take up to two hours, and at the conclusion, the priests drain all of the above secretions, which have been caught in the yoni base during the ritual, into a large copper container. Each member of the congregation receives a spoonful of the Panch Amrit (which means "elixir of five things") into a cupped right hand and sips it, imbibing the psychically charged, symbolic sexual fluid.

Many Westerners are likely to view such a rite as bizarre, perverted, and profane, and in fact, most Western literature about Hindu ritual espoused this notion until well into the twentieth century. Most of our perceptions about what is bizarre, perverted, profane, or immoral are the products of cultural prejudice and social conditioning. Swamiji taught in Papua New Guinea for a time, and he recalls that the indigenous people there considered it obscene for a woman to expose her thighs, for instance by wearing a bathing suit. At the same time, it was the height of good taste and style for women to appear in public with bare breasts, the direct opposite of what is acceptable on most beaches in the United States.

The word *moral* comes from a Latin root meaning "custom of the place," and this confirms our deepest intuitions; concepts of morality, and particularly sexual morality, are culture-specific and have no validity as universal truth. Certain ethical precepts may be almost universal, at least with respect to in-group behavior, but many of our moral judgments are strictly local prejudices.

Perversion is also largely relative. From the Tantric perspective, it is difficult to comprehend how humans could engage in cunnilingus or fellatio without being overcome by a sense of worship and adoration: you are either on your knees or prone and are physically attached to a living altar. The ramifications of oral congress are profound, and it can become a religious experience, producing mystical states for both worshiper and worshiped.

Oral intercourse can evoke primal archetypes from the unconscious of the participants, producing a blissful merging with the divine. In this state, both the clitoris and the penis become prototype nipples, and the associated fluids transubstantiate into galactic milk. Our bodies become conduits for surges of cosmic energy, and we are electrically locked onto a direct pipeline to the Goddess as pure Shakti. And yet, until very recently, virtually all Anglo-Saxon countries and many American states treated oral sex not only as a perversion but also as a criminal act.

Swamiji tells of a youthful, ecstatic dream of paying homage to a goddess with cunnilingus. When she reached her zenith, he felt something hard gush into his mouth. He spat into the palm of his hand the largest, most beautiful white pearl: "one pearl of great price."

The yoni, or vulva, forms a *mandorla*, or entrance, to a profound altered state of consciousness. Some identify the Latin root *valvae*, meaning "folding or double doors," as an antecedent of *vulva*; another etymological tree relates the word to the verb *volvere*, "to roll or to turn about." Both are perhaps correct; vaginal lips are the double doors of the temple or lodge, beyond which lie the deepest secrets of human existence.

The divine relationship of Tantric lovers is that of gardener and flower reenacting the celestial dance of universal cosmic creation. "As below, so above." This Tantric interpretation is a universal alchemical allegory in which the lovers become the instruments for the transmutation of consciousness. The conjugal (from the Sanskrit root *yug*) couple employs the laboratory of their bodies to work (labor) karmically and with mantra (oratory) toward the experience of consummate freedom.

To reiterate, the most important physical point about the genitals pertains to oral congress, cunnilingus and fellatio. This is a psychic short circuit, a bringing together of two primary zones. The erogenic zone in the mouth is not only physically hard-wired into every one of us, it is psychologically embedded at the deepest level. Infants often nurse with the tongue under the nipple so that when they suckle, the nipple actually stimulates the G-spot within the mouth, just in front of where the hard and soft palates meet. The satisfaction derived from sucking imprints on each infant a need for oral gratification that endures in all of us as adults.

Freud wrote extensively about oral gratification, and as we have discussed, he had some important insights. He went wrong, however, on a number of counts, particularly when he suggested that taking pleasure in oral congress is somehow infantile and neurotic, a product of oral deprivation or arrested development. The sucking reflex is the first gratification one can have, and the act of sucking on the lingam or the yoni can be very satisfying for both partners; for the person sucking, the genital becomes a nipple. Very gently sucking on the clitoris or the penis takes us back to a primordial state and leads to a cessation of the fluctuations of the mind.

The Tantric system we teach utilizes visualization with both fellatio and cunnilingus (the clitoris is also a prototype penis). The visualization is essentially the same as the one employed during nipple stimulation, but even more energy is exchanged, and the psychic effect is still more powerful. Thus, the partner performing oral sex imagines consuming a golden energy that is drawn from the cosmic storehouse down through the top of the receiver's skull, into the lingam or yoni, and then into the mouth, in endless supply. This is a very deep meditation that vivifies and energizes both participants. It can be complete in itself, or it can serve as a powerful precursor to genital intercourse, enhancing that experience immensely.

In conclusion, remember the following: oral sex represents a very primal pleasure derived from sucking; this can consume the conscious mind, producing a regression to a primordial state. Once this happens, at some level, you are psychically extracting milk. That milk becomes an astral, sexual secretion corresponding to the physical secretions—menses, semen, and vaginal fluids. And these sexual secretions produce an alchemical fluid, a sacred elixir (see chapter 15, "The Tantric Mass and the Secret of Amrita").

twelve

The Secondary Erogenic Zones

The secondary erogenic zones are so named because they are not as highly sensitive as the primaries. Nevertheless, they are replete with nerve endings, and stimulating them will produce a significant physiological response in most people. In addition, they are directly connected to the psychic channels. These zones should be stimulated first, because doing so will facilitate the flow of energy without shocking the system.

The secondary erogenic zones are five in number:

1. The Earlobes
2. The Nape of the Neck
3. The Sacral-Lumbar Junction
4. The Gluteal Folds
5. The Inner Thighs

Secondary Erogenic Zone 1: The Earlobes (*Karnapraanta Marma*)

Many of us discovered the earlobes' erotic potential back in our high school days, but adults often forget the power of youthful sensations. In Tantra, the earlobes have a very special significance, since they are directly connected to Ida and Pingala.

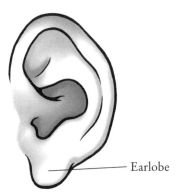

Earlobe

Secondary Erogenic Zone 1: The Earlobes

In most people, the earlobe is amazingly sensitive to stimulation—kissing, licking, and sucking. If you have forgotten about this sensitivity, just start experimenting; you may be surprised by the results. If you really focus on the earlobes and spend fifteen minutes having them stimulated, you will virtually lose your mind just from the sensation.

As a general rule, women are more sensitive than men and tend to be more in touch with their bodies. As with the nipples, men may have to train themselves to enjoy stimulation of their earlobes, but sensitive women will tell you that having their earlobes nibbled, licked, or sucked sends a flush directly down Ida and Pingala, and a tingling sensation goes to the small of the back and into the uterus. Men who have sensitized themselves may feel it in the testicles. This is a direct connection; the energy moves down the spine, following Ida and Pingala, which are analogous to the bladder meridian in acupuncture. During sexual excitement—even in the absence of direct stimulation and although they are not composed of erectile tissue—the earlobes will engorge, just as the nipples, lips, and genitals will engorge.

Many non-Western societies pay special attention to massaging the ears and earlobes to stimulate the internal organs throughout the body. The Balinese Hindus have particularly developed the art of ear massage. In this system, the ear represents an inverted fetus, with the reflex points for the head located in the earlobe. Both Ayurvedic Marma therapy and Chinese acupuncture have identified specific reflex points in the ear that directly relate to the genitals. Traditionally, Chinese

Taoist sexologists consider prominent earlobes (and full, swollen lips) in a woman to be a marker of orgasmic readiness.

The practice of piercing the ears exists in many cultures, often as a rite of passage in early childhood. This practice is widely believed to have a beneficial impact on physical and mental health. More important for our purposes is the fact that knowledge of the erotic power latent in certain points in the ears also exists transculturally. For example, a disembodied pair of ears pierced by an arrow is one of the most arresting images in the "Hell" panel of *The Garden of Earthly Delights*, Hieronymus Bosch's famous sixteenth-century triptych. Bosch's arrow penetrates the ears at points similar to those used by Chinese and Ayurvedic acupuncturists to stimulate the reproductive system and genitals.

The same reflexes also exist in animals. For example, when rabbits get sexually excited, their pink ears will flush vividly red. Flashing red ears is a female rabbit's sex signal. When she has red ears, she is sending out an invitation.

If you scratch a dog behind the ear and stimulate the right point, a neural reflex extends down the spinal column and produces movement of the back leg on the same side. *Mahouts*, or elephant drivers, use the analogous point on the elephant's ear to control the animal. So, ear reflexes are some of the most powerful and most accessible in the body. This is all solid neurology.

Secondary Erogenic Zone 2: The Nape of the Neck (*Krikatika Marma*)

This zone is located roughly where the growth of the hair ends. These very sensitive nerves are best stimulated with a long exhaled breath and light stroking; the old complaint about breathing down your neck has its roots in this sensitivity. When the nape of the neck is stimulated, particularly with the breath, the energy rebounds directly into Muladhara Chakra and then opens up Sushumna.

The power of breathing on the neck crops up in the most surprising ways in many different cultures; some of this is real "black magic" stuff. In the seventeenth century, a number of priests were burned at the stake for breathing down women's necks, thereby driving them into ecstasy and rapture. In both Eastern and Western traditions, if you make a sacred sign—the cross or the symbol OM with sandalwood—over the cervical vertebrae, it is supposed to seal you off from nefarious

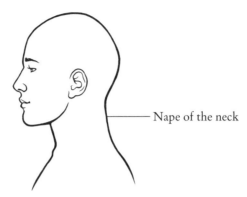

Nape of the neck

Secondary Erogenic Zone 2: The Nape of the Neck

psychic influences. And the French occultist Eliphas Levi claimed that anyone who breathes down the back of another person's neck is a vampire and is practicing "black magic." Of course, this vampirism and "black magic" stuff is rubbish, but there is a kernel of truth in it.

If you have studied zoology, you know that when cats, rabbits, or guinea pigs copulate, the male grabs the nape of the female's neck in his mouth, which drives the female wild. That is the standard guinea pig maneuver and the standard rat, cat, and rabbit maneuver. Of course, we are not rats, cats, or rabbits, but we are sometimes guinea pigs, and it does pay to experiment.

When a mother cat picks up a kitten by the nape of its neck, it doesn't bother the kitten at all. In fact, the kitten immediately relaxes, and this is a very significant spiritual symbol. In the Indian tradition, there is a distinction between Bhakti Yoga and Tantra. Bhakti Yoga is the path of devotional love. The transillumination comes from utter love and devotion to the Guru.

This concept of devotion is foreign and even frightening to many Westerners, but it is a subjective experience of transformation that can be very rapid and very profound. It can open a person up in many ways. If you are a Bhakti Yogi and you surrender to the Guru, the Guru is the mother cat who comes along and picks you up gently by the nape of the neck. Like a kitten, you surrender and go limp, and the Guru will carry you up to the mountaintop.

In Tantra, we take the opposite approach. We say that if you worship the Goddess Shakti, she is like the mother monkey. And the mother monkey doesn't carry her baby. The baby clasps tightly around her neck, clings to her back, and rides her from tree to tree. The Tantric Guru does not carry the disciple. Instead, he or she helps the disciple up onto the mother monkey's back for what can turn out to be quite a wild ride! And that is Tantra versus Bhakti: both are beautiful, both work, and both are effective. But each has its own approach. In one case, you are carried, and in the other, you climb up and hold on tight and the force carries you.

Secondary Erogenic Zone 3: The Sacral-Lumbar Junction (Nitamba Marma)

If you look at a sideways diagram of the spine, you will see a series of curves. These curves delineate the three sections of the spine: lumbar, thoracic, and cervical. At the very base of the spine are the four coccygeal vertebrae. The sacrum comprises five fused bones just above the coccygeal vertebrae. The five bones of the sacrum form a sacred, downward-pointing triangle, the symbol of Shakti, and the word *sacrum* means "holy bone." In both Eastern and Western traditions, the sacrum has great significance. It is said that the sacrum was ritually kissed in the Witches' sabbat, and in the Jewish tradition, some believe there is a bone in the sacrum that survives death and will crawl underground back to Jerusalem.

Folk wisdom in Australia holds that stroking this area will arouse your partner. This folk wisdom is absolutely correct. There is a reflex known as the cranial-sacral outflow. It is part of the parasympathetic nervous system, and it goes straight into the genitals. Esoterically, stroking the sacral-lumbar junction area opens up Muladhara and Swadhisthana Chakras.

Recent developments in medical technology bear out the essence of the folk wisdom regarding the sacrum. In 2004, Dr. Stuart Meloy, an anesthesiologist and pain specialist in Winston-Salem, North Carolina, conducted a study of eleven nonorgasmic women. He implanted electrodes from a pain-control device known as a spinal-cord stimulator in the lower backs of the women, six of whom had never before experienced orgasm. Ten of the eleven subjects had orgasms in response to electrical stimulation of the sacral nerves. The device was so effective that when the study came to an end, one of the subjects reportedly said that having the electrodes removed was like "losing my best friend."

Meloy's study was first presented to the general public on the popular American television program *Good Morning America*. The news account described Dr.

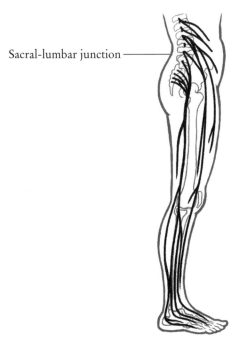

Sacral-lumbar junction

Secondary Erogenic Zone 3: The Sacral-Lumbar Junction
The profusion of nerves from the sacrum spread to the genitals and down the legs to the soles of the feet.

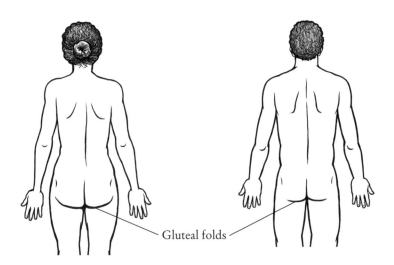

Gluteal folds

Secondary Erogenic Zone 4: The Gluteal Folds

Meloy's initial discovery as inadvertent and his reaction as having been one of surprise.[1] This is yet another instance in which Western medicine and technology are, in some ways, just beginning to catch up with ancient Indian Tantric knowledge. While some in the contemporary New Age movement might object to artificial devices as unnatural, it is important to remember that the Tantric approach is fundamentally a pragmatic one; it neither requires nor rejects the use of artificial means but only concerns itself with effectiveness and the degree of consciousness with which they are employed. Clearly, there are many benefits to stimulating the sacral area, with whatever tools are at your disposal.

Secondary Erogenic Zone 4: The Gluteal Folds (Shroni Marma)

This zone can be somewhat difficult to find and is less immediately sensitive than the other secondary zones. You should explore the area at the tops of the thighs, where the buttocks meet the legs. This area can become very sensitive once you have identified and grown attuned to it; stimulation here should be quite gentle. Soft kisses, licking, and breath are best. Again, stimulation of this Kama Marma is related to the bladder meridian in acupuncture, and stimulation on the left activates Ida while stimulation on the right activates Pingala. When stroking, start deep inside the thighs with the fingers radiating to the yoni or lingam, and stroke up and around the gluteal fold to the outside.

Secondary Erogenic Zone 5: The Inner Thighs (Lohitaksha Marma)

Remember to stroke upward, toward the genitals. As is so often the case, this knowledge is common folklore, but it was worked out 2,500 years ago and described in detail in the *Kama Sutra*. The insides of the thighs, of course, are very sensitive, so much so that certain medical tests involve stroking them.

The cremasteric reflex involves nerves that extend from the insides of the thighs into the spinal cord, and this reflex is tested to determine that the spinal cord, disks, and vertebrae are intact. The test is very simple; it involves stroking the insides of the thighs. In the healthy male, the scrotum will tighten up slightly. Erection of the

---

1 ABC News, "Doctor Discovers the 'Orgasmatron': Physician Working with Pain Relief Stumbles upon Delightful Side Effect," *Good Morning America*, ABC, November 9, 2004. (See a related report at http://abcnews.go.com/GMA/Living/story?id=235788&page=1.)

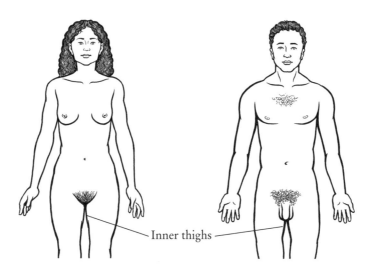

Secondary Erogenic Zone 5: The Inner Thighs

lingam may occur in response to prolonged stroking of the inner thighs. In women, vaginal lubrication indicates normal function, and higher levels of arousal can occur in a nonmedical context.

Thus, stroking the inner thighs can be highly stimulating and very erotic. The same applies to the other secondary erogenic zones, but the inner thighs, because of their proximity to the genitals, are particularly sensitive.

In examining these erogenic zones, these Marmas, we are building up a series of psychic pathways. Those who are interested in the Western esoteric tradition will discover that East and West are not so different after all. The Kama Marmas can be mapped out on the human body, and the end result is a rough diagram of the Tree of Life. The two are not quite identical—the diagram must be squared out a bit—but the similarities are striking.

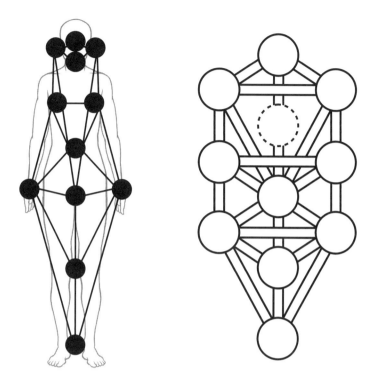

Map of the Kama Marmas and the Tree of Life

thirteen

The Tertiary Erogenic Zones

The tertiary zones are the final category. To reiterate, when we refer to tertiary zones, we are not suggesting they are of tertiary importance. We mean that these zones are even less responsive erotically, at least during the initial stages of arousal; however, once a higher level of excitement has been reached, stimulation of the tertiary zones can have a remarkable impact. The tertiary zones are also a bit more varied and individual in terms of the degree of sensitivity and the type of response that stimulation will generate, so the process of exploring them and discovering their erotic potential will be a far more personal and individual adventure.

As we move from most sensitive to least sensitive, the number of zones increases, so the tertiary zones are the most numerous. There are ten tertiary zones:

1. The Medial (Outer) Surface of the Little Finger

2. The Center of the Palm

3. The Navel

4. The Anus

5. The Anterior Nares (Nasal Openings)

6. The External Auditory Meatus

7. The Sole of the Foot

8. The Big Toe

9. The Thumb

10. The Back of the Knee

The tertiary erogenic zones have another very special characteristic. Tradition has it that one of them will be active at any given time, so at this very moment, stimulation of the correct tertiary zone would start to turn you on, no matter how unresponsive you might be feeling. This ancient Indian tradition, still alive among the Siddha practitioners of Tamil Nadu, holds that these points fluctuate with the phases of the moon.

Even though one of these zones will always be active, and stimulating the active zone would produce arousal, the inactive zones are relatively unresponsive until a higher general state of excitement is reached, and there is no way to determine which tertiary zone is active at any given time, unless you are a master of Tamil Siddha medicine. For this reason, it is important to bear in mind that the tertiary zones should not be brought into play before the primary and secondary zones have received considerable stimulation.

Tertiary Erogenic Zone 1: The Medial (Outer) Surface of the Little Finger (Kanistha Aghuli Marma)

In folklore, the little finger influences the gonads, and in acupuncture, the small intestine. Once you are in a sensitive state, the gentle stroking of the little finger will send a tingle. This area can actually be very sensitive when you reach a state of deep relaxation. In normal states of consciousness, we are so bombarded by crude sensations that we seldom notice such subtle sensitivities. The path of the stroking can extend from the wrist creases, where the outside of the palm under the little finger (ulna-percussion part) starts, continuing right up the side of the little finger to the tip.

The related acupuncture point is called Small Intestine 3, and it is one of the most painful points in the body. Acupuncturists insert a needle at the fold of the finger joint to relieve rheumatoid arthritis in the shoulder area. When that whole meridian—what Western medical practitioners call the brachial plexus—is stroked, the shivers go up the arm and to the spinal cord. As soon as the sensations reach the spinal cord, Sushumna starts flowing.

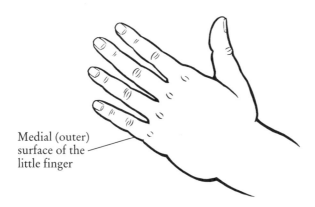

Tertiary Erogenic Zone 1:
The Medial (Outer) Surface of the Little Finger, or Hypothenar Eminence
Stimulation of medial edge of the little finger includes the "ulna-percussion" edge of the hypothenar eminence in a gentle stroking or caressing movement.

Tertiary Erogenic Zone 2: The Center of the Palm (Tala Hridaya Marma)

This second tertiary zone, the palm of the hand, is closely related to the first. It is a very special area, sometimes referred to as the "crucifixion chakra." If you do any kind of hands-on healing work or use palming techniques, you are probably familiar with the subchakra in the palm of the hand. In acupuncture, there is a point in the palm that stimulates the heart, Pericardium 8. The palm is very sensitive indeed. Gentle stroking will produce a kind of ticklish sensation.

Nearly all of the Kama Marmas begin to express themselves during the embryonic stage of development. For example, the grasp reflex develops in the womb and is elicited by placing a finger on the newborn baby's palm; this causes the hand to close tightly around the finger. Trying to remove the finger causes the infant to tighten its grip to such an extent that it can often be lifted from the table. This muscular reflex rapidly diminishes with age, but the neural sensitivity is embedded for life in the palm. This reflex is also present in the foot, and touching the sole will cause the toes to curl. Neurologists often refer to these two reflexes collectively as the palmar and plantar grasp.

Children are very ticklish—so ticklish that you just have to make the motion of going to tickle them and they are likely to burst out laughing. Ticklishness in children

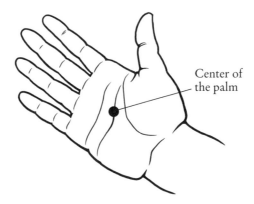

Center of
the palm

Tertiary Erogenic Zone 2: The Center of the Palm

is generalized sexual energy that has not yet become particularized. Most adults are
not nearly as ticklish overall, because the sexual energy has concentrated itself in certain zones.

If you start gently stroking your palm, you will discover that it is much more
sensitive than you would have ever suspected. Once you are in a state of sexual excitement, tickling the palm in a counterclockwise direction can be highly erotic. The
palm and the outer surface of the little finger fall into the category of what might be
called compatibility zones. If you find yourself attracted to someone, you can get a
good sense of your sexual compatibility by holding hands, stroking either point, and
observing the response.

Tertiary Erogenic Zone 3: The Navel (Nabhi Marma)

In the Tantric tradition, the best way to stimulate the navel is to stroke it in a clockwise direction or tongue-kiss it in a circular fashion. This awakens Nabhi Marma or
Manipura Chakra (Conception Vessel 8 in Chinese acupuncture). Although this is
often the least sensitive zone prior to arousal, it will respond to careful stimulation
at the appropriate time. To be more precise, the Nabhi Marma extends to the waist
for women and is limited to the navel itself in men. The female navel is an echo or
reflection of the vulva—"as above, so below."

Belly dancing probably originated back in an age when harem girls straddled
their masters and made vigorous pelvic movements to facilitate sexual consumma-

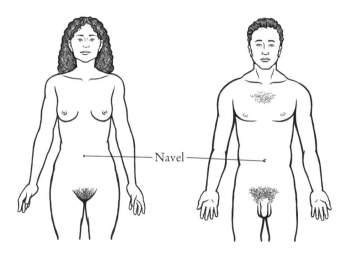

Tertiary Erogenic Zone 3: The Navel
The sensitive area extends out in a line to the crest of the hips in women but is limited to the navel itself in men.

tion. Today, the undulating, grinding, and thrusting actions of the dances present a formalized version of these ancient harem copulation movements. Although the actions are usually referred to as early folk-dance movements, the erotic element is unmistakable, and the dancer's costume draws attention to the navel, giving it special significance by alternately concealing it and revealing it.

For women, the best initial approach is not to stimulate the navel itself, but to stimulate out in a line toward and along the crest of the hips. The nerves in this area produce a very powerful abdominal reflex that is often used to test the integrity of the entire nervous system. The test involves taking the end of a neurological hammer and making some strokes from the navel down to the groin. The navel will jump, contracting sharply, if the reflex is intact. Embryologically, the navel and the genitals have a common tissue origin, and in some people this connection still exists so that stimulation of the navel will elicit a distinct tickle in the genitals.

Tertiary Erogenic Zone 4: The Anus (Guda Marma)

Anal stimulation is one of the most direct ways to activate Muladhara Chakra and induce or intensify the flow of Kundalini. In Tantra and Yoga, there are a variety of mudras and bandhas that involve anal contractions. These excite the physical

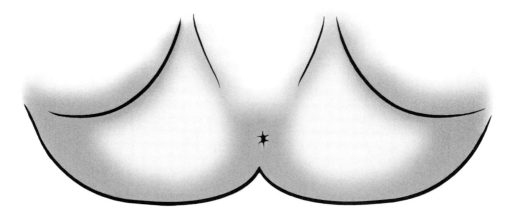

Tertiary Erogenic Zone 4: The Anus

nervous system and stimulate the flow of psychic energy. The anal area is very sensitive; this has long been well known in the East but has not always been well understood or appreciated in the West.

Analingus is the ultimate test for personal hygiene. Eastern personal hygiene is utterly immaculate. Here is a simple Tantric test: at any time of the day, would your partner want to kiss you anywhere on your body? If you can pass this test, then you are fulfilling an Eastern standard of personal hygiene—something few of us in the West can accomplish.

In traditional India, many people have virtually no concept of public hygiene. For instance, there is little public awareness that flies can carry disease. Indian public hygiene can be absolutely shocking to the first-time visitor. Even experienced travelers may have to go through a period of adjustment and may still be subject to overload after a few weeks. At the same time, Indian personal hygiene is absolutely immaculate. The situation is reversed in the West; we tend to emphasize public sanitation and sewage disposal. Garbage collections are perfect, but we forget about the garbage that is on our bodies. There is a lot of ecstasy to be gained if our bodies are kept as clean as a temple, but this entails far more than merely applying deodorant.

In many cultures, including most Western societies, the anus is considered a taboo point. This erogenic zone includes the anus and the surrounding area. In some people, this is one of the most powerfully exciting parts of the body, and virtually anyone can learn to enjoy anal stimulation. Contrary to popular belief, anal responsiveness in men has nothing whatsoever to do with homosexuality. The sensitivity is merely due to a concentration of nerves that all humans possess. Nevertheless, many heterosexual men are reluctant to explore the anal area, based on mistaken fears about what enjoying this type of stimulation might mean. This is but one of many unfortunate taboos about the anus that can influence both men and women, regardless of sexual orientation, and deprive them of experiencing the full range of sexual pleasure.

Taboos are so strong that some cultures view anal intercourse as psychically dangerous, and there is a popular view in the West that treats it as somehow degrading. Anal intercourse actually has some significant psychic benefits. Of course, it is important to use condoms for anal intercourse in this day and age. Anal stimulation need not include anal intercourse, however. For those who are uncomfortable about exploring this zone, external stimulation of the perineum can be an effective first step. In men, applying pressure to the perineum will also stimulate the prostate, and this is often a relatively unthreatening way for men to discover anal pleasure. The anus itself can be stimulated gently with the tongue or a well-lubricated finger. From the Tantric perspective, this type of exploration is profoundly valuable for contemporary men. Awakening the erotic potential of the anus means breaking a very significant taboo, and anal penetration of any kind is perhaps the best way for a man to have an experience that evokes the female role in intercourse and for him thereby to connect physically with his own feminine aspects.

Stimulation of the anus alone can arouse Kundalini in some instances. It instantly opens up the solar plexus center, Manipura Chakra. The ancient Indians understood the importance of anal stimulation. Some of the statues from the temple complexes at Khajuraho in central India depict it, and a careful examination of one of these statues reveals the depth of this understanding (see photograph at top of next page).

In Kriya Yoga, it is widely understood that a reflex exists between the anus and the solar plexus center. Immediately above the solar plexus center is the diaphragm; in fact, anal stimulation can be used to restore breathing. When the breathing has stopped, rapid anal dilation will restart the respiratory process immediately. Obstetricians in the nineteenth century discovered that using a finger to stimulate a baby's anus often triggered the respiratory reflex, thereby saving the lives of babies who stopped breathing immediately after birth.

Image of anal intercourse from the temple at Khajuraho

Nandi Temple, Khajuraho, circa 1000 CE. In this image, a Brahmin priest, identifiable by his shaved head and the sacred thread over his right shoulder, is engaging in anal intercourse, which instantly reflexes into the solar plexus. At the same time, he is manually stimulating Manipura Chakra with one finger directly opposite the navel and the other reaching around to the front of the navel. Photograph by K. L. Kamat, www.kamat.com.

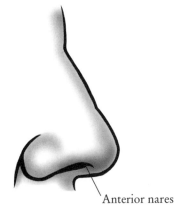

Anterior nares

Tertiary Erogenic Zone 5:
The Anterior Nares (Nasal Openings)

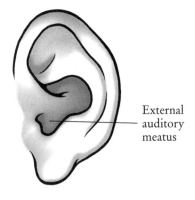

External
auditory
meatus

Tertiary Erogenic Zone 6:
The External Auditory Meatus

Tertiary Erogenic Zone 5: The Anterior Nares (Gandhanalalikaa Marma)

The anterior nares (nasal openings) means the very front of the nostrils. Nose rings have become quite popular, and it bears noting that frequently the points on the body where jewelry is utilized represent psychic zones, or subchakras. All of the Kama Marmas are subchakras that are specifically related to sexual energy. If you stroke the anterior nares, the nervous system will respond; you will feel that slight tingling sensation start to stir in you. This zone is usually worked with the tongue, sometimes the teeth, or stroked with the little finger. And once a person has gotten into a sensitive psychosexual state, nibbling the tip of the nose—very gently—starts to send tingles all over the face.

Tertiary Erogenic Zone 6: The External Auditory Meatus (Karnadhvanana Marma)

This is not to be confused with the earlobe; it is the ear hole itself. The ear has multiple layers of symbolic meaning. As we have so frequently pointed out, the correspondence is "as above, so below." First, recall that the shape of the ear reflects the shape of an inverted human fetus. The ear also evokes the yoni. Penetrating the ear with the tongue represents phallic penetration of the external auditory meatus, which comes to represent the vulva. That is the lock and key principle of a receptor and a stimulator. If Shakti places her tongue into Shiva's external auditory meatus, she is psychically reversing the roles, something that can have a very powerful effect. The tongue is the phallus, and the ear becomes the vulva . . . lingam and yoni . . . key and lock.

Physiologically, the tragus and area around the ear entrance are richly connected with a branch of the vagus nerve called Arnold's nerve, popularly called the Alderman's nerve by the young English aristocrats of the nineteenth century. The custom of the time was to attend very long, boring events known as Alderman's banquets, which included endless speeches and toasts and too much to eat and drink. The young medical students of that era discovered that if they splattered iced water in each other's ears, the reflex would kick over the stomach peristalsis, boost the heart rate momentarily, then settle and produce a peaceful but alerting response that would allow them to drink more and generally bear the situation to the bitter end.

The connection between the ears and the nervous system is so strong that when you insert your thumbs into your ears, you induce dominance of the parasympathetic nervous system, and this can accelerate entry into deep, introspective, meditative states.

For the same reason, penetrating the ear with a finger can have a powerful effect on sexual response. It is said you should never put anything smaller than your elbow into your ear, but we would add: except when you are making love. Very gently lick the little fingers (sex fingers, and also a tertiary zone), and when you are both in a responsive state, you can gently insert your moistened little fingers into your beloved's ears. This is likely to produce an ecstatic sensation. This technique can be particularly powerful during oral congress, for either the male or female. When your partner is making oral love to you, lick both little fingers and insert them into your partner's ears. This also enables you to guide the head gently and direct it so that the movements will give you the most pleasure.

Also, by inserting your moistened fingers into the ears during oral lovemaking, you take the active partner back to a primal state. This makes the sucking sensation even more psychologically profound. Blocking the ears in this way helps evoke the watery, prebirth state of womb life.

The little fingers are not only the sex fingers; they are also the psychic fingers. In traditional séances of the nineteenth and early twentieth centuries, participants sat around a table and joined little fingers because they were considered particularly psychic or potent. Thus, the use of the little fingers has a profound effect not only on the recipient but also on the person inserting them, and this creates a powerful psychic circuit.

The entire ear is replete with reflex points. Remember that cultures around the world pierce infants' ears as an early rite of passage and to insure the well-being of the child. The symbolic fetal eye, located in the earlobe, is often seen as the center for ailments of the eye. Thus, in some societies, that point in the ear is pierced to ward off or cure eye problems. According to one Chinese tradition, stimulating the little flap of the ear actually stimulates the genitals. We have already discussed Hieronymus Bosch's *Garden of Earthly Delights*, which contains the image of a pair of ears penetrated by an arrow at the genital reflex point (see chapter 12, "Secondary Erogenic Zones"). To reiterate, this is another among many absolutely astounding cross-cultural recognitions of the erotic power of the ear.

The mechanism of the middle ear is remarkable; it consists of three bones, which are the smallest bones of the body. They produce a 22x magnification of sound from the eardrum to the inner ear canal. Amazingly enough, there are twenty-two letters in the Hebrew alphabet and twenty-two trumps of the tower in tarot, and while we are on the subject, that golden chalice, that Communion cup, that essence of the human being—the skull from which we have a divine Mass each day—consists of precisely twenty-two bones.

If you wish to bring a person out of a deep trance state, blowing into the ear will do the trick. There is an Australian folk tradition for dealing with people who snore. Snoring occurs when a person is down in a delta state, which is characterized by a very low, slow brainwave pattern. The Australians believe that the way to stop someone from snoring is to blow into the ear. This interrupts the delta pattern and usually causes the person to stir without waking up and therefore to stop snoring.

Another folk tradition holds that you can tame a horse by blowing into its ear, and after that, it will follow you anywhere. In certain initiation rituals, a mantra may be blown into a disciple's ear, establishing a powerful psychic bond between Guru and disciple. A good Guru is not like a horse trainer, in that she desires freedom for the disciple, but the taming analogy is not entirely misplaced, especially during the earlier stages of the relationship. Mouth-to-ear transmission is an important aspect of the Hindu tradition; in fact, the word *Upanishad* can be translated as "ear-whispered teachings." A popular saying of the 1960s and '70s, "Blow in my ear and I will follow you anywhere," has an entirely different meaning that is more directly relevant to the subject at hand, since gently blowing in the ear can be a powerful erotic stimulant, as can whispering "sweet nothings."

Tertiary Erogenic Zone 7: The Sole of the Foot (Padaa Hridaya Marma)

The sole of the foot is analogous to the palm of the hand and also has a central area called the "crucifixion chakra." In addition, there is a subchakra in the sole of the foot that is associated with Muladhara. It is known as Malkooth in the Western tradition. In one Western magical practice, you start with visualizing a blazing golden or reddish brown ball between the soles of the feet. Many traditions state that you

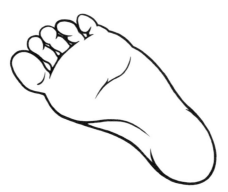

Tertiary Erogenic Zone 7: The Sole of the Foot

suck the apanic or earth energies up through the soles of the feet. Thus, the whole foot can be stroked, and doing so will send energy straight up the body.

In acupuncture, Kidney 1 is equivalent to Padaa Hridaya Marma. Acupuncture points and Ayurvedic Marma points correspond, with a few exceptions. There is a significant difference in that the area of an Ayurvedic Marma point is relatively large compared to the corresponding acupuncture point, which lies roughly at the center of the area circumscribed by the Marma point, and, as already noted, the Kama Marma encompasses an area that is larger still.

Acupuncturists also know this point as the fountain of life or the bubbling spring. There is another acupuncture point, known as the resuscitation point, that is also located in the sole of the foot. If you put a needle about two inches into that point and twist it viciously, you can revive people who have just drowned. It is quite effective because it jump-starts the whole cardiopulmonary system, but we don't recommend that you try it! The entire sole of the foot is powerful both psychically and erogenically, but this point is a particularly erogenic one in men. (For more on this point, see Swamiji's *A Chakra & Kundalini Workbook*, Appendix Two, "Loss of Consciousness During the Yoga Class.")

Another way of working with the soles of the feet involves tickling. When your partner is in a very sensitive state, you can tickle the sole of the foot. Not everyone will enjoy this kind of stimulation. The sole of the foot is one of the only ticklish areas left in most adults. A few individuals will not respond at all to stimulation while others may find it unpleasant, but in most aroused adults, the ticklish sensation is likely to become erotic. This is a very specific manifestation of the general principle that the childish sensation of ticklishness is transformed into the adult sensation of eroticism—and that is no laughing matter.

Tertiary Erogenic Zone 8: The Big Toe (Padaaghushtha Marma)

The big toe is to the foot as the thumb is to the hand. It is the phallic digit, and sucking the big toe will produce an orgasm in certain individuals, most of them women. In Tantric terms, the big toe reflexes to Ajna Chakra, the third eye, and to the pituitary gland. The experience of fellatio on the big toe will drive some people into another dimension, although sensitivity varies considerably. Of course, in this particular area, good personal hygiene is critical; you can't just walk around and suck anyone's big toe right off the street.

The neurological mechanism that makes the big toe so responsive is related to the Babinski reflex. Babinski was a neurologist who also happened to have a great interest in Sanskrit, and he devised a famous neurological test. In the Babinski test, a stimulus is applied to the outer surface of the foot and across it. In most circumstances, the foot will extend and the big toe will twitch, as will the other four toes, albeit to a lesser extent. The big toe twitches by itself, without the other four toes being involved, in only three circumstances. One is when the big toe is broken, another is during orgasm, and the last is in sleeping adults.

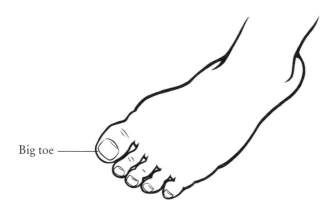

Big toe

Tertiary Erogenic Zone 8: The Big Toe

You have to train to be able to separate the big toe and move it without involving the others. In some of the Eastern traditions, this has been known for centuries, and they measure how intense the orgasm is by whether the big toe gives a convulsive twitch. Often the big toe will point up and out and the other toes will curl, hence the popular expression "toe-curling orgasm."

Tertiary Erogenic Zone 9: The Thumb (Angushtha Marma)

The word *thumb* comes from the same root as *tumescence*; it means "thick." The thumb is the phallus of the hand. Now, what does it insert into? It inserts into the hand's own mount of Venus or mons veneris.

Anatomically, this fleshy pad is called the thenar eminence. In Indian palmistry, it is known as *Shukra* (Venus), and it is said that when Shukra is full and fat, the subject has a high libido. People of this type are both tempted and tempter, the seducer and the seduced. If the thickness of the Shukra is medium, then it indicates fidelity and family type, and when it is thin, absent, and almost atrophied, it is said that this is a person with little or no libido. Many variations occur.

In Tantra, just as in foot massage or reflexology, massaging points on the hand affects the psychic nadis. Gentle massage of this fleshy pad stimulates the immune system and relieves tension. A rotation massage with the balls of the thumbs is considered particularly effective for cold or flu symptoms. You can also relieve tremendous amounts of tension by massaging the center of the Shukra with your thumbs. So, often, massaging the Shukra before making love will take away the day's tensions. It may not be erotic to dig into it, but you should stroke it and nibble it. While sucking the thumb is not quite as highly erotic as sucking the big toe, it can still be quite powerful.

Tertiary Erogenic Zone 10: The Back of the Knee (Janu Marma)

The back of the knee, or popliteal space, is a very sensitive point, well known in martial arts as a target for a disabling blow. The relevant acupuncture point is Bladder 54, and a major artery passes through the zone. The skin at the back of the knees is extremely thin and responds to gentle stimulation. In women, it is often particularly sensitive, generally when they are aroused. It opens up Manipura and Swadhisthana Chakras and reflexes into the sacral-lumbar junction. This is one of the slowest zones

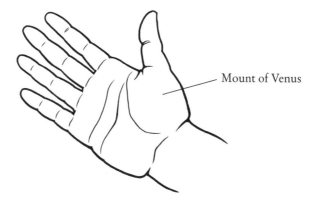

Mount of Venus

Tertiary Erogenic Zone 9:
The Thumb and Thenar Eminence, or Mount of Venus of the Hand

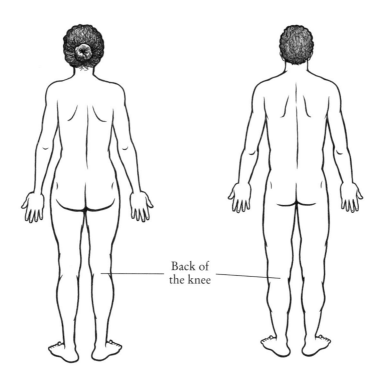

Back of
the knee

Tertiary Erogenic Zone 10: The Back of the Knee

to respond, and in most individuals, other zones must have been aroused before Janu Marma becomes active. Once a sufficient level of arousal is achieved, however, it can become exquisitely sensitive. It can be stroked, tickled, kissed, or tongued.

This concludes our exploration of the Kama Marmas. Westerners are generally un-accustomed to being systematic and methodical in their sexual encounters, and it will take some time and practice to become truly adept at working with the zones, but it is well worth the effort. Once you have developed a working familiarity with them, you will be able to employ them and bring your partner to new heights of pleasure. You will also be able to improvise and adjust for the individual within the context of this marvelous system that has never before been fully explicated in print and that had not been publicly taught to Westerners before Swamiji introduced it in 1976.

fourteen

Tantric Massage Magic

$\mathcal{J}$n the strictest traditional terms, there is no such thing as "Tantric massage." The phrase has gained currency with the increased popularity of Neo-Tantra in the Western world. In recent years, it has come to refer to prolonged genital massage, usually nonejaculatory for men and with ejaculation as a goal for women. In some cases, it can serve as a euphemism for mere prostitution; in other instances, it can be approached with considerable seriousness and can be a very valuable tool for learning about one's body and sexual response. We point this out not to make any moral judgments about current practice but only to suggest that anyone interested in purchasing a "Tantric massage" should bear the rule of *caveat emptor* in mind.

Massage, of course, is widely practiced in India, and there are a plethora of different approaches. Many of these practices are rooted in Tantra and the closely related fields of Ayurveda and Tamil Siddha medicine. In the past three decades, some of these Indian modalities have become better known in the Western world. Most of them are focused on relaxation, health, and healing; they are neither sensual nor do they directly address or seek to stimulate sexual energy, an approach that reflects the generally puritanical attitude of modern Indian society.

The system that Swamiji introduced at Gnosticon is based in the Tantric tradition and is specifically intended for working with sexual energy and the practice of Vama Marga Tantra. Swamiji's magical massage techniques can be a very powerful prelude to any form of sexual interaction, from Neo-Tantric genital massage to

Tantric maithuna. The material in this chapter is derived from Swamiji's original Gnosticon lecture on Massage Magic, supplemented by a lecture that he gave during the 1980s. The basic content of the lectures is the same, but bringing the two talks together makes it possible to provide a more comprehensive explanation of the techniques.

There are many different types of massage, and while any good massage is beneficial, there are significant differences between Eastern and Western approaches to massage or "bodywork." Generally speaking, traditional Western forms of massage, such as Swedish, work on the physical body and only indirectly affect the psychic anatomy and the flow of energy within the body. Conversely, Eastern techniques—shiatsu, acupressure, and Ayurvedic massage, for example—have a more explicitly energetic focus, so that while specific points on the body are worked, this is not necessarily done to produce a direct physical response, but instead to redirect or enhance the flow of energy within the body.

While massage has become far more popular since the 1970s, attitudes about it continue to be shockingly benighted, at least in the United States. It is still associated with prostitution in the public imagination, and a recent study by the American Massage Therapy Association estimated that twenty-one percent of Americans had experienced a professional massage in the previous year, an increase of thirteen points since 1997 but unchanged between 2003 and 2004.[1] Thus, massage remains a relatively exotic practice in mainstream society. It has unsavory associations in the minds of many, and we frequently encounter sophisticated adults who are afraid to receive one.

Etymologically, the word *massage* comes from the Portugese *amassar*, which means "to knead" and is itself derived from the Arabic *massa*, or "dough." The physical act of massage refers to a kneading of the tissue, the life energy, if you wish, the blood and lymph throughout the body. Like the kneading of dough, which prepares dough for leavening, massage works deeply in the body and effects a transformation, softening and stimulating all the tissues and reducing muscular tension.

So, a typical massage is a systematic kneading of the body that is going to enhance circulation of the blood and the lymph and induce muscular relaxation. When

1 The American Massage Therapy Association's eighth annual survey, conducted in 2004: "2004 Massage Therapy Consumer Survey Fact Sheet," published online at http://www.amtamassage.org/news/04consurvey.html.

we hold our tensions in our muscles, we are uptight, and massage will help us release tension. For this reason, regular massage is part of leading a well-balanced life. As we have already indicated, Eastern massage techniques do more than just knead the body and relax the muscles; they also directly address the flow of internal energy.

More importantly, extra-sensual perception often emerges during massage, whether Eastern or Western, and this is a critical Tantric element. Receiving massage is, on many levels, as intimate as a sexual relationship, and that is why massage is so commonly assumed to be sexual in the popular mentality. It is also why the practitioners of Swedish massage are so concerned about draping the body in such a way as to thoroughly negate any hint of eroticism. The sensual or erotic aspect of massage emerges from a transport of consciousness that frequently arises from intimate physical contact. Whenever you bring the sensual or the erotic into any aspect of existence, you can create an altered state—a transformation of the consciousness from the mundane to the arcane.

So, massage is sensuality—sexuality if you wish—in a very different context. Out of this sensual, erotic transformation of consciousness arises the Self, the Shakti forces that flow up and down the spinal column, or Sushumna. This is also the objective of Kundalini Yoga, of Hatha Yoga, and of Kriya Yoga. To say this is not in any way to negate the value of practicing Yoga; it is only to point out that extraordinary results can sometimes be experienced even without the physical discipline of Yoga. Yoga and other related physical approaches help prepare the body to experience the flow of energy and to manage it once it begins to move. Similarly, some forms of Western psychotherapy can be enhanced when the therapist works in conjunction with a massage professional.

Massage is one of the easiest and least threatening modalities in which people can begin working with the male and female polarities. It is one of the simplest and most direct ways to get the energy moving up and down the spinal column. We are going to explore several methods that are unique to Tantra for doing that very thing: opening Ida, Pingala, and Sushumna and moving the energy up and down the spinal column. For those more versed in acupuncture terminology, that means opening up the governing vessel and the double line of the bladder meridian down each side of the spine.

We have already suggested that the ultimate power of the human being dwells in the urogenital system (see chapters 6 and 7 for a discussion of this subject in the context of autoeroticism). It is important to bear in mind that virtually anyone can benefit from a urogenital massage—notwithstanding sexually repressive legal constraints—because this type of stimulation will release the vital hormones into the entire psychophysical complex. In addition, the subjective experience of sexual pleasure is beneficial in its own right.

Before considering massage for another person, we need to examine how we can massage ourselves internally and urogenitally. The next exercise is widely known in Tantric and Yogic circles and has been described comprehensively in other contexts. Swamiji has discussed it in some detail in *Ecstasy Through Tantra*, but it is less commonly considered in the context of massage. It is, in fact, a powerful inner massage technique, a way of stimulating both the internal organs and the whole energetic system. It works well as a prelude to massaging your partner or just as a way of stimulating your own inner energy. We are referring, of course, to Ashwini Mudra. You will recall that a mudra is a gesture, action, or posture that changes your mood, your consciousness, your psychophysical state.

Ashwini means "horse," and for our purposes, Ashwini Mudra is the gesture of the horse. Now, how do you know who is a Yogi and who is not a Yogi? According to Arthur Koestler in *The Lotus and the Robot*, "A Yogi is a man who blinks with his anus." And that is very good and very accurate, if not quite a comprehensive definition.

Both ends of the gastrointestinal tract are rife with nerve endings. We have the whole concept of anal fixation and oral gratification, central concepts in the Freudian model of psychosexual development. Freud built a system of psychology that he claimed was universal; however, much of it was based on his personal idiosyncrasies, many of which were connected with Muladhara and Swadhisthana Chakras. Nevertheless, Freud was a genius, and he made a profound contribution to the understanding of human consciousness.

It is interesting to consider various Western therapeutic approaches with the chakras in mind; Alfred Adler's psychoanalytic philosophy emphasized the will to power and the need for dominance; this is the realm of the "power trip" and "working from the gut level" and relates to Manipura Chakra. When you move up to the heart center, Anahata Chakra, you have Carl Rogers and the humanistic approach. The Jungian realm evokes Ajna Chakra and the opening of the world of visions, archetypes, and the collective unconscious.

In the years since Swamiji alluded to these parallels between the Tantric system and the Western psychoanalytic tradition, others have explored and elaborated on these issues in far more detail. Some would suggest that the correspondences are to be taken literally and should be understood as absolute and ironclad. We suggest that the linkages between East and West are interesting and that the transcultural symbolism can be quite stunning. At the same time, it would be a grave mistake to understand the chakras in strictly Western or psychoanalytic terms. Readers should be aware that many Neo-Tantric, New Age, and popular versions of the chakra system have little to do with the classical form, and that charlatans who will claim that your chakras are spinning in the wrong direction abound. Healers who work with the chakras and lack traditional training may or may not be gifted at what they do, but we are once again in the realm of *caveat emptor*.

To return to the internal massage, there is another term: *Mulabandha*. Mulabandha is static where Ashwini Mudra is dynamic. Mulabandha is useful for containing the internal energy, while Ashwini Mudra is useful for moving it. Ashwini Mudra is an ancient system of internal massage in which there are a series of dynamic anal contractions. Unfortunately, in our society, we think of the anus as a dirty place. If you wish to be a Tantrika, you need to understand that no part of the body—absolutely *no* part of the body—is dirty per se. The state of your body depends solely on your personal hygiene, but the body part itself is not dirty; it just is.

For thousands of years, people in the East have learned to control the whole pelvic floor through a series of anal contractions that are spread forward to the vagina or the scrotum and penis. Ashwini Mudra is dynamic because it involves contraction and relaxation, the basic life rhythm. This pumping action moves energy from below upward.

In the practice of Yoga and for general health purposes, Ashwini Mudra is an extraordinarily powerful and important technique. It is the most profound form of self-massage. It was developed because ancient Hindu culture had a very empirical orientation, unlike premodern Western societies, which tended to deny the importance of experience and observation, relying on scripture to determine the nature of reality. As a product of the Indian cultural matrix, Yoga is empirical. That means it is based on observation first, and theory emerges from observed experience. In such a system, theory is relatively unimportant; experience and action are what matter.

Ancient India was rich and luxurious enough to support great scholars, and diverse and tolerant enough to have a social structure that accepted even the most eccentric Yogis: those who appeared naked in public and devoted themselves to peering inside their own bodies. Legend has it that Ashwini Mudra was discovered by a Yogi who was out walking on a path. The Yogi saw a horse defecating as it walked ahead of him, and immediately after the horse had defecated, the Yogi noticed the action of the horse's anus. This Yogi had nothing better to do than to look at a defecating horse and contemplate it. He began to put two and two together and think, "Maybe what is good for the horse would be good for a human, if done deliberately," and that is why this practice is known as Ashwini Mudra, "the gesture of the horse." Ashwini Mudra is very important, and it is something Westerners would not discover for millennia, until Kegel exercises were introduced as an exercise for women after childbirth. Even today, its value for general health and well-being has not been fully appreciated in the West; men, in particular, are frequently unaware of its benefits.

Ashwini Mudra becomes especially powerful when it is repeated fifty or more times. In addition to affecting the flow of energy and the psychic body, it can help prevent hemorrhoids (varicose veins of the anus) and can prime up the whole urogenital tract, strengthening erections in men and vaginal musculature in women. According to the *Gheranda Samhita*, a seventeenth-century Yogic text, Ashwini Mudra "awakens the Sakti (Kundalini)" and "destroys all diseases of the rectum . . . gives strength and vigour and prevents premature death."[2] Yogic texts are often written in hyperbolic and metaphorical language and should not be taken literally, but this passage makes it clear that Yogis have long been aware of Ashwini Mudra's health-enhancing properties.

What follows is a simple, straightforward, and very powerful way of practicing Ashwini Mudra. You can do this in any comfortable upright sitting position. Re-

---

2 Rai Bahadur Srisa Chandra Vasu, trans., *The Gheranda Samhita* (Allahabad, 1914; repr., New York: AMS Press, 1974), 33. This translation has been widely reprinted and is a available in various editions. Another translation renders the passage in similar, if more puritanical, terms: "Aswini Mudra . . . generates strength and confidence . . . is an excellent exercise for curing secret disorders . . . builds up vigour and prevents premature death." Shyam Ghosh, *The Original Yoga* (New Delhi: Motilal Banarsidas, 1999), 134. Commentaries on other, more circumspect translations also make it clear that Ashwini Mudra is an effective technique for Kundalini arousal. For example, Parivrajika Ma Yogashakti, *Science of Yoga: Commentary on Gherand Samhita* (Bombay: Jaico Publishing House, 1966), 99–100. See also, Swami Digambarji and Dr. Mahajot Sahai, *Yoga Kosa*, vol. 1 (Poona: Kaivalyadhama S.M.Y.M. Samiti Lonavla, dist. 1972).

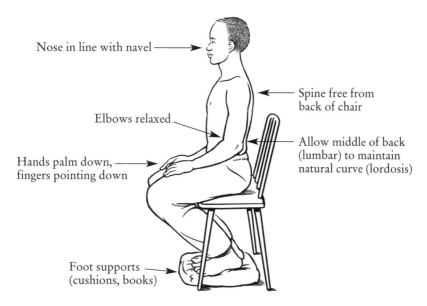

Nose in line with navel

Spine free from
back of chair

Elbows relaxed

Allow middle of back
(lumbar) to maintain
natural curve (lordosis)

Hands palm down,
fingers pointing down

Foot supports
(cushions, books)

Modified Vajrasana in a chair—a good posture for learning Ashwini Mudra

member, there are no sitting-down postures in Yoga, only sitting-up postures. For Ashwini Mudra, you can sit cross-legged or you can do it kneeling (*Vajrasana*), but for the purpose of this exercise, you should sit in a chair with your knees tucked underneath, emulating Vajrasana; be sure you are comfortable.

Close your eyes and put your knees together. Press the knees together as tightly as possible. Hold them, count to three mentally, and relax. Next, take your mind into the insides of your thighs, near the groin. Press your thighs in as if you were going to squeeze or massage your genital organs. Squeeze your thighs together as tightly as you can. Hold, count to three mentally, and then relax. Next, squeeze the buttocks together as if you were grasping a pencil in the crease. Hold, and repeat the process of counting to three and relaxing.

Take the mind down to the anus. You may never have delved into your body in this way, but keeping your eyes closed, mentally locate the anal region and bring your attention to it as fully as you can, even if it is an area you tend to avoid.

Next, you should try a very subtle experiment—"as above, so below." Do a tongue lock: close the mouth and press the tongue against the upper front teeth as hard as you can. Do this while keeping your mind on your anus. You may find that

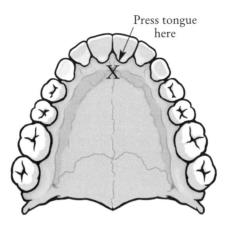

Position of the tongue for experiencing sahaja Ashwini Mudra

something very interesting happens. Just maintain your consciousness on your anus and put your tongue against your upper front teeth. Relax your body, press your tongue hard against the front teeth, and keep your mind on the anus. Relax, and repeat the process three times; then open your eyes.

About half the people who do this will feel a reaction in the anus on the first attempt. It is very subtle, but every time you press with the tongue, the anus will twitch. You can repeat this experiment several times over a few days. If you just sit down, relax, and push with the tongue, you will experience *sahaja*, or natural and easy, Ashwini Mudra. It is just a slight twitch.

The mouth and the anus are connected. They are at opposite ends of the gastrointestinal tract, which is thirty-two feet of tubing. Nothing in the gastrointestinal tract is in the body, because the gastrointestinal tract itself is a tube inside the body. So, everything inside it is not inside the body; it is inside the tube that is inside the body. If you create tension at one end of the tube (the mouth), you create tension at the other end (the anus). Tension in the mouth is a part of life; we do create a lot of tension with our mouths, and "as above, so below."

The next level is slightly more complex. It involves doing an anal contraction and sending that contraction forward across the pelvic floor. In women, the vagina will twitch, and men will feel the testicles move inside the scrotum. The sensation of movement in the genitals is the sign that you are doing it correctly. To reiterate, you begin with an anal contraction, and you bring the contraction forward to the perineum and the genitals. So, what begins as an anal-contraction exercise becomes one that encompasses the entire pelvic floor, starting at the anus and spreading forward.

Now put all the elements together. Close your eyes, concentrate, and repeat each step, holding for a count of three. Begin by squeezing the knees together, and relax. Move to the insides of the thighs, and relax. Then pull the buttocks together, as if you were holding a pencil, and relax. Next, go down to the anus and bring all of your attention to it. Squeeze the anus and move the contraction forward. See if you can feel your testicles pull in the scrotal sac, or the lips of the yoni tighten slightly. Relax and repeat the process.

Finally, fill a quarter to a third of the lungs with air and hold the breath. (Note that people with uncontrolled high blood pressure should not do this part of the practice.) Begin twitching the anus at a rate of approximately one twitch per second. When you get up to about twenty anal twitches, you may feel a desire to breathe. If so, just take in a sniff of air. That way, you don't have to stop and exhale; you just keep topping off the lungs. Sixty twitches is not an unreasonable number to start with. This is just like any other exercise: with practice, you will be able to increase the number of twitches and the length of time you can hold the breath.

The purpose of the preliminaries—of squeezing the knees together, pressing the thighs, and squeezing the buttocks—is just to create more awareness, to lead you in. Many of us are so disconnected from our bodies that we don't even know where or how to begin to feel the anus. Once you have learned how to breathe and twitch, you can dispense with the preliminaries.

Now that you have learned how to massage yourself internally, we can return to what is more conventionally defined as massage. We will begin with the trapezius muscle. The whole anatomical, muscular essence of a human being, the ability to keep the head and shoulders erect, depends on the trapezius. If you recall your geometry, the shape of this muscle resembles a trapezoid, and it is the source of a lot of trouble in the modern world. Most of us suffer from trapezius disease; that's not a precise medical term, but it is an extremely common ailment. We in the modern world are dying because we carry too much on our shoulders.

The trapezius muscle originates at the back of the skull. It shoots across the shoulder blades and ends up down at the twelfth dorsal vertebra, the last vertebra that is attached to a rib.

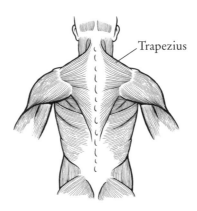

Trapezius

The trapezius muscle

Working on the trapezius muscle is a key element in almost all forms of massage, because tensions stored in the trapezius tend to radiate outward and manifest in other parts of the body. Therefore, relieving tension in the trapezius releases many of the tensions that may be felt elsewhere. Just grab your shoulder and squeeze, and you have got yourself a chunk of trapezius. Odds are that you will find it hurts.

There is a simple Eastern method for loosening up the trapezius that is also used in Western massage. Unlike the techniques described later in this chapter, this requires the use of a massage cream; oil can be used if cream is not available, but cream has the advantage of being absorbed more quickly and drying faster, which makes it more suitable in this context, since the next step involves dry massage. The receiver should be nude (at least from the waist up) and should lie face down. A massage table is ideal, and anyone interested in Tantric sexuality would be well advised to invest in one. If a massage table is not available, the receiver can lie face down on a bed or on the floor. If you are using a massage table, use a face cradle as well. If you are working on a bed or the floor, the receiver should do everything possible not to elevate the head, since raising the head tightens the trapezius. You can arrange pillows in such a way as to keep breathing free and keep the spine level.

Cross the thumbs; this short-circuits the Ida-Pingala energy. The left hand conveys the Ida energy. You are running the left thumb, which has a subchakra in it, up Pingala, on the right of the spine. On the other hand, there is a subchakra in the tip of the right thumb, and you are running it up Ida, the left-hand channel. It doesn't

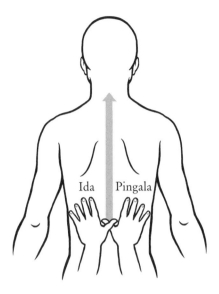

Technique for loosening the trapezius muscle
Position the thumbs as shown to short-circuit Ida and Pingala. Work upward to loosen the trapezius muscle.

matter whether the left thumb is over the right, but it does matter that they cross. We cross everything over; as usual in Tantra, we do everything the opposite way.

Cream or oil should be applied to the upper back, and the giver should work upward, letting the cream slip around. This is a preliminary loosener. It is a method that is quite commonly used in India. You work your way up the spinal column, the Tree of Life, the *brahmadandu*, God's staff. You just run your hands gently up the spinal column and spread the cream, moving into the trapezius muscle and gently loosening it up. Spend a minimum of ten minutes on this very important part of the body.

The next technique engages the psychic base of a human being. As we have already discussed, the sacrum is a triangular bone comprising five bones that are fused together, evoking the five tattwas or elements. This sacred part of the body contains the major nerves of the urogenital apparatus: the nerves to the penis, to the scrotum, to the prostate, to the uterus, to the vagina, and to the ovaries. Vibrating this area, using a technique known as percussion, turns on the "rest, recuperation, and relaxation" part of the autonomic nervous system and sends a very gentle stimulus all the way up Sushumna. This approach produces a state of physical relaxation and mild energetic arousal. It is more pleasant than taking an advanced Kriya Yoga course, in which you lift yourself about one foot off of the ground and bounce on your bottom to produce the same effect. It is a far more enjoyable way of getting the vibrations to move up the spine.

Bring your hands together and make a percussive vibration on the sacrum, striking gently with the side of the hand, as in a karate chop. This should create a soft vibration, a gentle drumming. It is important to keep your hands relaxed, and learning to do so requires some practice; you can experiment on your own thigh. The purpose is to get that vibration moving up the spine. It takes three or four minutes for the energy to move, and you only need to spend a total of about five minutes on this technique.

Next, dry your partner's skin and your hands thoroughly with a towel as a prelude to a traditional method that is used to awaken Ida and Pingala flows and keep the energy moving up Sushumna. This method requires great sensitivity and usually takes experimentation and practice. You use the breath and the lips. For men, a beard or mustache provides added tactile stimulus. Some people find this sensation delightful.

Place your lips parallel to your partner's spine so that one lip will track Ida and the other, Pingala (the left and right channels). The lips must be dry and should brush gently alongside the spine. Exhale, making sure that the breath is warm and that the exhalation is very slow and controlled. Work from the base of the spine to the base of the skull.

So, you start at the sacrum and you move up, very slowly. There are three requirements: that the lips are dry, that the lips remain in contact with either side of the spine, and that there is a steady, slow exhalation through the mouth. You move all the way up to the base of the skull, and as soon as you get to the top, you return to the base of the spine and repeat the process. Try to avoid touching your partner with your nose.

As you experiment, you are likely to discover a place on your partner that induces shaking. When you find that zone, which can be anywhere but most often is on the neck or between the shoulder blades, you work that area back and forth until the shaking subsides. This can take a couple of minutes. Interestingly enough, if you do this practice consistently with the same partner, you will find that the location of the responsive area varies from week to week, day to day.

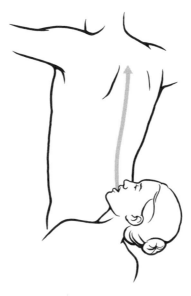

Tracking the spine along Ida and Pingala with dry lips

The next maneuver is known as "dry friction" in the West. It is a Shakti arouser, and it produces a considerable amount of heat. The classical Tantric scriptures describe two characteristic signs of Kundalini manifesting: trembling or uncontrolled shaking and a flush of heat. When the Goddess is fully extended into the cranial cavity, the rest of the body is often cold, yet there is burning in the head.

The epileptic seizure is one analogue to the classical model for Kundalini arousal. Where there is a convulsion, there is also an altered state of consciousness. There is a loss of control and a flush of blood. Unlike the epileptic seizure, however, the classical Kundalini experience is not accompanied by "swallowing the tongue" or spasms so uncontrolled as to endanger others. The key element is the altered state of consciousness accompanied by powerful body tremors.

The sexual response cycle is the other analogue to the classical Kundalini experience; this parallel is both relevant and more significant, since it lies within the scope of normal human experience. The sexual response cycle often includes shaking, convulsions of the muscles, and a flush that runs up the body into the head. In many ways, Yogic efforts to awaken Kundalini are attempts to duplicate one or the other of these analogues, and if we consider states of mystical ecstasy from other traditions, the same analogies apply.

One other naturally occurring state in which the human being has a cessation of the fluctuation of consciousness and does lose control is the uninhibited sneeze. The sneeze is a cranial orgasm, albeit a minuscule one. If we just take that sneeze down from the cranial cavity to the pelvic cavity, we have a climax. The two phenomena are more or less the same thing. A pelvic sneeze is a big loss of control, if we let it go. Interestingly enough, we have all heard that it is unhealthy to stop your sneezes, and yet people go to great lengths—conscious and unconscious—to squelch the sexual response.

Returning to the massage, take the dominant hand, usually the right hand, which the psychics say is the projecting hand (but if you are left-handed, use the left hand), place it on the base of the sacrum, and start moving up. It takes practice to be able to do this comfortably, but it will produce the most incredible sensations. You produce dry friction on your partner's back, working your way from the sacrum to the base of the skull by rubbing in an up-and-down motion on a small section at a time. This will build up heat; eventually, a wave will move right up the body. You should be able to feel the heat building up in the palm of your hand; remember, there is a sub-chakra there. When it gets so hot that neither you nor your partner can stand it, you have really gotten the hang of it.

Unlike many forms of massage, this approach requires that you move rather quickly in order to get results. After awakening the spine, begin to work between the shoulder blades, stimulating Anahata Chakra. There are people who don't want to meditate on anything below the heart, and so they focus on one of the higher chakras. Of course, the chakras are all connected, and Anahata Chakra links directly with Muladhara. The minute you open Anahata, you have automatically opened up Muladhara. And when you open up Muladhara, you open up Anahata. When you work between the shoulder blades at Anahata Chakra, it should be so hot that it feels like your hands are burning.

At this point in the massage, you will have built up enough energy to move into the Vama Marga meditative experience—the classical Tantric buildup. At this stage, the receiver is relaxed, the body's energies are moving, and the flush of heat is rising. This is a perfect opportunity to begin relating in a more overtly erotic way. One option would be to stimulate the Kama Marmas as described in chapters 9 through 12.

Before moving to the Kama Marmas, you may wish to experiment with some adjuncts to the basic massage that Swamiji described for a 1992 article in *Australian*

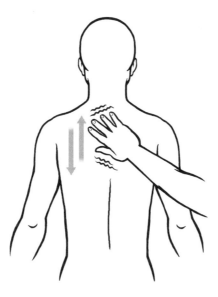

The dry-friction rub generates heat

Women's Forum. Take your partner's hand and work the mons veneris of each hand (the fleshy mound at the base of the thumb) with your own thumbs. Next, have your partner lie face down, straddle his thigh facing the feet, and use your thumb and forefinger to massage each ankle, just in front of the Achilles tendon.

This massage of the Achilles tendon stimulates the prostate and testicles in men and can be very tender in menstruating women. Both of these are very delicate areas, and you have to be sensitive to your partner's response and extra careful about the quality of touch. The next step is to apply a generous amount of warm oil to your partner's back and use your entire body as a massager, varying the pressure and direction of your movements as the spirit moves you. Needless to say, this can be an extremely erotic dance.

Finally, apply copious amounts of saliva to your thumb, forefinger, and middle finger and stimulate your partner's nipples. Spread the fingers around each nipple slowly and gently tug upward, sliding your fingers up as you tug. Release the nipple when you reach the tip. Be sure to stimulate both nipples. Some people will find this extremely exciting, and it can be done for up to half an hour, provided you keep the fingers well lubricated.

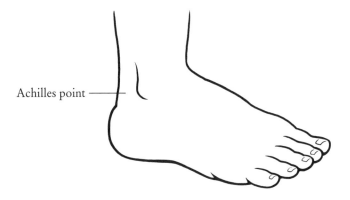

The Achilles tendon should be massaged gently

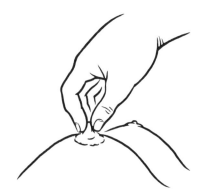

Stimulation of the nipples
Prolonged nipple stimulation can produce very high states of arousal. Be sure your fingers are well lubricated.

Whether you move directly to the Kama Marmas or incorporate the adjunct stages of the massage, you will have created relaxation and excitement, the optimum conditions for Tantric sexual practice. This will prepare you to increase the level of excitement and move on to plateau, peak, and resolution should you choose to do so. The Tantric sexual response cycle, with its prolonged excitement phase, is a paradigm for the meditative experience. That is why we come back to it again and again and again in Vama Marga Tantra. Vama Marga practitioners have long understood that sex is the form of mystical experience most readily accessible to the common person. The fundamental techniques of Vama Marga Tantra, including these massage methods, are designed to prolong the excitement phase and facilitate the circulation of energy within the body, thus maximizing the potential of sexuality so that this simple, natural experience can engender a mystical one.

To recapitulate, the massage includes the following steps:

1. Begin by loosening the trapezius; at this stage of the massage, use cream or oil. Cross the thumbs, working Ida and Pingala. Go up the spine to the trapezius, spreading the cream and gently working the muscle to loosen any tension.

2. Next, use percussion to vibrate the sacrum and start awakening the energy.

3. Use a towel to remove any excess cream or oil and start stimulating the spine with dry lips and warm exhaled breath.

4. Use a dry-friction rub with your dominant hand to produce the paradigmatic heat and flushing, indicative of the movement of Kundalini.

5. Continue the dry-friction rub rapidly between the shoulder blades. This affects Anahata and Vishuddhi Chakras, the heart and throat centers.

When this massage is done in sequence, it is a complete cycle. It will produce an altered state of consciousness, and it will enable you to get more deeply in tune with your partner. It can be employed independently or as foreplay leading directly to maithuna or other sexual contact. It can also be used, with or without the supplemental techniques, as a precursor to systematic stimulation of the Kama Marmas.

fifteen

The Tantric Mass
and the Secret of Amrita

Hindu tradition describes a precious fluid capable of imparting immortality to any being—demon, gnome, dwarf, or human—who drinks it. This precious elixir of immortality is known as *Amrita*. The prefix *a* in Sanskrit means "not or against," as it does in Latin and thus in English. *Mrit* is Sanskrit for "death," that ultimate initiation each of us must undergo. From the Sanskrit *mrit*, we have Latinate words in English like *moribund*, *mortality*, and *postmortem*.

This Amrita is a special substance produced in conditions of heightened ecstasy. The importance of Amrita is recognized transculturally: in Tantra, in Western alchemy and magic, and in the Catholic Mass, if one examines them from an esoteric perspective and discovers their hidden meaning. This is a profound subject, one that implicates the deepest levels of the human psyche and relates to matters of life and death.

Amrita is that fluid that is against, or will prevent, death. But what do we mean by *death*? Individual physical death is not at issue; it is inevitable. This is an esoteric question. The most terrible death is the death of the soul, the death of the spirit, the death of the spiritual courage that exists within each one of us.

According to a Hindu myth, the gods had a conference about this precious fluid, this Amrita, and they asked, "Where will we hide it? If these creatures called humans find it, they will become immortal, like us. They will become godlike, divine, *devas*, possessed of *vidya* [wisdom]. We cannot let them find it."

One of the gods said, "We will put it on top of the highest mountain." But the others objected, "No, one day man will reach to the very top of the world." So another proposed, "Let us sink it in the sea." But the other gods replied, "One day this human creature will even go into the very depths of the sea." "Well, then where will we hide it?" At last they decided, "Let us hide it deep within man himself, because this poor, foolish creature will never think of looking within." And by looking within, you can find this Amrita, this elixir of immortality.

Christian ritual—particularly, but not exclusively, Catholic ritual—centers on celebrating the Mass. The origin of the word *Mass* itself is significant. It is derived from the Vulgar Latin *messa*, for the dismissal at the end of a religious ceremony. *Messa* in turn is probably derived from *missa*, the feminine past participle of the Latin verb *mittere*, "to send." The words *missile*, *missive*, and *message* all share the same origins.

At the core of the Mass is the Communion, in which the bread becomes the body and the wine in the chalice cup becomes the blood of the *Christos*. Christianity and its mythology and ritual are deeply embedded in Western culture; the Christian tradition has helped shape the way any Westerner experiences the world, regardless of background or current spiritual orientation.

There is a mystical element that is also a part of any Westerner's spiritual and psychological heritage, and it lies in the Gnostic origins of Christian ritual. At one time, this ritual had profound esoteric meaning, and the Mass sent a message to the highest consciousness of the participants. It is sad to think that the very word *Catholic*, which originally meant "universal," has come to imply "narrow and parochial" and that Western culture has tended to alienate people from their inner, primal nature. The meaning of the ritual has not been entirely lost, but most have forgotten it; so today, when people talk about a Mass or a Communion, they are describing an external ceremony, symbolized by the Communion cup, which of course is an exoteric tool.

The Communion cup has a very important symbolic meaning, and the exoteric Communion has its esoteric counterpart. In the Tibetan equivalent of what is known as the *Panchamakara* in Hindu Tantric ritual, a skull bowl is used for the wine, so the Communion cup is actually a human skull.

Tibetan kapala, or skull bowl, used in Tantric ritual
Photo by Patricia Johnson (Devi Veenanand).

This too is an exoteric expression, but it brings us much closer to the hidden meaning. It represents how each one of us is subsisting and existing by virtue of a daily Communion. Our existence depends on a form of Amrita or elixir in which the brain floats like a fetus in the womb. This Amrita is called the cerebral-spinal fluid in Western physiology.

This elixir is produced in the brain, within the cavern, *Brahmanrandhra*, God's cave. The Amrita is manufactured in the heaven that lies within us and descends to bathe the earth below: the spinal cord and thereby the nervous system and the entire body. Each day, we drink our own Mass; we drink from the chalice cup of our own skull in order to exist, or perhaps we should say *sub*sist. This fluid, however, is not the true Amrita; it is only that Amrita that allows life to go on until the initiation death brings.

Somewhere within the human being, there is an elixir, and under a certain set of magical circumstances, this elixir can be transmuted or transformed into a potent, vibrant life force.

In Western mythology, the rose symbolizes the female genitals, the yoni. Not only is the image of the rose imbued with profound symbolism, the word itself has multiple esoteric implications and merits close examination. Out of the word *rose*, Eros, the god of love, arises, anagrammatically and associatively if not etymologically. Something that is hidden or esoteric, that is kept confidential or done in secret, is something *sub-rosa*—literally, "under the rose." And the fact that secret things are sub-rosa hints at the existence of a map, a guide to understanding this Communion.

Just as the rose in Western mythology symbolizes the yoni (in Tantra), so the cross stands for the lingam. The lingam is the phallic stake, and there is evidence that crucifixion was done upon a stake, not a cross. Hence, the rosy cross of the Rosicrucians, like so much other Western mystical and alchemical imagery, stands for the union of the yoni and the lingam.

In the East, the *padma,* or lotus, represents the yoni, the doorway through which all of us began our initiation into life. The lotus is a delicately perfumed flower that will only open its petals under the soft warmth of the sunshine. Eastern legend holds that when a bee visits the lotus, the bee experiences an orgasm, but the nectar yielded by the lotus flower can only flow, can only be distilled from her inner essence, when the bee has provided sufficient stimulation by probing deep inside and fully arousing the lotus. When this padma has been thoroughly stimulated and the nectar flows copiously, she opens and expands fully, and then the nectar can be extracted by the bee to manufacture this honey elixir.

This legend exists in both the Hindu and Chinese traditions, and it has profound and sweeping implications. At one level, it relates to oral sex, oral congress—cunnilingus and fellatio. Not only is oral sex frequently the most intensely arousing form of sexual stimulation, it also has a powerful psychological and spiritual dimension. In these terms, oral congress is an act of worship. It represents giving in, surrender, for both giver and receiver. This surrender is the gateway to a transcendent state of consciousness, the psychic union and energetic exchange of Shiva and Shakti, of Radha and Krishna. In some Eastern traditions, any form of oral congress is viewed as an act of worship. And this may sound strange to us, just as the Hindu custom of touching the feet seems strange, but again the power of oral congress lies in the psychological, unmitigated realization that this is not procreative sex. This cannot be sexuality, cannot be eros, or eroticism, for the reproduction of mankind; instead, it is erotic activity for the production of psychic children.

The rosy cross of the Rosicrucians evokes the union of lingam and yoni

One tradition holds that when the male (Shiva) performs oral congress or worship, he should follow a prescribed pattern so as to evoke the psychic forces. This
is a process of creating an expanding arc of energy. It is closely linked to the erogenic zones discussed in chapters 10 through 12. The ritual begins with Shiva gently nibbling the tip of Shakti's nose, the location of a specialized psychic center. He
proceeds by building a circle of force, always moving in a clockwise direction. The
stimulation passes down into the armpits, which are themselves an erogenic zone,
and then returns to the tip of the nose. Next, the circle is taken down to the nipples, closing again at Shakti's nose. Shiva then stimulates Shakti's nipples and circles toward the area around the navel, which is stimulated in clockwise circles with
the mouth. This circular descent builds continuing waves of energy.

Utilizing this pattern results in the subtle psychic essence being sucked out of the
chalice of the skull and led downward. From the navel, the force goes to the pubic
area—most beautifully named in western anatomy the mons veneris, or mount of
Venus—and from there to the yoni, the entire vulva itself, and finally to the clitoris,
the key to the nervous system.

This is a South Indian Tantric method of performing cunnilingus in a ritualistic
manner. It evokes the sacred relationship between Krishna and Radha, between
Shiva and Shakti, the love of the gods. The ritual is also described in modified form
in the *Koka Shastra*, a classical text similar to the *Kama Sutra* but of more recent
origin, dating to between the eighth and twelfth centuries CE. Although neither of
these texts are Tantric in the strictest sense, both emerged from the same cultural

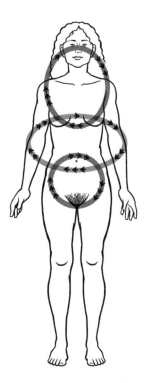

Pattern for performing ritual cunnilingus
While performing ritual cunnilingus, the clockwise progression downward to the yoni generates a wave of energy.

matrix, and the *Koka Shastra* was written at a time when Hindu and Buddhist Tantra were at their peak in Indian society. The *Koka Shastra* treats the yoni as an object of veneration, the doorway of life—the chalice cup below equal to the chalice cup above. The text describes the yoni as a power zone that may be perfumed, shaved, washed, and smeared with honey prior to cunnilingus.

Thus, under special circumstances, there is a vital fluid, essence, elixir of life, or Amrita that can be extracted from the yoni-chalice. The Western custom of drinking champagne out of a slipper evolved during the Middle Ages; this is really a symbolic version of drinking wine directly from the yoni and, at a deeper level, for imbibing this Amrita itself.

This Mass, this particular magical act—and we have only begun to touch on its total implications—has certain preconditions. In the Tantric tradition, there is a subtle force that must be present between partners if the elixir of life is to be produced. This force is called *bhava*. The term comes from the same Sanskrit root as *bhakti* (devotion). Bhava is a particular state; it implies love, and it implies serving. A Bhakti Yogi lives a life of service and devotion. When a state of devotion exists between partners—a state of love, a state in which you can fly high—that is bhava.

When the psychic bhava or interrelationship is built up, something extraordinary can happen. This state of bhava can transform the actual internal secretions into something very special, into the Amrita. But there are preconditions. The first precondition is that the bhava absolutely must exist; the emotions must be united with the body. Love must exist between the partners; that spark must be present. Western ideas about romantic love are not part of the classical Tantric tradition, but in the modern West, it is probably easiest to experience the bhava in the context of a committed relationship.

The bhava takes time to emerge, and as we have already discussed, prolonging arousal is an important aspect of Tantric sexual practice, because it produces an altered state of consciousness. In this altered state of consciousness, the full power of the bhava can be experienced. For men, this requires the delaying of ejaculation, even though the ejaculate itself is essential for the ritual.

In order to extend the excitement phase and delay ejaculation in sustained Tantric ritual, the man may find it helpful to drink two to four glasses of water approximately an hour and a half before the ritual commences. This will vary somewhat from individual to individual, and you will have to fine-tune the timing and quantity of water you consume. The aim is to go into the excitement phase with a half-full bladder. In the upright postures of Tantric intercourse, this is not uncomfortable. You should feel that you could urinate if you wanted to but not have an urgent need to do so.

This partially full bladder confuses the ejaculatory mechanism, since the semen comes out through the same tube as the urine. There is a two-way valve that prevents urination when the penis is erect. When the bladder is partly full and the penis is erect, the nervous system receives conflicting signals; thus, the presence of urine in the bladder can help delay the ejaculatory response. There is an added benefit: urinating after any sexual act cleans the urethra and thereby reduces the risk of infection. This is true for both men and women.

A second condition often flows naturally from the first, so that once the state of bhava has evolved, one's mental attitude changes. When working with a partner, the state of mind must be such that your partner's bodily secretions are absolutely stimulating and pleasant to you. This can be challenging for many in the West, and in addition, one must be mindful of the health issues related to the exchange of fluids. The body's secretions are intrinsically powerful, as we have discussed in the context of Perfume Magic (see chapters 8 and 9), and the secretions—perspiration, semen, vaginal dew—must be fresh. A very high level of personal hygiene is essential. As the level of sexual excitement increases, the stimulating power of the secretions starts to reinforce itself, creating an upward spiral of sexual excitement.

If we examine the Western Mass in esoteric terms, it is really a magical ceremony; as a consequence of an act of will, by the priest saying the Mass, the bread becomes the body and the wine becomes the blood of the *Christos*. This is called transubstantiation. Consider the literal meaning of the word *transubstantiation*. *Trans* implies "transform," and *substantiate* means "that which stands under." So, transubstantiation is the transformation of that which stands under or supports phenomenal existence, just as legs stand under and support a table. Without the legs, the tabletop cannot exist as a table in the phenomenal world.

And what is the one thing that stands under and supports all of us? It is that essential act, that primal union of lingam and yoni—the substantial basis of existence. Without that first Yoga, none of us would manifest, just as a tabletop would not be, at this level, without the legs. Transubstantiation implies that the substance upon which all else stands—namely, our very existence—can be transformed into something more.

Embedded in this symbolism is the recognition that we have lost touch with the source of our existence. The bread and the wine are the elements of transubstantiation. The bread is the body of Christ; the word *Christ* comes from a Greek root meaning "oil," and if you trace the roots of the word back far enough, it means not only "oil," but that most precious of oils—semen. So, literally, the bread is the semen. And the wine is the vaginal dew, the fluid that is secreted in heightened ecstatic states.

The chalice itself symbolizes the entire process. The lingam is the base or stem of the chalice. It stands under, supports, and holds the chalice cup, or yoni. (Note that this relationship is reversed in Indian representations, in which the yoni is the base that supports the lingam.) In symbolic terms, the hollow stem is not only a lingam, it is also an alchemist's retort. A Mass can be performed within this alchemist's retort and chalice cup, and in the esoteric sense, this Mass is the production of the elixir of life.

Indian folk medicine holds that forty drops of blood equal one drop of semen, or *shukra*. In other words, semen is distilled blood. The secretions that are carried through the lingam are manufactured in the secret alchemical retorts within the body, the testicles, which form a testament to human existence. In the case of the yoni, the vaginal cup is filled with an Amrita, or dew, that is produced by the blood vessels and glands surrounding it, distilling it. Just as the semen can be said to be distilled blood, this fresh vaginal dew seeps through from the blood vessels and glands surrounding the vaginal chalice cup to form a layer, a sweat, perspiration from within.

Perhaps a better and more Tantric word for *transubstantiate* would be *transudate*. *Sudate* comes from the Latin word for sweat, and *transudate* means "a sweat or distillation of something that is carried across a permeable mucous membrane." Female ejaculate is also produced through transudation, entering the urethra, as it does, from glands contained in the urethral sponge.

The Western magical tradition has recognized the importance of this Amrita, from the days of the medieval alchemists through the modern era. Israel Regardie helped translate the more abstruse aspects of Aleister Crowley's thinking and the work of the Golden Dawn into more readily comprehensible form. In chapter 16 of *The Tree of Life*, which was reprinted in its entirety as Appendix A in Swamiji's *Ecstasy Through Tantra*, Regardie shared some profound insights into Western magical imagery; however, even Regardie had certain puritanical attitudes about sexuality and could not avoid connecting it with so-called black magic.

Regardie wrote, "The method of which it is proposed to speak is so puissant a formula of the Magic of Light and one so liable to indiscriminant abuse and use in Black Magic, that if a conception of its technique and theory is to be presented at all, then the original intent of the writer must be discarded."

But this Amrita cannot be produced for or used in any form of black magic. The production of this elixir requires both the mingling of the alchemical elements of the male and female and the existence of a state of mind, the bhava, because it is the bhava that alters or transubstantiates the secretions, which are secreted in the secret cavities of the participants' own bodies. The bhava can only come into being within a framework of love and reverence, emotional and sexual ecstasy, and without the emotional state, the mechanical act cannot produce the transubstantiation. So, this is not "Black Magic," whatever "Black Magic" may be. Regardie himself called the ritual the "Mass of the Holy Ghost."

Regardie also described a very interesting set of alchemical symbols and secret symbols of the Rosicrucians. He refers to a mermaid with breasts with "two streams returning to the sea"; this represents Anahata Chakra with the nipple reflexes, or nadis, running straight down to the uterus, to Muladhara and Swadhisthana Chakras. According to Regardie, in Rosicrucian symbolic language, it is said that "if you torture the eagle, the lion will become feeble," and that "the 'Eagle's Tears' and the 'red blood of the lion' must meet and mingle. The eagle and lion bathe, eat and love each other. They will become like the Salamander and become constant in the fire."

In the image of the salamander lies the essence of the teaching. It refers to oral congress with the lingam or yoni, fellatio or cunnilingus. The mythological salamander, it was believed, could survive sustained heat, could live in fire, and that ability to live in fire is the Tantric state, a state of prolonged excitement in which the fire of passion can be sustained so that the transubstantiation of the physical substances can take place. This is true bioenergetics. This is true "mind over matter": using your mind, your mental state, your emotional state, and transforming the secretions of your own body, the matter of your own body, into something supernatural, the Amrita. Ultimately, it is the mental and emotional state that produces the change.

According to Regardie, alchemy required "one circular crystalline vessel, justly proportioned to the quality of its contents" (the yoni), and a "caballistically sealed furnace" (the lingam). With these tools, "the manufacturer of the alchemical gold which is the dew of immortality" conducts "a peculiar operation having several phases. Through the stimulus of warmth and spiritual fire to the Athanor [furnace] there should be a transfer, an ascent of the Serpent from that instrument." In the end, "the conclusion of the Mass, consists in either the consumption of the transsubstantiated elements, which is the Amrita or the anointing and consecration of a special talisman."[1] Regardie was aware of the Tantric tradition, which indirectly

---

1 Israel Regardie, chapter 16 in *The Tree of Life* (London: Rider and Company, 1936). Reprinted in Dr. Jonn Mumford, *Ecstasy Through Tantra* (St. Paul, MN: Llewellyn Publications, 1995), 139–150. Quoted with the kind permission of Llewellyn Publications.

influenced Western alchemy, hence his use of the term *Amrita*, but this awareness does not negate the importance of the transcultural symbolism involved.

Similarly, Robert Anton Wilson has observed that alchemical writing, like the *Tantric Shastras,* relies on a secret language, commonly referred to as a "twilight language" in Tantra. The purpose of this twilight language is to obscure the meaning of secret rituals and prevent the uninitiated from understanding them. Wilson described a practice that has come down to us from the Gnostic tradition and then was quickly disguised by the transformation of Gnosis, or a state of knowing, into so-called Christianity, or really Church-ianity. In this ritual, the man was advised "to obtain some of his own semen by performing cunnilingus after coitus has been completed. Some of this he himself swallows, and some he transmits to the lady, who swallows it via a kiss. This curious rite, which goes back to the Gnostics around 300 CE, has always been highly regarded by European Occultists."[2]

In Tantra, in the Catholic Mass, in alchemical symbolism, and in the more modern Western magical tradition, the essential elements are the same: the relationship between the lingam and the yoni—the alchemical marriage—the transformation of the body and its substances into a sacrament, and the consumption of the bodily secretions, just as the bread and the wine, the blood and body of Christ, are consumed by the congregation. In the manufacture of this Amrita, two substances of opposite polarity come together to form a new substance, and this substance can be retrieved by cunnilingus.

Regardie also understood the importance of mantra. He wrote, "it should be in the nature of a short mantram appropriate to the nature and type of working, rhythmical in composition." This means any couple that undertakes to manufacture this Amrita should be using a chant. In India, for hundreds of years, a specific chant has been employed for all Tantric acts of transubstantiation. There are variations of this chant, and one form can be found in a seventeenth-century Tantric textbook, the *Shiva Samhita,* in the hidden chapters, which are often omitted in whole or in part from English translations. Near the end of this text, you will find the following mantra: "OM Aim Kleem Streem," and that is the mantra to use.[3]

2 Robert Anton Wilson, *Sex, Drugs and Magic* (Tempe, AZ: New Falcon Publications, 2000), 77–92, 110–142.

3 These bija mantras are not always readily discoverable by the uninitiated. English translations may include the relevant sutras while omitting a transliteration of the bijas. In *The Original Yoga*, for example, the translation reads, "Within the four-petalled Muladhara Lotus is the Seed of Speech, glowing like a spark of electricity. The Seed of Desire is in the heart . . . blooming like a red bandhuka flower. In the Ajna lotus . . . shines the Seed of

There is a variant on this mantra that is very special and should only be used once ritual contact has been made with the Guru. The vibrations resonate to form a triangle in which magic can be worked. Then the mantra we use is "OM Aim Kleem Streem OM." If you think about the words in either mantra, they cannot be translated from the Sanskrit into English. Indeed, they are meaningless in Sanskrit; however, they are onomatopoeic, universal statements.

To paraphrase a very eloquent explication of the word *OM* by Dr. David Frawley (Pandit Vamadeva Shastri): *OM* is the universal sound that produces ascent and assent; it leads to both the "ascent" of consciousness and the "assent" of the psychic forces of the cosmos. *Aim* suggests direction and is also a *bija* (seed) mantra that invokes Saraswati, the goddess of learning; *Kleem* educes the power of Kama, the god of love, and Krishna, the channel of worship, and suggests *clean*, implying purity—to purify like a stream; *Streem* stands for the flow of Shakti force and is an ancient bija mantra that flushes away all obstructions. So, substitute the English word *stream* and what happens? To invoke this mantra during maithuna, during intercourse, during Tantric ritual, is to direct a pure force of Shakti through Sushumna into the chalice, the Communion cup of the skull, into which the Shakti will spray and, whether consciously or unconsciously recognized, fall back down the alchemical retort of your body to produce Amrita, or a specialized state of transcendent consciousness. We offer this to you as one of the most powerful Tantric mantras to be utilized in this magic of wand and cup, lingam and yoni, rose and cross.

The most important aspects of this Mass are the sustained state of excitement and the emotional intensity. It is the emotion, or passion leading to compassion, that brings about the actual transubstantiation. The ritual is exactly as Wilson describes. First, the Shakti must be aroused to such a high pitch that the yoni exudes its precious fluid. Then the lingam and the yoni, the pedestal and chalice, perform their union. So, that precious magic substance, that ojas, that semen or bindu, is transformed in the alchemical retort of the chalice.

The two fluids are allowed to mingle, and out of two come one, provided the requisite emotional state has been achieved. Then the man drinks from the yoni that

---

Force, like ten million moons." Shyam Ghosh, *The Original Yoga: As Expounded in the Sivasamhita, Gheranda Samhita and Patanjala Yogasutra* (New Delhi: Manushiram Manoharlal Publishers, 1980), 96. *Aim* resides in Muladhara, *Kleem* in Anahata, and *Streem* in Ajna. Since the *Shiva Samhita* states that the bija mantras must be kept secret, it is perhaps not surprising that some translators have obscured them.

Yab Yum with kiss

fluid, that shukra, that *rajaska*, the male and female essences combined into a new substance. One plus one, father plus mother, produces child. That child is Amrita, or alchemical dew, and it is passed from one partner to the other in a kiss.

The magic can also be performed through cunnilingus or fellatio alone. This requires a more profound state of concentration. In this method, one partner uses the mouth to transform the pure sexual fluid, mixed with the saliva, into another form of Amrita and again transfers it in a kiss.[4]

One final symbolic point: in Hindu Tantra, Western alchemical symbology is reversed. The male is always represented by white. So, on a Tantric altar, we always place a white rose or flower. Alongside it, the *maharsja*, or female fluid, is represented by the Goddess's essence—a red flower. Every woman is a flower—a *flow*-er. That is how we got into the habit of calling women flowers; they are the flowers of the human race, or the flow-ers, literally, physically, and psychologically, through which the human continuum perpetuates itself. The maharsja, the female fluid, is symbolically red. The male fluid or essence, *Soma,* is white. So, a Tantric altar always includes the two elements: positive and negative, yang and yin, wand and cup, Shiva and Shakti, Krishna and Radha, male and female, white and red.

---

4 When safer sex is a consideration, it is possible to enact the ritual exchange symbolically by using a substitute fluid, or by means of visualization alone.

Shiva and Shakti

Shiva and Parvati (Shakti) from Moor's Hindu Pantheon, *1810. The river Ganges flowing from Shiva's head represents the Amrita.*

The performance of this Mass involves the worshipful invocation of the Goddess in the body of the Shakti; working from the tip of the nose down to the armpits and to the breasts, and then circling down to the navel and to Venus's mound; the invocation "OM Aim Kleem Streem OM"; and the uniting of wand and cup, pedestal and chalice. In this ritual, the alchemical or Kundalini fire is built up within, and at that moment of discharge, at that moment of Yoga, or union, the semen, the bread of the body of this Christ, is visualized as white light flecked with sparks of blue, charged with pranic blue energy, and this charged host impregnates and in turn charges the chalice cup of the yoni. And at the same time, Shiva visualizes the vaginal dew as wine, and the chalice, the vaginal cup, is seen as ruby red flecked with sparks of golden light.

The great Yoga—of which each and every one of us is a physical byproduct—occurs at the moment Shakti visualizes the power of white light pouring into her, flecked with blue sparks, and Shiva visualizes the chalice, into which he is pouring his essence, as ruby red flecked with sparks of gold. At that moment, the true Amrita, or nectar of immortality, is created. This true Amrita can be utilized for magical purposes and rejuvenation.

This, then, is one of the deepest esoteric teachings of Tantra; this is the complete mystery of the wand and the cup, the lingam and the yoni—the true transubstantiation. All else is mere outer, exoteric recognition, just as a physical church is merely the outer form of the cathedral of that true church, that true place of worship: your own mind-body complex, for the kingdom of heaven lies within each and every one of you.

Swamiji and Swami Umeshanand
Initiation day in Sydney, Australia, October 2003. Photo by Patricia Johnson (Veenanand).

Afterword

by Dr. Jonn Mumford (Swami Anandakapila Saraswati)

Nearly thirty years have passed since I lectured at Gnosticon in 1976. In those more innocent days, I never dreamed that Vama Marga Tantra—or, to be more precise, its Western stepchild, Neo-Tantra—would become a big business. At that time, Bhagwan Shree Rajneesh (Osho) was (for better or worse) still a relatively obscure Indian teacher attracting a small cadre of Westerners to his ashram in Pune, and only a few years earlier, in his spiritual classic *Be Here Now* (1971), Ram Dass devoted a brief section to sexual energy and just over a page to sexual Tantra, concluding that he and his collaborators were not "sufficiently evolved in the use of this method to present this section in a more definitive form at this time." So, it is stunning, if not entirely surprising, that just three decades later there are dozens of books on the subject and a plethora of schools (many of them influenced by Rajneesh) offering costly workshops, "initiations," and teacher trainings.

In retrospect, Ram Dass was probably more right than he knew—and more right than I realized at the time. For the most part, Western Neo-Tantra has little (and sometimes nothing) in common with the tradition from which it claims to originate. I should add that this characteristic is not limited to Vama Marga Tantra; Hatha Yoga, as it currently exists in the West, is frequently little more than a form of physical exercise, sometimes with a dash of relaxation thrown in, and the whole concept of "power yoga" is bizarre and laughable from a traditional perspective.

Western attitudes toward sexuality are unbalanced and might even be called insane. Western culture uses sexuality as a tool for marketing, for inspiring prurient interest and titillating the public before condemning it as immoral. Sex is something that is dirty and disgusting, so much so that you should only do it with someone you love. Sexuality is "naughty," and a woman who embraces sexual pleasure is still a "slut" in the minds of many.

At the same time, popular magazines are filled with articles promising to reveal sexual secrets: how to drive your man wild in bed, how to have male multiple orgasms, and on and on. So, the attitudes veer between the puritanical and the salacious, with little room for wonder, awe, or even intentional and conscious exploration of sexuality. Even the most serious Western student of Tantra cannot avoid being influenced by this cultural milieu.

In addition, Western culture elevates the pursuit of wealth, status, and power, treating this pursuit as nearly a spiritual obligation. Our economy depends on consumerism, which is inevitably accompanied by an ethic of disposability and a never-ending quest for instant gratification and novel experiences. Thus, we Westerners (and, sadly, many Easterners as well) are little more than voracious consumers, not only of material things but also of ideas, experiences, and indeed of spirituality. In this context, Sacred Sexuality and Tantra may be little more than this year's model, to be discarded when the next new style emerges.

It could not be otherwise. The modern world is not ancient India, and Western values are often antithetical to Indian values. At the same time, I respect but cannot fully embrace the wholesale rejection of Neo-Tantra that some purists have advocated. In the past, I have argued that Neo-Tantra is better than no Tantra. I stand by that assertion, although I do think some of the ideas that are current in Neo-Tantric circles have the potential to be quite damaging. I hope that this book can help correct some of those misconceptions and guide Westerners into the tradition a little more deeply than they otherwise might have ventured, and thereby help them synthesize the authentic principles of Vama Marga Tantra with their own modern, Westernized lives.

Despite the obstacles that Westerners face, and despite the fact that culture prevents Westerners from fully appreciating the beauty and richness of the Tantric path, there remains something to be gained. Even if we Westerners can only attain a very limited experience of Vama Marga Tantra, sincere and committed efforts can yield profound rewards, and honest, sustained attempts to lead one's life as a Tantrika can function as a powerful antidote to the dominant consumerist paradigm.

So, how to go about experiencing even a drop of the divine nectar of Tantra, how to go about breaking free from the bonds of culture, language, and tradition? The first step is finding a form of sadhana, or spiritual practice, that works for you. For many, the most powerful sadhana may be relationship. If we can go through all the struggles of day-to-day living and still approach our partner with an attitude of reverence and worship, we can begin to taste that nectar.

Another key to understanding the Tantric attitude toward both sexuality and relationship can be found in an extraordinary—if most unlikely—place: seventeenth-century England. For centuries, Catholic marriage ceremonies had been performed on the steps, not within the doors, of the church. Only after exchanging vows could the couple go inside for the wedding Mass, ensuring that physicality was kept separate from the realm of the spirit. In 1662, the archbishop of Canterbury, Thomas Cranmer, issued the revised *Book of Common Prayer*, which included a new, Anglican marriage ceremony. The crux of Hindu Tantra in regard to sexuality may be summed up with this single phrase from the English marriage ceremony in the *Book of Common Prayer*: "With my body I thee worship." Nothing more and nothing less! Few among us succeed in sustaining an attitude of worship for a few minutes, let alone a lifetime.

This is not a path for the thrill-seeker, the weekend warrior, or the faint of heart.

I am grateful to my students, Swami Umeshanand and Devi Veenanand, for their commitment to Tantra as a spiritual path and to communicating the material I presented at Gnosticon to a new generation of seekers. Although this book conveys the essence of what I taught nearly three decades ago, at a time when Tantra was an obscure, esoteric subject, it has also been enriched by their insights and experiences. They are striving to live and teach Tantra as authentically as any Westerner can. For many years, I was reluctant to allow this material to appear in print, but when they expressed an interest in writing this book, I knew the information would be in good hands, and the results have more than validated my confidence in them.

Hari OM Tat Sat
Swami Anandakapila Saraswati
Sydney, Australia, 2005

Acknowledgments

$\mathcal{J}$t is deeply humbling to consider the impact others have had on the creation of this book.

I am profoundly indebted to Swamiji. This book began as a mere adaptation of his Gnosticon lectures. Had it remained that and nothing more, the content would have been significant in its own right. Because he has so generously supplemented the lectures with additional material from his personal archives, it has become even more valuable. Those who are familiar with the original tapes will recognize that the chapters devoted to the Kama Marmas, in particular, are far richer in detail than the original lectures. Beyond his direct contributions to the content, his encouragement and support sustained us as we worked through the material.

I am equally grateful to Devi Veenanand. This book was her idea, and she began transcribing the Gnosticon tapes even before Swamiji gave us his blessing. She has been my collaborator, muse, and inspiration from the first. She has also been my toughest and most trusted critic, taking time to read the entire text aloud with me with infinite patience, make changes to the manuscript, and select and organize the material for the illustrations, even as she pursued her primary career as an opera singer, indeed while preparing for a role.

Bruce Anderson (Somananda), our good friend, gurubhai, author of *Tantra for Gay Men*, and an accomplished teacher, provided much-needed moral support, helpful critiques, and valuable suggestions. Thanks to Michael Chase Walker for his feedback, particularly on the early chapters, for his friendship, for our spirited debates, and for introducing me to vetiver, which has become my personal scent. We are also grateful to Paul Skye (Swami Ajnananda Saraswati) for his very helpful observations, corrections, and careful reading of the manuscript. Dr. Judy Kuriansky very generously went above and beyond our request for a blurb by closely reviewing the manuscript, making detailed and useful suggestions, and providing very valuable information about current research in sexology.

There are a few others who deserve mention for the important role they have played in making this book possible. My first Tantra teacher, Anna Harvey, was always nurturing, supportive, and totally grounded in our work together. Anna guided me into a new universe, and I look back on my training with her with great fondness and appreciation. Marci Javril led me to Sunyata, who in turn led me to Swamiji. In vastly different but equally important ways, Bhagavan Das and Dr. Rudy Ballentine have helped shape and deepen my understanding of Tantra and my approach to this material.

Special thanks to Carl Llewellyn Weschcke for permission to reprint his 1976 Gnostica article and for his support, to Wade Ostrowski for his careful editing, and to all those at Llewellyn who have contributed to bringing this book into the world.

Finally, my parents have always supported me and encouraged my eclectic interests, even when those interests seemed incomprehensible and perhaps somewhat threatening. They raised me to be a questioner, and that is a rare thing in this society. While my approach to the spiritual life is quite different from theirs, the humanist values they instilled in me are not so distant from the Tantric ideal of finding the divine in others and in oneself; the difference is not nearly as great as I used to imagine. I am forever grateful.

MARK A. MICHAELS
(SWAMI UMESHANAND SARASWATI)

I join Umeshanand in thanking those who provided us with such valuable feedback. On a more personal note, I would like to thank my dearest Swamiji (Dr. Jonn Mumford) for giving me the opportunity to transcribe this material. Working through the more than ten hours of tapes left me feeling almost as if I had been in a front-row seat at Gnosticon. Swamiji is an extraordinarily dynamic and engaging public speaker, and the excitement and enthusiastic response of the audience reached beyond the confines of space and time.

I also wish to thank Umeshanand for his virtuosic ability with words. At various points during the writing of this book, I struggled to find the right words to express my ideas. Virtually every time I felt stuck, he was able to transform my ideas and suggestions into clear and coherent prose.

My parents taught me that one's spiritual quest is a personal journey of self-discovery, not to be dictated by anyone else. This attitude is a fundamental aspect of the Tantric approach, and I am grateful to them for instilling this value in me.

Seven years ago, I stepped into my first Tantra workshop. Little did I know that step would lead me to my beloved Umeshanand, who would become my partner on this journey of Tantric exploration. Our sadhana is our relationship, and I am awed by each moment and opportunity to see yet a new aspect of this divine being. Our union (Yoga) and our ever-deepening love is a sweet mystery; there is always more to discover.

PATRICIA JOHNSON
(DEVI VEENANAND)

"East Meets West in Dr. Jonn Mumford" by Carl Llewellyn Weschcke, Gnostica, 1976

As this article, "East Meets West in Dr. Jonn Mumford," by Carl Llewellyn Weschcke (from Llewellyn's magazine *Gnostica,* Issue 37, 1976), makes clear, Swamiji's Gnosticon lectures covered a number of topics not included either on the original tapes or in this book, among them Mantra Anesthesia and Yoga Nidra. The article also gives one a sense of the galvanizing impact Swamiji's lectures had on his audience and makes evident just how novel these teachings were at the time. It is too bad that only about half of the lectures seem to have been recorded. Fortunately for those with an interest in Tantric sexuality, most of the crucial material was taped, but a few gaps remain. This article is a very important supplement that fills in some of those gaps and provides additional insights. It will reward the careful reader with a deeper understanding and with techniques for making the practices discussed in the preceding chapters even more effective.

East meets West

in Dr. Jonn Mumford

by Carl L. Weschcke

One of the most exciting persons lecturing during the third week of Gnosticon 5 was Dr. Jonn Mumford of Sydney, Australia. Born in Canada, educated in both the United States and Canada, trained in psychology and chiropractic medicine, he was initiated at the Ashram of Paramahans Satyananda Saraswati in Bihar, India, where he was declared a Swami. Today, he practices chiropractic medicine in Australia, and constantly teaches and lectures about Tantric Yoga.

At Gnosticon 5, Swami Anandakapila gave sixteen lectures introducing his students to effective Tantric practices utilizing *Trataka* (blinkless gazing) on projected symbols of the chakras, visualizations of the externalization of consciousness as in astral travel, *Yoga Nidra* (psychic sleep), and Circle Meditation. He opened the sessions with a public lecture and demonstration of yogic achievement through *mantra anaesthesià*, inducing insensitivity to pain in volunteer subjects from the audience through the shouting of a mantra. At other times during the sessions, he encouraged members of the audience to *sew* his limbs together, and demonstrated *neti* (nasal cleaning with a string passed up one nostril and down the other).

When in the role of teacher, Swamiji dressed in the robes and beads of his order; as Dr. Jonn Mumford, attending the various banquets and giving newspaper and radio interviews, he dressed as a professional man of the Western world. As a man of East and West, he spoke to the needs of his students, and met all on common ground. I was so impressed with the effectiveness of his teaching methods that I immediately asked him to return to America for Gnosticon 6 to repeat his introductory lectures, and then give a second advanced series of lectures for those who completed the first sequence either at Gnosticon 5 or during the first days of Gnosticon 6. He has promised to do so.

To attempt to summarize his lectures in a few thousand words and a couple of pictures is, of course, an impossibility.

Yet, Dr. Mumford/Swami Anandakapila presented his material so well that I feel that I can give you a worthwhile overview.

Tan-tra

Like many modern teachers, Swamiji uses an approach of linguistics to help his students. *Tantra* is shown to contain two essential ideas: *Tan*—relating to "tangible": solid; and *Tra*—relating to "transcend": liberating. So *Tantra* works toward liberation through the physical. The *tango*, a sensuous dance, contains the same idea of being in touch with the physical—as does *tangled* and *tangent*.

The actual Sanskrit words combined in *Tantra* are *Tanoi*, meaning "to expand," as in the sexual sense of "tumescence"; and *Travati*, meaning to liberate, as in "detumescence." And, of course, the common conception of *Tantra* in the West is "The Sex of Yoga."

It is true that *Tantra* can be defined as "Two people using the mind/body complex to liberate each other," and it is this interpretation that perhaps has the greatest interest and application to the present time—for not only does it offer an efficient way of psychic development, but it also directly treats the sexual problems of most people, whether they have resulted from repression or from loss of emotional content through "over-liberalization."

In *Tantra*, the excitement phase of the sexual cycle, expansion and arousal, is emphasized and continued through mutual adoration and worship of the sexual partner. The female is an altar, or Goddess, through which the male may unite with the Divine. But in this sense, all bodies are feminine—whether male in sex or not—and all minds are masculine. So the female participant achieves union with the Divine just as the male participant does. (The comparison with various practices of Western Wicca should be quite striking to the reader.) Tumescence is maintained for long periods of time to expand the aura and increase the in-flow of *Prana*, life-energy.

In this manner, as Swamiji puts it, "The pair in sex accomplishes the repair of physical and psychological damage."

Kama Marmas

While the sexual aspects of *Tantra* were not developed until late in the lectures, it seems somewhat easier to describe each of the main techniques that are used separately. In sexual yoga, or worship, the various love points, or erogenous zones of the male and female bodies, are stimulated to bring the physical bodies into peak condition and to nourish the psychic bodies!

At the primary level:

1. The lips (and the labia). Tongues must unite as well as lips.
2. Breasts, nipples. The nipples both radiate psychic energy, and can "breathe energy in" to nourish the heart chakra. Nipple stimulation also opens the Ajna Chakra.
3. Genitals. In woman, the vulva and the clitoris. Stimulation of the vulva is evolutionary, while the clitoris is described as the "key" to the autonomic nervous system. In man, the penis.

At the secondary level:

1. Earlobes. Stimulates the Muladhara Chakra. Start with the right earlobe to open Ida, then the left to open Pingala. These are the channels of energy on either side of the spine.
2. Nape of the neck. Stimulation, as with the breath, opens up Vishuddha Chakra.
3. Sacral-lumbar area. Opens up Manapura Chakra.
4. Gluteal fold. Opens up Muladhara.
5. Inside of thighs. Stroking up to the genitals opens up Swadhisthana Chakra.

At the tertiary level:

1. Edge of the little finger.
2. Palms of the hands.
3. Navel. Actually a sub-chakra, Nabhi. It is related to Manapura.
4. Anus. Stimulates Muladhara.
5. Anterior mares (inside of nose). Opens up Ajna.
6. External auditory meatus (ear orifice). As an aside: a trance can be broken by blowing sharply into the ear.
7. Sole of foot.

In sex worship, these various *Kama Marmas* are kissed, caressed, anointed with oils and perfumes, adored by the eyes, etc. To proceed "properly," one should start with the secondary zones, then the primary, then the tertiary, and back and forth.

—continued on page 19

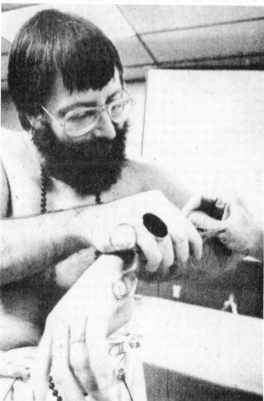

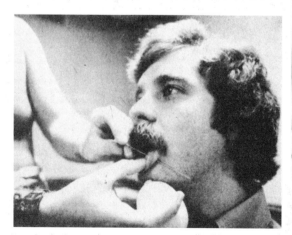

Top: Preparing for a demonstration. *Bottom:* Mumford passes a threaded needle through his forearm with the help of a volunteer. *Left:* Demonstration of *Mantra Anaesthesia*. Needle has been inserted without any sensation of pain.

A bad feeling has developed regarding the word "ritual" in the West, particularly when it is applied to love-making; yet, in Tantra, a ritual is made of sex because it brings us into contact with the life-force of the universe. In Tantra, the conscious is used to affect the unconscious, to create the superconscious.

A Psycho-Sexual Exercise

As will be explained later, the visualization of symbols and the moving of these visual images in the mind are extremely important parts of the training. One of the exercises taught by Swamiji that can be used both individually and by couples is given here.

1. In the imagination, form a golden circle the size of thumb and forefinger joined, and inside place a red glowing point.
2. Move this image about the body, starting at Ajna (brow chakra), then to right ear lobe (to stimulate Pingala), then to left (Ida). Then down to left nipple, and then to right. And finally down to penis or clitoris.

In each case, you may anoint the part of the body involved with saliva to aid concentration. You should first form the golden circle, and then add the red spot (Bindu). In the case of couples, partners can visualize upon each other. The man should anoint first, and then the woman, and then both visualize the images.

With this emphasis on sex, it is interesting to look at the word *virgin*, which actually means "a perfected person," an integrated man/woman. *"Vir"* relates to virile, or masculine power. *"Gin"* relates to gynecology, feminine. So the idea of a mass performed upon the body of a virgin, as in the old myths about Witchcraft, takes on a new possible meaning.

Chakras

I have already used the word *chakra* several times without offering an explanation of the concept involved. Most students of magick and of Yoga will have a satisfactory understanding of the subject, and know of the seven main chakras, but there may be some who are coming into contact with the word for the first time.

The word itself means "a spinning disk," and it describes the clairvoyant vision of this whirling center of energy that can be contacted with the mind. Each chakra, and there are a great many, relates to a specific physical center in the body; but the seven main chakras, and also the eighth, which is considered in this particular system, all have their "root" on the spinal column, and then have a "stem" and a "blossom." Because of their resemblance to flowers, they are symbolized by the Lotus in the Eastern tradition, and by the Rose in the Western.

NAME	LOCATION	GOVERNS
1. **Muladhara** "The Center at the base of the spine."	Basal root center at the coccyx. In male, blossom ½ inch inside the perineum. In female, at the cervix.	All the skin surfaces.
2. **Swadhisthana** "The Sacral Center."	Root in the Sacral, i.e., "sacred" area of the body. Blossom 1½ inches below navel.	All the fluids of the body.
3. **Manapura** "The Solar Plexus Center."	Root in lumbar area of spine; blossom in the navel.	All the flesh, and the pancreas.
4. **Anahata** "The Heart Center."	Root between shoulder blades; blossom midway between the nipples.	All the fat, cholesterol, ketones, and fat products of the body.
5. **Vishudda** "The Throat Center."	Root in lower cervical area; the blossom at the jugular notch.	All the bones; the calcium balance of the body.
6. **Ajna** "Brow Center."	Root at the bump at back of head (occipital protuberance); blossom at nasion (point between eyes where extended eyebrows would cross.)	Mind.
7. **Bindu**	The place of the hair whorl. The posterior fontanelle.	
8. **Sahasrara** "Thousand Petaled Lotus."	Root at the flat spot at top of head, the anterior fontanelle. Blossom is whole brain.	

Each of these chakras, or psychic centers, has associated with it a geometric symbol and an archetypal scene that arises in the unconscious mind when contact is made. One of the teachings of Tantra is that contact can be made with the chakra by visualization of the symbol. Swami Anandakapila projected a number of colored slides, and by teaching his students to concentrate their attention and to stare without blinking upon the geometric symbol in colors complementary to those desired, he made the visualization process become a vivid experience.

–continued on page 20

NAME	SYMBOL	UNCONSCIOUS SCENE
Muladhara	Yellow Square	Red feminine triangle with a green serpent coiled 3½ times, head upward.
Swadis-thana	Silver Crescent	Moonlit night with surf breaking upon beach.
Manapura	Red Triangle with point down (female triangle)	Yellow lotus or sunflower with flower upward.
Anahata	Blue Hexagram	Flame burning in total darkness.
Vishudda	Violet Oval	Violet nectar, with a sensation of cold.
Ajna	Grey Circle, a "Pearl"	Golden coin the size of a silver dollar with an OM symbol on it.
Bindu	Red "Dough-nut"	A white drop of semen.
Sahasrara	None	Red Lotus flower filling entire head, with a golden egg at center.

The practice of *Trataka,* gazing upon the symbol without blinking, was used effectively in every lecture. Visualization is not easy; yet it is the key to all occult progress. One must learn to actually *see* the symbol in color, floating in space outside one's body! This is done in dreams, and yet people find great difficulty in learning to do it in conscious life, except through experiencing "after-images"—closing the eyes and looking outward through the eyelids.

You can experience something of what we did by purchasing sheets of colored paper, or using poster paints, and making up the geometric diagrams indicated below. Try to get fluorescent, "day-glow" colors, and draw, paint, or paste them onto white cards about 4 by 4 inches in size. Remember that when Swamiji said to gaze without blinking, concentrating the attention of the "Bindu spot" at the center, he meant this to be absolute for at least a minute. If you have trouble, hold your eyelids open with your fingers, as this method requires that the optic nerves must become extremely fatigued for the after-image effect in complementary colors to be striking. After you have experienced this several times, you will know what you must achieve in visualization.

**Diagrams to facilitate
"after-image" visualization
of the chakras**

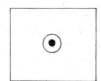

Muladhara
Blue Square
White Bindu
Black Spot

Swadhisthana
Black Crescent
White Bindu
Black Spot

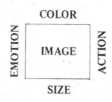

Manapura
Green Triangle
White Bindu
Green Spot

Anahata
Red or Orange Hexagram
White Bindu
Red or Orange Spot

Vishudda
White Egg
Black Bindu
White Spot

Visualization

Swamiji gave several little formulas for the use of visualization techniques in magical work. All of these were intended as aids to help the students bring all the factors together in a single concentrated endeavor.

One example of this was a drawing of a "case," such as a suitcase, showing all the elements that must be contained in the visualization effort. The point is that the visualized image must include *color, action,* i.e. movement, *size* (exaggerated), and *emotion* (you must have a feeling for the image.)

Again, you must learn to see the image *outside the body.*

	COLOR	
EMOTION	IMAGE	ACTION
	SIZE	

One of the points at which Tantra and occult psychology depart from common ideas about the mind and body is in the emphasis with which the former state that "the mind is outside the body," i.e., the body is contained within the mind! The mind is not something located within the brain somewhere, but is present throughout the body and outside of it. It is with the use of the trained imagination that we move into the world of magick.

We are familiar with the three dimensions of space and the concept that the fourth dimension is time. Tantrics and occultists have said for thousands of years that the fifth dimension is the imagination. Man's purpose in the Aquarian Age is to learn to function in the fifth dimension.

Another of Swamiji's formulas for visualization work is contained in this word: *Images.*

I = Irridescent colors. Form the mental images in fluorescent colors. Astral colors glow with a light of their own.

M = Magical. The fifth dimension of imagination is the world of Magick, where you have the ability to "cause changes to occur in conformity with will."

A = Active. A moving image holds the attention; so keep it in motion.

G = Gigantic. Make the image very large.

E = Emotion. You must have feeling about the image.

S = Simplicity ("KISS—Keep It Simple, Sweetheart!"). Too much complexity in details will occupy the attention, and take it away from the overall image.

—continued on page 22

The Third Eye

Several simple visualization exercises for "the opening of the third eye" were given.

See the third eye as a mental image floating in front of you. Then see *through* this third eye. The third eye, also known as "Shiva's Eye," is located at the point on the brow where the eyebrows would meet if they were extended, and it is here that the *Tilak,* or cosmetic caste mark, is placed. In this second exercise, place some saliva on this brow point. In the center of the head, directly between the ears, "see" a glittering red ruby, and from this ruby project a "laser beam" of red light through the *Tilak* point and feel that the saliva is being evaporated by the heat of the laser beam.

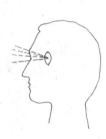

The third eye is, of course, *Ajna,* and its opening means that the emotional and mental natures are merged, or integrated. When you understand what is involved in the activation of a chakra, it is easier to understand the function of the exercises in Tantric practice. Merely concentrating with crossed eyes on the end of the nose, while perhaps a useful *adjunct,* will not open the third eye! Life must be lived and fulfilled, but Tantric rituals all are intended to accomplish this growth in a controlled and accelerated manner.

Yoga Nidra

The highlight, for all students attending these lectures at Gnosticon 5, was the daily practice of Yoga Nidra, "the sleep of the yogis." Dr. Mumford has prepared a special cassette tape for this: on one side he gives instructions and an understanding of the technique itself, and on the other side one of his students, Jasmine Riddle, narrates a "guided trip" of some 40 minutes designed to bring about an activation of all eight chakras in a safe and positive manner.

Yoga Nidra involves a deep physical relaxation, with concentration upon specific parts of the physical body, and the experience of the integrated mind/body complex. Psychological imagery is used to awaken aspects of the unconscious mind—to be repeated a number of times—for a slow release of the psychic scarring, traumas that we have all accumulated in our growth. While Yoga Nidra has characteristics of the states of consciousness induced by hypnosis or psychedelic drugs, it differs radically from these situations in that you are always in full control of your mental state. As various psychic scars, *samskaras,* are brought to the surface from the deep unconscious, emotional energies are released, bringing images with them, and sometimes unusual physical sensations. If these become disturbing at any time, you can bring the experience under direct control, ending the session.

Sex Magick

In his bridging of East and West, Jonn Mumford/Swami Anandakapila has written *Sexual Occultism* to show how the powerful sexual dynamic is used as the most efficient method of psychic-spiritual development available, and how it is com-

bined in the ancient and modern practices of Tantra Magick to integrate the Kundalini Power with other techniques.

In this book, he illustrates the positions for sexual intercourse that facilitate the arousal and direction of the Kundalini, or Serpent Power. In his lectures at Gnosticon 5, Swamiji spoke with the power and conviction of a person who had realized the great potential within "Holy Matrimony" for the fulfillment of individual spiritual destiny. He explained that it is this great power lying within the sexual act that is responsible for the many taboos on sexual life in primitive societies, for in sex there is the power of the creative force itself—and this is the foundation of all magical work and spiritual development.

It is in the *tangibleness* of physical sex, combined with the exercises in visualization and psychic stimulation of the chakras, that *transcendence* can be achieved. The electrical and magnetic natures of the male and female bodies complement each other to release the energies that can be directed by the trained imagination for physical health, astral travel, magical work, opening of the chakras, and more. In Tantra, the exchange of energies between male and female bodies is prolonged and used to bring into the merged bodies cosmic and planetary forces and to establish direct contact with the Deity.

In his culminating lecture, Swamiji arranged a Circle Meditation to demonstrate the method of using group energies in a magical way. Using the many techniques he had taught for concentrating energies within the body, he guided us to a blending of our individual selves and energies together in the one common vision. Together we saw a magical image to be realized in the renewed opportunity to learn ancient knowledge.

For many, it was an initiation. For all of us, it was a beginning. □

Swami Anandakapila's Books/ Distance Learning Programs

Swamiji has retired from public teaching, except for an annual advanced intensive at Ananda Ashram (which was founded by Dr. Swami Gitananda Giri Guru Maharaj) in Pondicherry, South India. Our company, Kailash Center for Personal Development, Inc., sponsors online OM-Kara Kriya® courses taught by Swamiji. These courses, which focus on Dakshina Marga practices, are a distillation of his lifetime of study and are a wonderful way to learn under his personal guidance and supervision. Information about the courses and details about online registration are available at www.jonnmumfordconsult.com.

Swamiji's books include the following:

Psychosomatic Yoga: A Guide to Eastern Path Techniques (1962)

Sexual Occultism: The Sorcery of Love in Practice and Theory (1975)

Ecstasy Through Tantra (1987)

A Chakra & Kundalini Workbook: Psycho-Spiritual Techniques for Health, Rejuvenation, Psychic Powers & Spiritual Realization (1997)

Magical Tattwa Cards: A Complete System for Self-Development (1997)

Mind Magic Kit (1998)

Karma Manual: 9 Days to Change Your Life (1999)

Death: Beginning or End?: Methods for Immortality (1999)

For details about our classes, information about our online Fundamentals of Tantric Sexuality course, or to subscribe to our newsletter, visit our website, www .tantrapm.com.

Selected Bibliography

Tantric Scriptures and Classical Indian Texts

Avalon, Arthur (Sir John Woodroffe). *The Serpent Power: The Secrets of Tantric and Shaktic Yoga; Being the Sat-Cakra-Nirupana and Paduka-Pancaka, Two Works on Laya Yoga.* Translated from the Sanskrit, with introduction and commentary. London: Luzac, 1919. (Available in the United States as a reprint from Dover Publications.)

Board of Scholars, A. *Sarada-Tilaka Tantram.* Delhi: Sri Satguru Publications, 1988.

Comfort, Alex. *The Koka Shastra and Other Medieval Indian Writings on Love.* New York: Stein and Day, 1964.

Digambarji, Swami, and Dr. Mahajot Sahai. *Yoga Kosa.* Vol. 1. Poona: Kaivalyadhama S.M.Y.M. Samiti Lonavla, dist. 1972.

Dvivedi, M. N. *The Yoga-Sutras of Patanjali.* Delhi: Sri Sat Guru Publications, 1992.

Ghosh, Shyam. *The Original Yoga: As Expounded in the Sivasamhita, Gheranda Samhita and Patanjala Yogasutra.* New Delhi: Motilal Banarsidas, 1999.

Magee, Michael, trans. *The Yoni Tantra.* Harrow, UK: Worldwide Tantra Project, 1995. (Available for purchase online in PDF format at: http://www.clas.ufl.edu/users/gthursby/tantra/booksold.htm)

Singh, Jaideva. *The Yoga of Delight, Wonder and Astonishment: A Translation of the Vijnana-bhairava.* Delhi: Motilal Banarsidass, 1979.

Tirumular. *Tirumantiram: A Tamil Scriptural Classic.* Translated by Dr. B. Natarajan. Mylapore, Madras: Sri Ramakrishna Math, 1991.

Vasu, Rai Bahadur Srisa Chandra, trans. *The Gheranda Samhita.* Allahabad, 1914. Reprint, New York: AMS Press, 1974.

Yogashakti, Parivrajika Ma. *Science of Yoga: Commentary on Gherand Samhita.* Bombay: Jaico Publishing House, 1966.

Western Sexology and Psychology

ABC News. "Doctor Discovers the 'Orgasmatron': Physician Working with Pain Relief Stumbles upon Delightful Side Effect." *Good Morning America.* ABC, November 9, 2004. (See related report at http://abcnews.go.com/GMA/Living/story?id=235788& page=1.)

Braun, Saul, ed. *Catalog of Sexual Consciousness.* New York: Grove Press, 1975.

Dodson, Betty. *Sex for One: The Joy of Selfloving.* New York: Harmony Books, 1987.

Gay, Peter. *The Freud Reader.* New York: W. W. Norton and Company, 1989.

Groddeck, Georg. *The Book of the It.* New York: Random House, 1961.

Lewis, Thomas, Fari Amini, and Richard Lannon. *A General Theory of Love.* New York: Random House, 2000.

Masters, R. E. L., ed. *Sexual Self-Stimulation.* Los Angeles: Sherbourne Press, 1967.

Masters, William H., and Virginia Johnson. *Human Sexual Response.* Boston: Little, Brown and Company, 1966.

Sargant, William. *The Battle for the Mind: A Physiology of Conversion and Brainwashing.* Cambridge, MA: Malor Books, 1997.

———. *The Mind Possessed: A Physiology of Possession, Mysticism and Faith Healing.* New York: Penguin Books, 1975.

Weller, Sheila. "Inside Betty Dodson." *Penthouse Forum: The International Journal of Human Relations* 5, no. 5 (1976): 39–43.

Tantra, Yoga, and Western Occultism

Bharati, Agehananda. *The Tantric Tradition.* London: Rider and Company, 1965.

Dass, Ram (Richard Alpert). *Be Here Now.* San Cristobal, NM: Lama Foundation, 1971.

Garrison, Omar. *Tantra: The Yoga of Sex.* New York: Crown Publishers, 1964.

Koestler, Arthur. *The Lotus and the Robot.* New York: Macmillan, 1961.

Regardie, Israel. *The Tree of Life.* Saint Paul, MN: Llewellyn Publications, 2000.

Saraswati, Swami Janakananda. *Yoga, Tantra and Meditation in Daily Life.* York Beach, ME: Samuel Weiser, 1992.

Wilson, Robert Anton. *Sex, Drugs and Magic.* Tempe, AZ: New Falcon Publications, 2000.

Paramahansa Satyananda Saraswati

Saraswati, Swami Satyananda. *Kundalini Tantra.* Monghyr, Bihar: Bihar School of Yoga, 1984.

———. *Sure Ways to Self-Realization.* Compiled by Swami Gaurishankara Saraswati. Monghyr, Bihar: Bihar School of Yoga, 1980.

———. "Vama Marga: The Practice of Left Hand Tantra." *Yoga Magazine* (March 1981).

Dr. Jonn Mumford (Swami Anandakapila Saraswati)

Mumford, Jonn. *Psychosomatic Yoga: A Guide to Eastern Path Techniques.* London: Thorsons, 1962.

———. *Sexual Occultism: The Sorcery of Love in Practice and Theory.* Saint Paul, MN: Llewellyn Publications, 1975.

———. *Ecstasy Through Tantra.* 3rd ed. Saint Paul, MN: Llewellyn Publications, 1987.

———. *A Chakra & Kundalini Workbook: Psycho-Spiritual Techniques for Health, Rejuvenation, Psychic Powers & Spiritual Realization.* 4th ed. Saint Paul, MN: Llewellyn Publications, 1997.

———. *Magical Tattwa Cards: A Complete System for Self-Development.* Saint Paul, MN: Llewellyn Publications, 1997.

———. "Kriya Yoga: Internal Alchemy for the Soul." *JOY: Journal of Yoga* 3, no. 6 (2004). http://subscriber.journalofyoga.org/kriya.htm (subscription required).

Reid, Vince. "Seventh Heaven: The Art of Erotic Massage; A Guide to Sensual Massage in Words and Pictures." *Australian Women's Forum* (December/January 1992): 36. (About and based on Dr. Mumford's work.)

Index

☾ LLEWELLYN ORDERING INFORMATION

Order Online:
Visit our website at www.llewellyn.com, select your books, and order them on our secure server.

Order by Phone:
- Call toll-free within the U.S. at 1-877-NEW-WRLD (1-877-639-9753). Call toll-free within Canada at 1-866-NEW-WRLD (1-866-639-9753)
- We accept VISA, MasterCard, and American Express

Order by Mail:
Send the full price of your order (MN residents add 7% sales tax) in U.S. funds, plus postage & handling to:

Llewellyn Worldwide
2143 Wooddale Drive, Dept. 0-7387-0900-X
Woodbury, MN 55125-2989, U.S.A.

Postage & Handling:

Standard (U.S., Mexico, & Canada). If your order is:
$49.99 and under, add $3.00
$50.00 and over, FREE STANDARD SHIPPING

AK, HI, PR: $15.00 for one book plus $1.00 for each additional book.

International Orders (airmail only):
$16.00 for one book plus $3.00 for each additional book

Orders are processed within 2 business days. Please allow for normal shipping time.
Postage and handling rates subject to change.

Ecstasy Through Tantra

Dr. Jonn Mumford

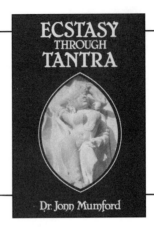

Dr. Jonn Mumford makes the occult dimension of the sexual dynamic accessible to everyone. One need not go up to the mountaintop to commune with Divinity: its temple is the body, its sacrament the communion between lovers. *Ecstasy Through Tantra* traces the ancient practices of sex magick through the Egyptian, Greek, and Hebrew forms, where the sexual act is viewed as symbolic of the highest union, to the highest expression of Western sex magick.

Dr. Mumford guides the reader through mental and physical exercises aimed at developing psychosexual power; he details the various sexual practices and positions that facilitate "psychic short-circuiting" and the arousal of Kundalini, the Goddess of Life within the body. He shows the fundamental unity of Tantra with Western Wicca, and he plumbs the depths of Western sex magick, showing how its techniques culminate in spiritual illumination. Includes fourteen full-color photographs.

0-87542-494-5
190 pp., 6 x 9 $16.00

To order, call 1-877-NEW-WRLD
Prices subject to change without notice

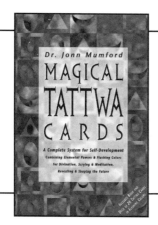

Magical Tattwa Cards
A Complete System of Self-Development

Dr. Jonn Mumford

Tattwas—the ancient Hindu symbols of the five elements (earth, air, fire, water, and ether)—act as triggers to the psychic layers of our mind through the combined power of their geometrical shapes and their vibrating primal colors. Tattwas are amazingly potent "psychic elevators" that can lift you to ever higher levels of mental functioning. The Hermetic Order of the Golden Dawn has used the tattwas for meditation, scrying, astral travel, and talismans. Now, with this new kit, you can use the tattwas yourself for divination and for bringing yourself into altered states of consciousness.

The twenty-five tattwa symbols are printed on 4" x 4" cards in flashing colors (colors that when placed next to each other appear to flash or strobe). Although the geometrical shapes of the tattwas have long been an integral part of the Western Magical Tradition, the flashing colors and their divinatory aspects have never before been available as the complete integral system presented here.

1 56718-472-3
Includes 26 full-color cards, and 5³⁄₁₆ x 8, 288-pp., illustrated book $29.95

A Chakra & Kundalini Workbook

Psycho-Spiritual Techniques for Health, Rejuvenation, Psychic Powers and Spiritual Realization

DR. JONN MUMFORD

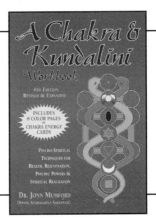

Spend just a few minutes each day on the remarkable psycho-physiological techniques in this book and you will quickly build a solid experience of drugless inner relaxation that will lead toward better health, a longer life, and greater control over your personal destiny.

Furthermore, you will lay a firm foundation for the subsequent chapters leading to the attainment of supernormal powers (i.e., photographic memory, self-anesthesia, and mental calculations), an enriched inner life, and ultimate transcendence. Learn techniques to use for burnout, mild to moderate depression, insomnia, general anxiety, and panic attacks, and reduction of mild to moderate hypertension. Experience sex for consciousness expansion, ESP development, and positive thinking. The text is supplemented with tables and illustrations to bridge the distance from information to personal understanding. In addition, the author has added a simple outline of a twelve-week practice schedule referenced directly back to the first nine chapters.

A Chakra & Kundalini Workbook is one of the clearest, most approachable books on yoga there is. Tailored for the Western mind, this is a practical system of personal training suited for anyone in today's active and complex world.

1-56718-473-1
296 pp., 7 x 10 $17.95

9 Days to Change Your Life

KARMA MANUAL

DR. JONN MUMFORD
(Swami Anandakapila Saraswati)

Karma Manual
9 Days to Change Your Life

DR. JONN MUMFORD

Many Westerners talk about karma, but few really know much about it. Now Dr. Jonn Mumford provides a clear, practical guide, featuring the traditional yet innovative approach of his first guru, Dr. Swami Gitananda Giti of India.

Karma is a simple law of consequence, not of moralistic retribution and penalty. It's a way of viewing existence that results in increased mental health and self-responsibility.

Discover the different types of karma. Process your personal karma by clearing out unwanted automatic actions—thus lessening the amount and rate at which new karma accumulates. Finally, learn a very direct method for "deep frying" the karmic seeds in your being through the Nine-Day Karma Clearing Program.

1-56718-490-1
216 pp., 5³⁄₁₆ x 8

$9.95

Death: Beginning or End?
Methods for Immortality

DR. JONN MUMFORD

This book is an exhilarating celebration of life—and death. It is a thought-provoking and interactive tool that will alter your perceptions about death and prepare you for reincarnation. Explore the history of death rituals and attitudes from other ages and cultures. Uncover surprising facts about this inevitable life event. Moreover, discover the ultimate truth about death, knowledge that is guaranteed to have a profound impact on how you live the rest of your life!

Learn how your experience of life after birth will impact your experience of life after death. Personally engage in five "alchemical laboratories"—five of the most crucial "stocktaking" exercises you will ever do. Learn a traditional Hindu meditation that will provide a psychic and mental refuge as well as deep physical relaxation. Practice a mantra that can liberate you from the endless wheel of blind incarnation. Use the tools provided in the book and avoid the death's biggest tragedy: to not ever discover who you are in life.

1-56718-476-6
216 pp., 5³⁄₁₆ x 8 $9.95

To order, call 1-877-NEW-WRLD
Prices subject to change without notice

Audiotapes
Dr. Jonn Mumford

Autoerotic Mysticism

Learn how to get in touch with yourself using massage. Focused autoerotic activity will lead to control and deep understanding of your sexual nature.

0-87542-514-3 $9.95

Psychic Energizer

This is a mental reconditioning tape, utilizing both Western and Eastern techniques of tension release and fractional relaxation. Introduced and then narrated by Mumford, with special musical effects for deep psychic response.

0-87542-547-X $9.95

Yoga Nidra

Yoga Nidra is a developmental technique that allows you to progress into a refined state of psychic sleep. The twin elements that Tantric yoga utilizes are body sensation and visualization. Dr. Mumford and Jasmine Riddle guide you through developmental stages by moving your consciousness through different parts of your body.

0-87542-548-8 $9.95

Sex & the Erotic Lover

MABEL IAM

How can one sustain ecstasy in a long romantic relationship? Can the magical art of sexuality solve a couple's problems? *Sex & the Erotic Lover*—now available in English—explores how sex magic can be used to improve relationships both physically and spiritually.

More than a guide to great sex, this book presents many techniques for rejuvenating romance and achieving spiritual harmony through the magical art of love. Readers learn the magical capabilities of the body's erotic zones, how to overcome sexual blocks, develop magnetism, be sexually creative, and build an erotic space at home.

0-7387-0825-9
240 pp., 6 x 9 $17.95

Spanish edition:
El sueño del amor
0-7387-0578-0 $14.95

Taoist Yoga and Sexual Energy
Transforming Your Body, Mind & Spirit

ERIC STEVEN YUDELOVE

The ancient Taoists believed that in order to connect to the energies of the outer universe, you first had to be able to control the energies of your inner universe. In *100 Days to Better Health: Good Sex & Long Life,* Eric Yudelove provided a basic foundation course in the practices of the Tao. Now he builds upon that foundation and takes you to the next level of Taoist practice: "Beginning Internal Alchemy."

Beginning Internal Alchemy is about gathering the energies from the five major internal organs, harmonizing it, and changing it from negative to positive. It's a process of refining yourself so you are capable of absorbing energy from nature and the cosmos, thus becoming a universe in miniature.

Taoist Yoga and Sexual Energy uses the same three-pronged approach first presented in *100 Days.* Each week, for another 100 days, in fourteen weekly lessons, you will learn more advanced practices for the Three Treasures of Taoist Yoga: Chi (breath), Jing (body), and Shen (mind).

1-56718-834-6
288 pp., 7 x 10, illus.   **$19.95**

To Write to the Authors

If you wish to contact the authors or would like more information about this book, please write to the authors in care of Llewellyn Worldwide and we will forward your request. Both the authors and publisher appreciate hearing from you and learning of your enjoyment of this book and how it has helped you. Llewellyn Worldwide cannot guarantee that every letter written to the authors can be answered, but all will be forwarded. Please write to:

Mark A. Michaels and Patricia Johnson
℅ Llewellyn Worldwide
2143 Wooddale Drive, Dept. 0-7387-0900-X
Woodbury, MN 55125-2989, U.S.A.
Please enclose a self-addressed stamped envelope for reply,
or $1.00 to cover costs. If outside U.S.A., enclose
international postal reply coupon.

Many of Llewellyn's authors have websites with additional information and resources. For more information, please visit our website at:
http://www.llewellyn.com